# THE NORTHERN BARBARIANS

## 100 B.C.–A.D. 300

ARCHAEOLOGY EDITOR
John M. Coles
M.A., Ph.D.
*Lecturer in Archaeology
in the University of Cambridge*

Silver beaker with gold leaf ornament
from Himlinghøje, Zealand, Denmark

# The Northern Barbarians

## 100 B.C.–A.D. 300

MALCOLM TODD

*Senior Lecturer in Classical
and Archaeological Studies
University of Nottingham*

HUTCHINSON
UNIVERSITY LIBRARY
LONDON

Hutchinson & Co (Publishers) Ltd
3 Fitzroy Square, London W1

London Melbourne Sydney Auckland
Wellington Johannesburg Cape Town
and agencies throughout the world

First published 1975
© Malcolm Todd 1975

Set in Monotype Times
Printed in Great Britain by The Anchor Press Ltd
and bound by Wm Brendon & Son Ltd
both of Tiptree, Essex

ISBN 0 09 122220 6 (cased)

To my family

# Contents

# Plates

# Figures

# Preface

In recent years there has been a welcome rise of interest, both general and scholarly, in the peoples who lived outside the bounds of the Roman Empire. This book deals with the most important group of these peoples in Europe, the early Germans, from the time of their first contacts with the Mediterranean world to the beginning of those migrations which carried them over most of Europe. The subject has been surprisingly little regarded in England (the interest of scholars here in the early Germans always lagging far behind that in the Celts) and the contributions so far made to it have tended to come from classical historians rather than archaeologists. The immense amount of work done by German archaeologists in particular has never been discussed at any length in England and in consequence our university students find it difficult to comprehend the place occupied by the Germanic peoples in the development of early European society and culture. This book has been written primarily with the needs of such students in mind, and for those who wish to go further into the subject the bibliography should provide the vehicle.

A full study of this immense subject would be beyond any one writer. I have attempted a general survey of early Germanic material culture, not a history of the peoples and their external relations, emphasizing those aspects which seem to me the most important. Inevitably in such a short treatment, some themes fare better than others, but I hope that nothing vital has been omitted. The book begins in the later stages of the pre-Roman Iron Age and extends down to the beginning of the fourth century A.D. This is a tantalizing place to stop, but to have gone further would have required another volume on the complexities of the fourth- and fifth-century Franks, Alamanni, Goths and Saxons.

Obligations incurred in the writing of books are not always easy to define, but two particular debts are outstanding. My former colleague Professor D. A. Bullough read the manuscript and corrected much in it. Miss Ann Douglas of Hutchinson

University Library has greatly assisted me over the format of the work as well as on innumerable points of detail. The book was largely completed in the congenial surroundings of the Römisch-Germanische Kommission in Frankfurt-am-Main, thanks to the kindness of its director Professor Hans Schönberger. Finally, to that same institution and to the Society of Antiquaries of London I am much indebted for access to incomparable library resources.

# Glossary

*agri decumates* (Lat.): Wedge-shaped tract of land between the upper Rhine and the Danube.

*Bandkeramik* (Ger.): Linear Pottery culture, a Neolithic pottery type named after its distinctive linear decoration.

*Bezirk* (Ger.): Administrative district approximately equivalent to a county or large borough.

*biconus* (Lat.): Pottery vessel of biconical form.

*Brandgrube, Brandgrubengrab (-gräber)* (Ger.): Cremation grave, containing objects and material from the pyre as well as the ashes of the dead.

*Brandschüttungsgrab (-gräber)* (Ger.): Cremation grave, in which the urn containing the ashes was covered by the remains of the pyre.

*cingulum* (Lat.): Roman military belt.

*denarius* (Lat.): Roman silver coin. The denomination was used as money of account in the early Empire.

*Einkorn* (Ger.): Species of hulled wheat (triticum monococcum).

*Einzelhof (-höfe)* (Ger.): Single farmstead, as distinct from a hamlet or village.

*en cabochon* (Fr.): Term used of precious stones, especially garnets, when smoothed or polished but not cut into facets.

*Flachsiedlung* (Ger.): Settlement on level ground, as distinct from one raised on an artificial platform.

*Formenkreis* or *Kreis* (Ger.): Assemblage of pottery and metalwork types occurring in a distinct geographical region. Frequently used by German scholars as an equivalent for culture.

*Fürstengrab (-gräber)* (Ger.): Princely, i.e. richly furnished, grave.

*futhark* or *futhork*: Runic alphabet, so named from its first six letters.

*Geest* (Ger.): Ancient alluvial deposits on the land surface, especially in the sandy regions of the North German plain.

*Grabgarten* (Ger.): Square earthwork enclosure containing burials in the southern Eifel region of W. Germany.

*Grubenhaus (-häuser)* (Ger.): Small timber house or hut erected over a depression in the ground.

*hängende Bogen* (Ger.): Decoration on pottery, in the form of hanging curves or swags.

*Herrenhof* or *Herrensitz* (Ger.): Dwelling of the leading man or family in a community or area.

*Kampfmesser* (Ger.): Short sword or dagger, mainly of the pre-Roman Iron Age.

*Kreis* (Ger.): See *Formenkreis*.

*Landkreis* (Ger.): Official term for area or district of land.

*limes* (Lat.): Strictly, a path or track. Commonly used as an equivalent for Roman frontier.

*Loess* (Ger.): Fertile, loamy soil deposited by wind, ranging from clay to fine sand.

*negotiator* (Lat.): Trader or businessman.

*powiat* (Polish): Area or district of land.

*Ringknaufschwert* (Ger.): Sword of Roman origin, its distinctive feature being a ring at the end of the pommel.

*Schalenurne* (Ger.): Flattish pottery bowl, often with upright neck. Common in the late Roman Iron Age.

*Schwarzerde* (Ger.): Fine fertile soil consisting of loess and humus.

*Spangenhelm* (Ger.): Form of helmet in which the cap is composed of several iron or bronze panels riveted to a metal framework.

*spatha* (Lat. from Ger.): Long, two-edged slashing sword.

*Standfussgefäss* (Ger.): Pottery bowl with pedestal foot.

*stehende Bogen* (Ger.): Decoration on pottery, in the form of standing arches or curves.

*Terp* (Dutch): Artificial mound or platform, heightened by continued occupation, on which dwellings and farm buildings were erected. German equivalent is *Wurt* or *Wierde*.

*terra sigillata* (Lat.): Name commonly applied to a glossy, red, slip-coated pottery produced in many workshops in the Roman Empire, especially in Gaul, Italy and the Danube provinces.

*Terrine* (Ger.): Large, wide-mouthed vessel tapering from the shoulder to a narrow base.

*Trichterschale* or *Trichterurne* (Ger.): Literally, funnel-bowl or funnel-urn. A wide-mouthed vessel tapering sharply towards the base.

*Viereckschanze* (Ger.): Square earthwork enclosure, occasionally enclosing deep ritual shafts. Best known examples lie in Bavaria.

*Wurt* (Ger.): See *Terp*.

# 1 | Germania and the Germans

## Germania

To Roman writers Germania meant that extensive part of Europe which stretched from the Rhine and Danube valleys to the North Sea and the Baltic. The eastern limits of the territory held by Germanic peoples were never clearly defined in antiquity. Tacitus was aware that to the south-east the Germans were bounded by the Sarmatians and the Dacians, and other evidence places these in the plain between the middle Danube and the Theiss, and in Transylvania respectively. But all the ancient authorities are vague about the north-eastern limits of the early Germans. Most modern scholars (at least those in western Europe) accept the broad valley of the Vistula as marking the most easterly zone of Germanic settlement and culture during the Roman period and this is the boundary observed in this book.

The geographical setting of the early Germanic peoples thus comprised a substantial part of the northern European plain, across which the great rivers Weser, Elbe, Oder and Vistula flowed towards the northern seas (fig. 1). Archaeology and philology allow us to add southern Scandinavia to the Germanic territories, so that in modern terms Germania covered most of West and East Germany, northern Holland, Denmark, southern Norway and Sweden, most of Poland and most of Czechoslovakia. But the early Germans observed no fixed bounds. During the Roman period the Germanic horizon was considerably extended towards the south-east, notably into south Russia. Even the frontiers with Rome were no Iron Curtain. On the contrary, there was a great deal of movement across these frontiers in both directions, setting in motion processes which were to transform Germania and, in due course, the Roman world as well.

Large tracts of this immense territory were very little known to the writers of the classical world. Even the better informed made the mistake of treating it as a single geographical unit, inhabited by people whose culture was entirely homogeneous. Most of the remainder of this book is devoted to the material culture of the Germans during the Roman Iron Age and this is not the place to anticipate its general conclusions. The first task must be to outline the physical character of Germania itself.

The heart of the territory occupied by Germanic peoples in the earlier Roman Iron Age falls into two natural physical divisions, the Northern Lowlands and the Central Uplands (the *Mittelgebirge*). The Uplands form plateaus rather than ranges of hills, their heights often attaining 1000m and occasionally as much as 1700m. Some of these hilly areas, for instance, the Harz mountains and the Bohemian hills, rise abruptly from the plain. Others, like the Łysa Gora hills of south Poland, swell gently from the lowlands with no marked change in the relief. The main river systems drain north and north-west from the Uplands across the Northern Lowlands, which form part of the great plain stretching from France to northern Russia. There are no heights here over 300m and most of the terrain is less than 100m in altitude. There is, however, considerable diversity in relief and in soil conditions. Several areas, such as the Lüneburg Heath and the Schleswig–Holstein uplands, have marked hilly characteristics.

The Lowlands fall into two broad zones which are parted by the Elbe. In the west the land lies almost at sea-level and is characterized by heaths, moors, bog, meadow, coastal marshland and extensive areas of fertile terrain. The eastern region is much more complicated. Close to the shores of the Baltic there lies a flat and fertile plain. Further inland, in Mecklenburg and Pomerania, there is an extensive area of undulating upland, well wooded now and strewn with lakes. Brandenburg is largely covered by broad marshy valleys containing many small lakes, but between the valleys lies better drained and more desirable land. Finally, a huge crescent of higher ground, with a covering of heath and forest, sweeps from the lower Elbe across the Fläming and Lusatian heathlands into Silesia and central Poland.

Towards the Central Uplands, the lowland gives way to an intermediate region, well drained and rolling country, a tillage zone of long standing. From it, three huge embayments stretch southwards into the Uplands: the Cologne, Leipzig and Silesian bays. This important zone is commonly given its German name

*Börde*. The Central Uplands are in no sense a barrier to communication from north to south and much of them can support settled agriculture. Three main areas may be distinguished among the Uplands. In the north lie the wooded upland blocks of the

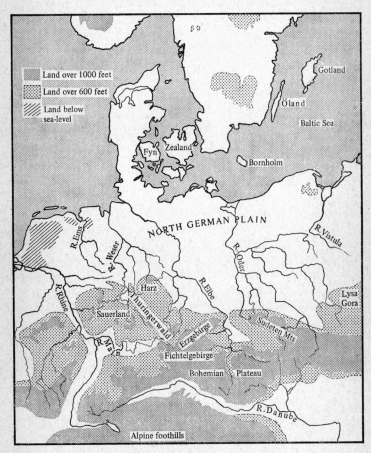

Fig. 1 Physical geography of Germania

Middle Rhine plateau, and immediately east of them the Weser uplands, drained by the Weser and the Leine. Further east still there are the complex ranges which radiate from the Bohemian plateau, the *Fichtelgebirge*, and *Thüringerwald* and the *Erzgebirge*, with the Harz mountains forming an isolated block to the north of them. To the south of these higher areas lie extensive and fertile lowlands, stretching across the valleys of the Main and Neckar to the upper Danube valley.

In these regions lying south of the borders of the ice sheets, the great rivers laid down enormous masses of gravel. These gravel deposits are particularly evident in the terrace gravels of the Central Uplands. The most interesting of the deposits in central Germania, however, is loess, which produces a light loamy soil, extremely fertile and much sought after by the early settlers of central Europe. A belt of loess lies along the northern edge of the Central Uplands and several tracts occupy the Upland valleys. Some of the larger valleys, notably between the Netze and Warthe, are occupied by extensive deposits of blown sand, again producing light soils which attracted early colonization.

Turning to the more northerly areas of Germanic settlement, Denmark, southern Sweden and the islands of the western Baltic have much in common with northern Germany, the whole region owing much to glacial deposition. Most of the Danish peninsula is a low plateau, the relief rising to only 173m in central Jutland. The boulder clay of Skåne and eastern Denmark produces the best soils. Central Jutland offered less attraction to the agricultural settler, while along the west coast runs a zone of sand dunes and behind it a belt of marsh.

Sweden north of Skåne is a region of great physical contrasts. The lowlands in the centre of the country have been much affected by faulting, which has left behind a maze of horst, troughs and steep-sided ravines. The larger troughs are occupied by considerable lakes and arms of the sea, but others, especially in Västergötland and Östergötland, have preserved level sediments over the limestone, resulting in plains of good cultivable soil. The limestone soils of the islands of Gotland and Öland are also productive and easy to work.

The coastal lands of northern Holland and north-western Germany originally offered the least inviting environment to the Iron Age settler. Along the North Sea coast from Friesland to Schleswig-Holstein lay clay marshes, now almost entirely drained and very productive. Paradoxically, much more is known about the settlements in this region than in any other part of Germania (see p. 97). Inland the marshes are overlooked by higher ground formed from old alluvial sands and gravels or *Geest*. Despite the forbidding problems they presented to cultivation and settlement, the coastal marshlands were extensively colonized during the Roman Iron Age and the communities concerned, as we will see, reached a high level of social and economic development.

Roman writers give an overall picture of Germania as a land dense with forest and festering with swamp.[1] This was substantially true for large areas, but by the first century A.D. clearance of the forest cover was well under way in many regions. In Schleswig–Holstein, for example, although a good deal of woodland continued to exist until well after the Roman period, numerous islands of cleared land had been created in the forest by the early Roman Iron Age. Elsewhere, there are hints of other extensive clearances. But it is doubtful whether in any region the population was large enough to necessitate wholesale removal of woodland. In any case, the forest constituted an important economic resource as pasture for cattle and pigs, and its elimination was unthinkable.

Various estimates of the total Germanic population during the Roman Iron Age have been put forward,[2] all of them scarcely more than guesses. By modern, or even medieval, standards the population at any time must have been small. The largest Germanic confederacy of the period, the Marcomanni and their allies, put only about 75 000 warriors into the field in a crucial campaign against the Roman armies in A.D. 6. The Marcomanni themselves probably provided the greater number of those men, but even so their population is unlikely to have been more than about 100 000 at this time. It is probable that the total population of Germania at the beginning of the Roman Iron Age was more than one million, but less than two. By the fourth century the figure had increased, but probably not beyond three million. Even by ancient standards, then, Germania was sparsely populated. The Roman armies which confronted the Germans on the Rhine–Danube frontier during the early Empire alone numbered some 200 000 men, and they sheltered twenty to thirty million souls in the European provinces.

## The origins of the Germanic peoples

The theme of *Ursprung und Verbreitung* has had a long and not always distinguished career in the historiography of the early Germans. In the eighteenth and early nineteenth centuries many scholars believed that the tribes mentioned by Tacitus and

Ptolemy were directly descended from the original inhabitants of northern Europe, not least because Tacitus said so. Later, in the mid-nineteenth century, the Celts were seen as the original settlers of Europe beyond the Rhine and, still more important, as the main agents of culture, craftsmanship and trade. The Germans were viewed at this time as savage interlopers, blundering about the northern lands, destroying Celtic cities, cultivating their land with the help of Celtic prisoners and taking whatever else they needed from their Celtic neighbours.[3] This phase of Celtomania did not last long. In the political climate of Bismarck's Germany scholars sought a nobler prehistory for the German people. By the 1880s the time was ripe for the wider deployment of archaeological evidence in the elucidation of Germanic origins. The task was taken in hand by several young scholars, notably Rudolf Virchow, Albert Voss, Alfred Götze and, above all, by a young pupil of the great philologist Karl Müllenhoff, Gustav Kossinna. Kossinna's views on the genesis of the Germanic peoples were to determine the main stream of thought on the subject until the Second World War and thus are worth more than a passing appraisal.[4]

Kossinna's method of study was founded on the principle (which he never permitted to be critically examined) that tribes or groups of tribes could be readily identified in the cultures distinguished by archaeologists. Applying the principle to the problem of Germanic origins, Kossinna convinced himself, and most of his contemporaries, that there was an ethnic continuum in northern Europe from at least the Bronze Age (and possibly from the late Neolithic) down to the Roman Iron Age and the emergence of the Germans in history, and that therefore the genesis of the Germans was to be sought in the brilliant Nordic Bronze Age culture which covered northern Germany from the Weser to the Oder, Denmark and the west Baltic islands. The idea of an ethnic continuum which was the basis of Kossinna's view will not bear close scrutiny. It rested on the assumption, apparently supported at the time by philological evidence, that a people and its culture remained in essentials an autochthonous unit over many centuries, now and again absorbing influences from outside, but remaining unaltered at the core. Major archaeological culture-provinces could thus be distinguished by the study of artifacts, and these culture-provinces must be taken to represent distinct peoples or tribal groups. As Kossinna wrote

in 1911, 'Sharply defined archaeological culture-provinces invariably correspond with clearly defined peoples or population-
groups.'[5]

Kossinna's views of Germanic origins were very much a product
of their nationalist time, and because they could easily be accom-
modated alongside prevailing ideas about the racial background
of northern Europe they were widely accepted in the earlier
twentieth century, especially during the Third Reich. Although
they had their critics from an early time, they continued to
influence European prehistorians to the 1940s.

Since the Second World War there has been an understandably
sharp reaction against this line of thought. The fallacy of
Kossinna's fundamental assumption about the identity between
archaeological cultures and peoples has been fully exposed and
can no longer play a part in serious prehistory. In the relevant
books published in the past twenty-five years there is an evident
reluctance to discuss Germanic origins at all, or to use the term
'Germanic' of anything which dates before about 100 B.C. The
reaction has gone too far. The material culture of those peoples
whom classical writers term *Germani* can be traced back with fair
certainty to the early phases of the northern Iron Age, that is to
the fifth and fourth centuries B.C., only about a century at most
before the first reports of the northern peoples were received in
the Mediterranean world. The contribution of three extensive
culture-provinces of the earlier Iron Age, namely the Face-urn
culture (*Gesichtsurnenkultur*) in Pomerania, the Jastorf culture in
northern Germany and Denmark,[6] and the Harpstedt culture in
the north-west, were probably of major significance for the
formation of the loose ethnic association to which the name
German was later given. But the details are denied to us and it
must not be assumed that the peoples of northern Europe were
conscious of any ethnic or cultural unity in the middle of the first
millennium B.C., any more than they were in the time of Julius
Caesar or Charlemagne. 'German', it will be well to remember,
was a term applied to the barbarians beyond the Rhine by the
Romans. It was never, so far as we know, applied by the early
Germans to themselves.

Philological evidence has always played a major role in the
discussion of when the Germans first appeared as a distinct
grouping of people. In the nineteenth century the emergence of a
recognizably Germanic language, in which certain sound-shifts

had occurred, was dated to the second half of the first millennium
B.C. Later, under the influence of Kossinna and his school, the
date was moved back to before 2000 B.C. Now, philological
opinion tends to favour the last five centuries B.C. for this development,[7] another pointer towards the formative character of the
period in which the three great early Iron Age cultures flourished.

The expansion, however, of the Germanic peoples from their
heartland in northern Germany and the lands about the western
Baltic was a long drawn-out process and we can glimpse in our
sources only a few episodes in it. In the late third century B.C., a
Germanic grouping called the Bastarnae suddenly appeared north
of the Danube and threatened the Greek cities of the Black Sea
coast. Where they came from is unknown. One authority suggests,
on the basis of certain pottery types, the area between the Elbe
and the Oder.[8] They were the first Germanic people to appear
in the Black Sea lands, foreshadowing the later Gothic migration.
A century later there are signs of widespread migration on a large
scale. Germanic settlers began to move up the Elbe valley into
Bohemia, a route followed by others in the first century B.C.[9]
To the late second century belongs that extraordinary migration
headed by Cimbri and Teutones from the Jutland peninsula,
which brought the Romans into such dire straits. After some
notable successes against Roman armies, these northerners were
beaten back and dispersed. They left no archaeological traces
behind them.

It was probably also in the second century B.C. that there were
movements across the Rhine into Belgium and the Rhineland.
Between the Belgae and the Rhine, Caesar encountered a group
of tribes who laid claim to a Germanic origin.[10] He names five of
these, Eburones, Condrusi, Caerosi, Paemani and Segni. These
people, we are told, had crossed the Rhine into Gaul at some
remote date well before Caesar's time, but still maintained a
conscious pride in their trans-Rhenane origins. The *Germani
cisrhenani* mentioned by Caesar still provoke controversy.
When did they cross the Rhine? Were they really Germans or
did they belong to some other grouping east of the river? Archaeologists and philologists have long been searching for traces of
them in Belgium and in the Eifel, without conspicuous success.
Attempts to identify assemblages of pottery with elements from
east of the Rhine have not been convincing, but this failure is
mainly due to the inadequacy of purely archaeological evidence

for revealing movements of population. Archaeology will not always identify, or even recognize, invaders if the potters and smiths whom those invaders employed were indigenous. There may well have been a crossing of the Rhine by westward-moving warriors and their followers without archaeologists being any the wiser about it.

A recent analysis[11] of the place and personal names of the *Germani cisrhenani* suggests that their origins were mixed. The names of the tribes include Celtic elements alongside Germanic, and others which are neither Celtic nor Germanic. Other peoples who laid claim to German ancestry, or to a German element in their composition, such as the Treveri, Aduatuci, Baetasii, Nervii and Tungri, also appear from their names to be of mixed ancestry. None of this philological evidence conflicts with the statement of Caesar that there had been a migration across the lower Rhine. The date of this crossing, however, is still uncertain; the most likely general context appears to be the second century B.C.[12]

In the earlier decades of the first century B.C., Suebi from the Elbe basin moved south-westwards towards the upper Rhine, setting in motion other peoples, probably including the Helvetii south of the Main. The major consequence, however, was the attack in 61 B.C. of an alliance of Suebi and Celtic Sequani under Ariovistus on the Aedui of central Gaul, an attack which led to the intervention in central Gaulish affairs of Julius Caesar.[13] The advancing Suebi had probably pushed back some of the Celtic population east of the middle Rhine, and this pressure by Germanic groups was intensified during the latter part of the same century. By the time of the Augustan invasions of Germania, Germanic peoples had begun to occupy most of the land between the Weser and the Rhine.[14] The latest major Germanic movement into territory hitherto held largely by Celts was that of the Marcomanni under Maroboduus into the Bohemian plateau.

In the east, meanwhile, there had been a corresponding expansion of the Germans. Traditions recorded mainly by western writers from the sixth century onwards derived several of the largest east German tribes from Scandinavia: Goths and Gepids from southern Sweden, Burgundians from Bornholm, Vandals from Jutland, Langobardi from Gotland and Rugii from Norway. The view is gaining strength that these traditions must not be accepted literally. That which derives the Goths from Scandinavia has come under the closest scrutiny, and the absence of any archaeological or other evidence in support has been ably demonstrated.[15] But the belief that the Scandinavian lands were a 'womb of nations' was both persistent and deeply felt, and it surely reflects actual events at some remote period. Specific traditions, however, cannot be relied upon and we must not assume that all the peoples whose legendary history derived them from the north actually originated there. But that there had been movements of settlers across the Baltic in the last three centuries B.C., in particular into the Oder–Vistula regions, appears highly probable. The details of date and occasion will probably never be known.

### The discovery of the Germanic peoples[16]

When the Germans first came into contact with the literate civilization of the Roman world they had no knowledge of writing, and there is no certain evidence that the literary arts were practised among them until after their settlement in the Roman provinces. German chiefs and other leaders did, it is true, send letters on various occasions to Roman emperors and commanders, and these letters were written in Latin. But not a single word of them need have been penned by a literate German. Roman travellers, merchants, prisoners, slaves and, later, Christian priests will usually have been called on to do this. Thus the early Germans could produce neither history nor the kinds of documents from which history might be written, and the available literary sources for the Roman Iron Age in northern Europe are confined to the surviving works of Greek and Roman writers. These are of inestimable value, but only if their inevitable limitations are appreciated. None of them should be regarded as a sacred text incapable of emendation.

The earliest reported journey by a Mediterranean traveller in northern Europe was that undertaken by the Massilian navigator Pytheas at some unknown date in the later fourth century B.C. His account of his travels, which also included a coasting along the western side of Spain and France and a circumnavigation of Britain, roused some ancient geographical writers to apoplectic fury, but has been, with good reason, more kindly received by moderns. From various passages in Strabo, Diodorus and Pliny, we hear that Pytheas sailed along the northern continental shore as far as the estuary *Metuonis*, which may be the Elbe, and the island *Abalus*, possibly Heligoland or one of the North Frisian group. He named two tribes, the Gutones or Guiones and the Teutones, the latter specializing in the collection of amber from the beaches. All this is credible and, like so much else in the surviving fragments of Pytheas, remarkably free from exaggeration. How far to the east he penetrated is unknown. Probably he did not reach the Baltic and he certainly did not get as far as the mouth of the Vistula, as some have claimed.

After Pytheas the record is a virtual blank for more than a century. The long tradition of Greek ethnographical composition, reaching back to Herodotos, apparently gathered no information about the northern inhabitants of Europe until the first century B.C. The Germans were first distinguished from their Celtic and Scythian neighbours in the *Histories* of the Syrian philosopher Poseidonios (*c.* 135–51 B.C.), a work now lost and represented only by fragments quoted by later writers.[17] Apart, however, from distinguishing the Germanic peoples for the first time, Poseidonios tells us nothing about them. It has, all the same, been widely accepted, following the great work of Eduard Norden on the sources of Tacitus' *Germania*,[18] that the tradition in which Poseidonios wrote was a powerful formative influence upon the great Latin historians who tell us most about the barbarian world. Norden's own influence, like that of many imaginative pioneers, worked too strongly on his successors and his excellent book has been misused in the attempt to sap credence in the accounts of Caesar and Tacitus in particular. We are asked to believe that most of what the later Roman historians said about the Germans was lifted from Poseidonios and his fellows. There is no discoverable basis for this view. The influence of the Greek ethnographers was certainly felt, but it was not all-pervasive.

Julius Caesar, the first Latin writer known to have dealt with the Germans at some length, included several chapters on them in his *Commentaries*.[19] The writings of a man who himself campaigned against the Suebi in eastern Gaul and in the Rhine valley would seem a promising source and the mere fact that Caesar's account is the earliest of any size is enough to compel a fair measure of respect. But Caesar's passages on his adversaries must be treated with care. He was probably only acquainted with the peoples living close to the Rhine valley, and thus what he writes about social organization and the allotment of arable land, to

name two notoriously controversial matters, should not be regarded as typical of all Germanic peoples. There is a more profound reason for treating Caesar's account with some reserve.
A general with high political aims and no leisure is unlikely to
make a dispassionate ethnographer. What he does say about the
ethnic situation in the regions about the Rhine is as definite as it
could be. He draws a sharp distinction between the Gauls or Celts
west of the Rhine and the Germans east of the river. The Gauls
were, as barbarians went, relatively tractable material in Caesar's
picture, but the Germans were simply savages. Caesar may have
genuinely believed that the peoples east of the Rhine were
different from those to the west (though he knew that some
peoples had crossed from east to west before his own day) and
there can be no doubt that they posed a major threat to the new
province of Gaul and perhaps to Italy. But it is reasonable to
suspect that Caesar actually drew an entirely spurious distinction
between Celts and Germans along the Rhine in order to justify
his own activities in northern Gaul.[20] To convince opinion in
Rome that those activities were essential in the military sense, the
peoples across the Rhine must be shown to be very different
from the Gauls and inimical to them.

This sharp distinction between Celts and Germans in the
*Commentaries* is one of the most striking and influential aspects
of Caesar's account of the barbarians; it became part of the
stock-in-trade of later writers and was generally accepted until
about a decade ago. Now, philologists and archaeologists agree
that Caesar either wholly misunderstood the ethnic situation on
the Rhine or for his own political purposes misrepresented what
he observed there. For it is now apparent that the inhabitants of
the lands immediately east of the Rhine in Caesar's day were
neither German nor Celtic, but a pre-Celtic grouping, probably
speaking a pre-Indo-European language.[21] The archaeological
culture of these people, however, is indistinguishable from that
of the inhabitants of the Rhine valley and the lands to the
west, whereas it is clearly marked off from that of the Germanic
peoples further north. We must return to this group of people
later when considering the relations between the Celts and the
Germans.

The invasions and temporary occupation of Germania up to
the Elbe by the Augustan armies greatly increased knowledge of
the western and northern Germanic peoples. Army officers will

have brought back to Italy first-hand accounts of the barbarian tribes and the dramatic increase in trade contacts between the Roman world and the north (see p. 35) opened up wide areas for the first time. The new knowledge was utilized by Livy, whose Book civ, now lost, contained a description of Germany, and by the Greek Strabo, whose *Geography* fortunately survives. Augustus' friend and lieutenant Marcus Agrippa presumably included data on Germania in the material on which the famous world map was to be based, but, apart from the fact that the Vistula was now known, we have only the sketchiest idea of what the Roman map of Germania looked like in the reign of Augustus.

During the first century A.D. the flow into the literate world of knowledge about the northern peoples was constant as diplomatic and trading contacts developed. A most regrettable loss from this period are all the twenty books of the Elder Pliny's *German Wars*. Pliny had served on both the lower and the upper

Fig. 2   The major Germanic peoples about A.D. 100

Rhine frontiers and his indefatigable curiosity about everything
no doubt made his books a vast store of information about
barbarian institutions, customs and culture. The work was probably a major source of the information supplied by Tacitus in
the most extensive and important surviving ancient text which
treats of the early Germans, the *Germania*. The publication of the
*Germania* in A.D. 98 is the high water mark of written sources
on the early Germanic peoples. Renaissance scholars called it a
Golden Book, and it remains so for anyone interested in the early
history of Europe. There is no need to describe here this extraordinary work and stress, as many others have, its outstanding
importance for the student of Germanic society and tribal
geography[22] (fig. 2). It will be assumed that the reader has read the
book, and preferably keeps it at hand.

After the *Germania*, the documentary sources fall away drastic-
ally in quality. From the middle of the second century we have
one of the most ambitious and comprehensive of ancient geographical works, the *Geography* of Claudius Ptolemaus, or Ptolemy, who worked in Alexandria.[23] His book, of which there is
still no well edited text, consists mainly of lists of places and
tribes, the places being given their latitude and longitude, so that
an overall map of a kind can be drawn up. Whether Ptolemy
himself actually published maps to accompany the *Geography* is
uncertain. Although the work undoubtedly contains much that
was new, even the sections dealing with the Mediterranean lands
contain many glaring errors, so that we can scarcely expect an
accurate account of northern Europe. The text locates major
rivers only by their sources and their mouths, and positions
tribes, sixty-nine of which are mentioned, 'above' and 'below'
them. Of the ninety-five places, or *poleis* (cities), which are named,
most are named by no other source so that it is particularly
regrettable that the positions given by Ptolemy are not reliable.
Not surprisingly, modern scholars have taken Ptolemy to task.
Schütte, for example, thought that many of the names listed
were inventions, doublets or garbled forms. This is too hard a
judgement on a scholar living in remote Alexandria, although it
contains a fair amount of truth. A high proportion of the tribal
names are supported by the evidence of Tacitus and Pliny, and
most of those which lack that support are credible name forms.
It is much more difficult to leap to the defence of the places
although even here there is an occasional gleam of improving

knowledge. The best instance of this is the place *Kalisia*, which Ptolemy places near the source of the Vistula. This should be Kalisz in central Poland (though this is not near the Vistula), an identification now supported by unusually good archaeological testimony.[24]

On the whole the reader is struck by the looming deficiencies of Ptolemy's lists rather than by anything else. The course of the Rhine was imperfectly understood, for the sharp northward bend on the upper course is omitted, as is Lake Constance. The Vistula is given a hopelessly short course and rises in a non-existent or misplaced mountain range. The Baltic coast is shown to run due east–west and 'Scandia' is shown as a small island. Other islands placed in the North Sea do not really exist. But inadequate as the maps constructed on Ptolemy's data must be, the *Geography* remains the latest extensive source for the geography of northern Europe available to us. After the mid-second century, the curtain descends and when it lifts once more, it is upon a changed scene. The later second and third centuries were a period of upheaval and movement. Major new groupings of people emerged and the beginnings of the great migrations may be sensed. Unfortunately, the sources available to us for this period are no match for these themes. The civilized world had little idea of what was happening in Germania beyond the clear fact that it spelled potential disaster. The third century is the Dark Age of northern Europe.

With the fourth century, we are again on surer ground, chiefly due to the surviving books of Ammianus Marcellinus' Roman history.[25] These are of immense importance for the light they throw on the frontiers, the relations between Romans and Germans, and on the contests with the Franks and Alamanni. Ammianus was personally acquainted with the problems besetting the Rhine frontier in particular, and thus gives a clear, soldierly view of what was going on. The state of Gaul in the late Empire is particularly well known, thanks to the remarkable flowering of poetry and letters in the late fourth and fifth centuries. Ausonius and Sidonius Apollinaris[26] tell us a good deal about relations between the Gallo-Romans and the barbarian intruders, but little about Germanic society and culture. A valuable source for Visigothic society at this time is the *Passion of St Saba*.[27] Later writers, if used with care, can reveal much about the barbarians at the time of the late Empire. Procopius contains much of value on barbarian warfare and a little on other matters, and Agathias has a most useful excursus on the Franks.[28] But with the sixth century, much had changed within the order that Tacitus had described. A few much later authors, such as Adam of Bremen and Saxo Grammaticus, occasionally provide information which is strikingly parallelled in earlier sources, some of it, of course, being citation. By and large, however, it is safer to suppose that what early medieval writers say about the Germanic peoples proves nothing for the Roman Iron Age.

### Germans and Rome

Julius Caesar's conquest after 58 B.C. of the rich lands of Gaul could only be secured if a satisfactory frontier could be established against the barbarians east of the Rhine. The problem was already serious when Caesar arrived, for those barbarians, notably the Suebi and their allies under Ariovistus, had no intention of accepting the Rhine as a frontier between themselves and the Gauls and indeed a considerable number of them were already ensconced west of the upper Rhine. Caesar's main task on the north-east frontier of Gaul was therefore to break the growing power of Ariovistus and his Suebic confederacy west of the Rhine. He had no serious intention of advancing eastward. In fact, such an advance was not within his power. His two crossings of the Rhine (in 55 and 53 B.C.) were little more than raids, another 'first' for this collector of 'firsts'.

The form of the Roman frontier system on the Rhine in Caesar's day and for thirty years afterwards remains unknown. No permanent bases of the period 50–20 B.C. have yet been revealed either by excavation or by air photography. Probably the line was held by auxiliary troops for the most part, the legions remaining in the interior of Gaul. Here and there, there are signs that friendly barbarians were settled in strategic situations to assist in the defence of the frontier. The barbarian community at Diersheim across the Rhine from Strasbourg,[29] for example, must have been settled there with the consent or the encouragement of Roman officers.

After 19 B.C. the attention of Rome again turned towards the peoples east of the Rhine. The intent was no longer to establish a defensive frontier along the Rhine, but to invade and occupy a huge area to the north-east of that valley.[30] The armies of Augustus had secured the Alpine passes by 15 B.C. and forts were then established on the territory of the Helvetii. Shortly afterwards the legions were moved up to the Rhine. Their destination was the Elbe and the next four campaigning seasons were spent in the pursuit of this goal. The river was reached and crossed in 9 B.C. and the Romans then set about the fearsome task of occupying the vast territory they had overrun. Roman discipline and organization were kept at full stretch by opportunist German tactics, and their commissariat taxed to the limit by the immense and arduous terrain. The invader had to bring with him his own supplies and blaze his own roads. Large as the Roman armies were, they could not take full control of the whole territory between Rhine and Elbe. The scale of the task which Augustus had undertaken must have been all too clear long before the loss of three legions in A.D. 9. It must also by then have been clear that there was little or nothing to gain by the occupation of the lands east of the Rhine. After further campaigns in A.D. 14–16, Tiberius, who knew the area at first hand, cut Rome's losses in Germany and pulled the armies back to the lower and middle Rhine.

After this time there were never again serious attempts to reduce to Roman control large areas east of the Rhine and north of the upper Danube. But the Roman High Command faced a major problem in the huge re-entrant between the upper courses of those two rivers and the only possible solution lay in annexation. The emperor Domitian began the systematic garrisoning of the area immediately beyond the middle Rhine after a great offensive against the Chatti in 83–5, and to these campaigns belong the origins of the great artificial frontier which, in its developed form, was to link the Rhine north of Coblenz with the Danube valley near Regensburg. This *limes* was, like Hadrian's Wall in northern Britain, a strongly garrisoned line of demarcation, and not a barrier which would have to be constantly defended. The area immediately in front of the *limes*, which consisted in its ultimate form of an earth bank, palisade and ditch, was also under military surveillance, as was the strip of territory immediately east of the lower Rhine, and the barbarians settled in these areas may well have been bound by some treaty relationship similar to that resorted to by the Romans in the late Empire.

The Rhine–Danube *limes* was one of the shorter-lived of Roman frontiers. It weathered the Marcomannic Wars of 166–75 and 178–80, but new groupings of barbarians resulted in the emergence of powerful new enemies. Early in the third century the Alamanni began their raids and were with difficulty held off. From 231 their attacks were incessant and devastating. The frontier garrisons were progressively weakened by the withdrawal of troops to deal with emergencies elsewhere and ultimately, in 259–60,[31] the Alamanni and their confederates compelled the Romans to evacuate the frontier and abandon the area behind it (the *agri decumates*). The barbarians had destroyed a Roman frontier on the continent of Europe for the first time.

The river frontiers of Rhine and Danube were much more difficult to breach. Indeed, the Germans were less concerned with destroying them than with raiding the rich lands behind and settling there if possible. The middle and lower Rhine was in the mid-third century exposed to the people known as the Franks. Roman writers were never quite sure who the Franks were and where they had originated. Probably the Franks themselves had no clear ideas about this either, for their own traditions, as recorded by Gregory of Tours, are clearly of no great antiquity. The Franks were a loose confederacy of several tribes welded together during a time of change in tribal geography in the early third century. Possibly an early impetus was given to the new grouping by the real chance of rich pickings as the Roman frontiers began to show signs of strain. The Franks demonstrated their growing power to terrifying effect in the 270s when they fell upon the provinces of Gaul. There were virtually no garrisons to confront them and few towns with walls. Gaul suffered more in material damage at this time than she did at the breakdown of Roman rule in the fifth century.

Like most of the barbarians with whom earlier Roman provincial administrators had had to deal, the Franks came seeking land and a livelihood. Some of them won possession of land within the Imperial frontiers by gaining recognition as federates (*foederati*). Other barbarians were settled on the land as semi-free peasants (*laeti*) in areas devastated in the late third century.[32] Many others entered the Roman army and some found their way to the highest ranks (see p. 34).

It is now a commonplace that long before the final collapse of Roman authority in the Rhineland, the provinces behind had received a very substantial influx of barbarians. These immigrants learnt to value many things in their new homes. They may have come seeking land but they found much else: better homes, secure supplies of food, the amenities and allurements of town life. Small wonder that the Franks maintained several of the established Roman industries when they became masters of the Rhineland, principally the production of wine, glass-making and the manufacture of wheel-made pottery. Some of them found city life much to their taste. Later, fifth-century Cologne and Trier may be described as Romano–Frankish communities, with some of the old public buildings being converted to the seats of Frankish leaders. At Cologne, for instance, one of the halls inside the Roman governor's palace became the residence of a barbarian leader,[33] though not necessarily as early as the fifth century. Late in the day these barbarians were becoming Romanized. Prolonged contact with the frontier provinces had taught them something of Roman values and they prized these highly.

From the times of first contact between the barbarian peoples of the Rhine and Danube lands and the expanding power of Rome, large numbers of barbarian warriors willingly took service with the Roman army. Julius Caesar used Germanic auxiliaries during his campaigns in Gaul and thereafter Roman rulers continued to find service for barbarians in all parts of the Empire. In the early days, separate bands of barbarians were often organized as individual units and led by their own chiefs, as were the Batavians serving under their chieftain Chariovalda in the army of Germanicus. From the time of Augustus to the late first century A.D. the outsiders were enrolled in auxiliary *alae* and cohorts named after their tribes, but from the Flavian period, if not earlier, they were increasingly employed in the general run of auxiliary formations. Picked men also formed the emperor's bodyguard (*corpore custodes*) from the time of Augustus to the reign of Galba and again from the early third century. Their influence went far beyond that of the hired thug. In later times this corps from time to time formed a useful political counterweight to the influence of the Praetorian Guard. Aside from the enrolment of groups of Germans, there was a constant stream of individual entrants into the Imperial service and some of these were men of influence in their tribes. Not infrequently they returned to their own people after years of service in the Imperial forces, and several demonstrated what apt pupils they had been of Roman military discipline and organization by prosecuting vigorous anti-Roman policies. The most effective of Rome's opponents in the first century of Empire were German war-

B

leaders who had learnt their craft with the Roman army: Maroboduus, Arminius, Gannascus, Civilis. The practice of employing such chieftains did also work to Rome's benefit sometimes. A chief of the Ampsivarii, Boiocalus, fought in the Roman army under Tiberius and Germanicus, in all serving the Romans faithfully for fifty years.

From the later second century the number of barbarians in the Imperial forces increased appreciably. Marcus Aurelius was compelled by the pressures on the Danube frontier to stiffen his armies with drafts from the very barbarians who were presenting the threat. As well as the Germans who were now enrolled in auxiliary formations, huge droves of barbarians, including prisoners taken in the Marcomannic Wars, were settled in lands which had been devastated by the plague. The succession of third-century rulers raised forces where they could, and a ready supply lay just beyond the frontiers. Aurelian began again the practice of raising purely German units and opened the way to still freer access by barbarians in the reigns of Diocletian and Constantine.

The new field army which emerged from the reforms of Constantine consisted primarily of highly mobile infantry, the successors of the largely barbarian auxiliaries of the third century. German tribal names now loom large among contingents of the field army and the numbers of Germans continued to increase during the fourth century until the greater part of the regular army was composed of barbarian troops.[34] The officer ranks too, including the highest posts, were open to men from beyond the frontiers. Despite the anti-barbarian feeling of many senators, the great names among the generals of fourth-century courts are German: Merobaudes under Valentinian I and Gratian, Bauto under Valentinian II, Arbogast, Stilicho. Some twenty Germans are known with certainty to have attained the rank of *magister militum* during this century, and the true total was probably much higher. We naturally cannot know how many members of the officer corps were actually brought into the Empire from outside, but the proportion was clearly very high. Franks and Alamanni appear to have been the most prominent element in military circles down to the time of Theodosius I. Thereafter, Goths and their associates came more into favour, until, about 400, a general anti-barbarian reaction in the eastern Empire dislodged many Germans from the highest posts.[35]

Beyond the frontiers the Romans were always prepared, and often anxious, to establish treaty relations with the barbarians who lay immediately outside. It was hoped that these treaties would help to build a screen against the remoter peoples and deter the immediate neighbours of the frontier provinces from raiding them. In return, the barbarian chieftains received Imperial recognition, often an asset in the shifting fortunes of tribal politics, subsidies in the form of money or precious gifts, and the promise of protection against their neighbours. These federate peoples (*foederati*) could be called upon to supply troops for particular campaigns or emergencies. As early as the second century, barbarian groups were from time to time settled within the Empire, whether they were federates or not, often on land which had been depopulated by warfare or pestilence. In the later fourth century federates were increasingly employed as the manpower of the regular army declined and as it became more and more difficult to prevent barbarian groups from crossing the frontiers and seizing territory on which to settle. Once they had established themselves within the Empire, the Romans found it expedient to use them in their armies, since, left to their own devices, they would surely create mischief.

Roman traders did not wait until an area had been annexed to the Empire before they began to exploit its commercial potential. Already before Caesar crossed the Rhine in 55 B.C., venturesome businessmen were plying a busy trade among the peoples of Germania. 'The Suebi give access to traders, to secure buyers for what they have captured in war rather than to satisfy any craving for imports.'[36] Caesar adds that they would not allow wine to be imported, 'believing that men are thereby rendered too soft and womanish to endure hardship'. Not all barbarians felt able to adopt this hard line on Mediterranean wine, and certain other luxury goods produced by the Empire had an immediate appeal for many of the wealthier barbarians.

Presumably this traffic in luxuries was welcomed by both sides. To the Roman traders a vast new market was opened up, while the Germans themselves were not slow to develop their commercial activities. Some peoples did so more readily and with more success than others. The Hermunduri beyond the upper Danube traded with Romans not only on the Danube bank but deep inside the Roman province of Raetia at the town of *Augusta Vindelicum* (Augsburg). 'They come over when they please and without a guard. To other peoples we only show off our arms and our camps. To them we display our palaces and our villas and they do not covet them.'[37] Although Tacitus' words imply that the Hermunduri were the only Germans to establish trading contacts of this kind in the first century A.D., this was certainly not the case. The Marcomanni in Bohemia were in the earlier first century engaged in a lively trade across the Roman frontier, as archaeology clearly testifies, and no doubt enterprising traders from other tribes were not slow to seize the new opportunities.

Some of the trade routes used in this early period can be mapped. The most famous were the tracks known collectively as the Amber Route. This led from *Aquileia* in north Italy to the Danube in the vicinity of *Carnuntum* and *Vindobona* (Vienna). Thence, two ancient tracks led northwards to the upper valley of the Oder: the better known of these was the road up the valley of the March from *Carnuntum*. The two tracks converged near the modern Polish town of Kalisz, fairly certainly to be identified as the *Kalisia* mentioned by Ptolemy, and from here the route led into the lower valley of the Vistula and on to the Baltic shore of Poland. In the same valley the Amber Route was joined by tracks running along the valleys of the Bug and the Dniestr, thus establishing a link between the lands bordering the Black Sea and the Baltic shores. A westward branch of the system led by way of the Oder across Pomerania and thence into Denmark, the Baltic islands and Sweden. There were several other approaches into free Germany, for merchants as well as Roman expeditionary forces. Two further routes led eastwards from the Rhine up the Lippe and the Main towards the Weser and the Elbe, meeting in Thuringia a track running northward from Bohemia. Coastal trade may also have played an important role, although archaeology will rarely reveal it. The Frisians, who were to prove themselves skilled seamen in early medieval Europe, and the Chauki were probably the leaders in this traffic.

Not all areas of Germania shared equally in the traffic with the Roman world.[38] As was noted earlier, the Hermunduri and Marcomanni took a leading part in these activities, but probably at different times, the Marcomanni in the early decades of the first century A.D., the Hermunduri later. Trade between Bohemia and Italy seems to have lapsed or seriously declined in the later first century, no doubt as a result of fresh markets opening in western and northern Europe. Roman imports remained incon-

spicuous in Bohemia until the later fourth century, by which time
the political scene had been transformed by the threat of the Huns.

The peninsula of Denmark and the adjacent islands evidently
had much to offer the Roman world, for the soil of Jutland,
Zealand, Fyn and Laaland has yielded up an astonishing wealth
of Roman silverware, bronze, glass and pottery vessels, especially
from the first two centuries A.D. Presumably the highly prized
amber of Jutland made a substantial contribution to the wealth
of the peninsula, but other commodities must have been available
to attract so many southern goods. It is difficult to see what these
were, apart from agricultural products and slaves.

A third major market area for Roman goods in the early
Empire was the lower valley of the Vistula and the adjacent coast.
The most conspicuous objects of trade in this region were bronze
buckets, bowls and skillets, and silver and bronze coins. Again,
amber from the coast was the attraction, followed by, one may
guess, slaves and possibly furs. An episode recorded by the Elder
Pliny suggests that most of the amber trade was conducted by
Germanic traders. In the reign of Nero, a Roman merchant
charged with the task of equipping gladiatorial shows for the
emperor made the journey to the Baltic lands. He visited native
commercial agencies and brought back with him among his other
acquisitions a great stock of amber.[39] Obviously, this man was a
pioneer and there is no evidence that his enterprise led to a
Roman takeover of the Baltic amber trade. The collection and
transport of amber from the Baltic coast was in full swing before
the end of the first century B.C., and this must have been the work
of Germanic traders, perhaps operating with the Baltic peoples.
Three pits containing in all 28 cwt of amber in a settlement near
Breslau give some impression of the scale of the enterprise before
any Roman trader came upon the scene.

In the late Empire trade contacts with other areas are evident.
Glassware and bronzes were now coming up the valleys of the
Dniestr and Bug from the Black Sea hinterland, that melting-pot
of many cultures, Greek, Goth, Sarmatian and Slav. Several
regions imported little from the Mediterranean. One of these
was southern Sweden and Norway, which in the earlier Roman
period received only humble pottery, glass vessels and coins.
In the late Empire this situation changed and high-quality bronzes
and glass began to reach the peninsula, reflecting new movements
of trade.

The categories of goods imported by the Germans were varied. The most striking are the items of Graeco–Roman silverware, and the occasional vessel of gold, found in hoards like that from Hildesheim and in the graves of chieftains and their families.[40] Tacitus protests that although the Germans possessed silver vessels, they held them of no higher account than vessels of pottery. It is impossible to reconcile this with the finds of superb silverware in Germania and Tacitus' statement must be seen as a Roman cliché of barbarian contempt for the civilized life. Some of the silver objects acquired by Germanic leaders, whether by trade, plundering raids or as diplomatic gifts, are among the finest examples of the silversmith's craft to survive from antiquity. From a superb range it is necessary to mention only the treasure from Hildesheim and the cups from the Hoby grave.

The quality of the imported bronzeware is also high, including a multitude of items from Campanian factories as well as from workshops nearer the frontiers. The greater part of this fine metalwork consists of bronze containers for liquor, especially wine: buckets, bowls, skillets, jugs, strainers and ladles, all the furniture of the chronic feasting in which the warrior retinues submerged themselves. To the early Empire belong fine buckets of several types and skillets with opposed swans' heads at the end of the handle. Later, the varied forms of bucket gave way to bowls and wine-pails with fluted sides and to the well known 'Hemmoor' type of bucket. The last-named was probably made in the frontier provinces: the Aachen and Cologne areas have been suggested. The fluted vessels are not so easy to place and may not be products of the Empire at all, but have issued from the fertile workshops of the Black Sea coast. Many other elegant table vessels crossed the frontiers to grace feasts in Jutland, the Elbe basin and Thuringia: shallow basins, handled bowls, trays and jugs with elaborately decorated handles. All this recalls the import of Greek and Etruscan metal wares into the Celtic world in the fifth and fourth centuries B.C., and like that earlier traffic must be associated with the import of southern wine.[41]

An essential accessory to metalwork of this high quality was fine glassware from which the wine might be drunk, and this too is well represented, especially in the Baltic islands and along the coast between the Elbe and Vistula. Glass vessels did not form a common feature of Roman trade in free Germany until the heyday of the provincial factories, notably that of Cologne, and thus the bulk of the finds of glass date from the third and fourth centuries. Among these are some of the most splendid products of the glass factories, for instance drinking cups with painted human and animal figures.

Unfortunately, not enough attention has yet been paid to the more humdrum objects which passed into Germania, so that it is not yet possible to estimate how lively the trade in mundane items actually was. The great number of finds of such things as pottery, especially *terra sigillata*, brooches and other kinds of ornaments, iron tools and instruments, weapons, and even so basic an item as the domestic quern (imported from the lava quarries of the Eifel) gives the impression that the Roman contribution to daily affairs was profound. One or two surprising imports have been recorded, the most remarkable being a complete set of Roman surgical instruments found in a grave of the late Roman Iron Age at Aschersleben near Halle.[42]

It is worth making a clear distinction between the luxury goods which penetrated deep into free Germany and those of humbler character which tend to be found closer to the Roman frontiers. To the latter category belong the thousands of Roman coins, including more than 400 hoards, found in Germania.[43] Tacitus commented on the barbarian possession of Roman currency so that we have a rare opportunity of testing the statement of a Roman author against archaeological statistics.

The Germans nearest us value gold and silver for their use in trade, and recognize and prefer certain types of our money. The peoples of the interior stick to the old ways and employ barter. They like money that is old and familiar, *denarii* with the notched edge and the two-horsed chariot design [i.e. *denarii* struck in late Republican times]. They also try to get silver in preference to gold.[44]

The archaeological evidence supports what Tacitus says on almost all these points. Republican *denarii* were certainly favoured by the barbarians, reasonably enough since they contained more silver than those of the early Empire. We might add that they also greatly preferred the *denarii* struck before Nero's coinage reform of A.D. 64 to later issues for the same reason. In hoards ending with early second-century coins, pre-Neronian silver coins are often commoner than those of the later first century. On the circulation of gold coinage, archaeology again supports Tacitus. Gold issues of the early Empire are rare in Germania, and it was not until the massive Imperial subsidies to barbarian leaders in the fourth and fifth centuries that this situation was radically changed.

The distribution of early Imperial coins is fully in accord with the distinction drawn by Tacitus between the peoples near the Roman frontiers, who used the imported currency as a means of

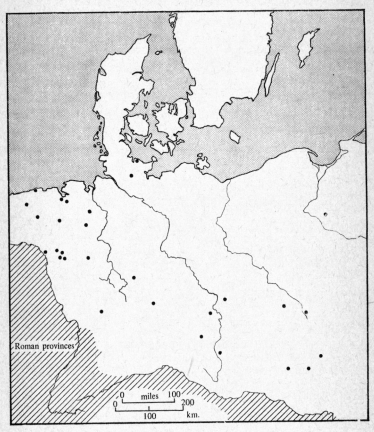

Fig. 3    Distribution of Roman coin hoards of the first century A.D. in Germania

exchange, and the remoter barbarians, who preferred barter. When the coin hoards of the first century A.D. are mapped, it is apparent that almost all of them lie within a belt some 200km wide immediately in front of the Rhine–Danube line (fig. 3).[45] It was not until the second century that coinage began to penetrate northward into the Danish peninsula and Sweden. This is all the more surprising in view of the quantity of luxury goods reaching the north as early as the reign of Augustus. This evidence definitely indicates that in the areas closer to the frontiers Roman coinage was appreciated as a means of exchange, whereas barbarians further removed from regular contact with Roman traders accepted coinage for its bullion worth, as a material from which fine ornaments might be made.

Not all the goods exported by the Romans into Germania have left traces which the archaeologist can expect to discover. The export of food from the Empire to the northern peoples was of great importance to them. In the late fourth century, grain was included among the subsidies paid by the Romans to keep the Visigoths quiet, and this practice had been established much earlier. The importance of the trade in food supplies to the barbarians is well illustrated by the events of a war in which Valens engaged the Visigoths (A.D. 369). The Roman emperor ceased all trade with the Visigoths and by this means reduced them to such hardship that their resistance quickly crumbled.[46] A similar tactic was later employed by the Romans, again with success, when they blockaded the Visigothic settlers in Gallia Narbonensis and starved them into defeat.

Information is sketchy about goods and commodities travelling from Germania into the Roman world. The trade in amber has already been mentioned. Though important, it will scarcely weigh in the balance against the flood of Roman imports. The coastal areas of northern Germany and Holland, and perhaps the Jutland peninsula, could offer supplies of animal products and these may have been exchanged for the Roman goods found in the native settlements. The Romans were always interested in acquiring such supplies, as the terms of the tribute they imposed upon subject peoples like the Frisians show.[47] Another important export from Germania was that of slaves, possibly the most costly export commodity which the barbarians could offer. Although slavery was not highly developed among the Germanic peoples, prisoners taken in inter-tribal warfare could be easily and profitably disposed of in the Roman frontier provinces. In the late Empire the main Visigothic export seems to have been slaves, including concubines of both sexes, agricultural labourers and domestic servants.[48] The traffic was organized, however, not by the barbarians themselves, but by slave-traders and Roman officers commanding the garrisons on the Danube.

These trade contacts not only affected to a certain extent the material lives of the northerners. They also contributed to the shaping of later events. Apart from providing furniture for the feasts of chieftains and domestic equipment which German craftsmen could copy but not invent, the northern peoples recognized from Roman imports that beyond the Roman frontiers lay a treasure-house, no remote El Dorado but well within their reach. A most potent influence was thus being exerted upon the Germans from an early date by Roman commercial activity, turning their faces towards the south and the wealth of the Empire.

## Germans and Celts

The relations of the Celts with the Germanic peoples have stimulated a major controversy with a rapidly growing literature of its own.[49] There is space to air only a few of the more important aspects of the controversy here.

The scanty evidence offered by Hekataios and Herodotos combines to show that by the later sixth century B.C. the Celts were a clearly recognizable major group of barbarian peoples inhabiting the region about the upper Danube and parts at least of France and Spain. The richly furnished cemetery found at Hallstatt in Austria has given its name to the robust culture centred on this region, a culture which introduced the extensive use of iron into central and western Europe. Some philologists would accept the bearers of the Urnfield cultures of the middle and later Bronze Age as Celtic-speaking, thus taking the Celts back half a millennium or more, but this is not certain. Whether or not the Urnfielders were Celts or proto-Celts, the society which the archaeological record outlines in the late Bronze Age is akin in its fundamentals to the barbarian societies later described by Caesar and Tacitus. Despite the many regional differences, barbarian Europe between the eighth and first centuries B.C. displays a marked homogeneity in such basics as economy, social structure and kingship. Celts and Germans were of course derived from the same Indo-European stock.

What of the later spread of the Celts and their dealings with the Germanic peoples? From the fifth century B.C. it is possible to detect the origins of a new phase in the Celtic cultures, named after the lakeside settlement of La Tène on Lake Neuchâtel. The heartland of this culture early comprised an area which reached from the upper Danube over the middle Rhine and into the Marne basin of north-eastern France. Ultimately, the Celtic La Tène culture was to cover most of western Europe from Spain to the Channel and beyond, and from the Bay of Biscay to southern Poland. Beyond the limits of the Celtic world proper the influence

| | | |
|---|---|---|
| – – – – – Northward limit of -apa river-names | ● | La Tène oppidum |
| | ⊗ | Late La Tène cart burial |
| —·—·—·— Northward limit of La Tène culture | ◎ | Other finds |

Fig. 4   Germans and Celts

of La Tène craftsmen was felt in Germany east of the Rhine, in Scandinavia, Poland, and far to the east among the peoples of the lower Danube. Our immediate concern is particularly with those areas where Celts encountered Germans.

One of the most fruitful meeting grounds of Celts and Germans was Bohemia. A Celtic culture flourished here from Hallstatt times and continued throughout the La Tène period. The most striking features of Celtic power at its height in this region are the superb iron weapons and tools, and the great *oppida* of the later phases of La Tène: Stradoniče and Zavist in Bohemia, Stare Hradisko in Moravia. Among the middle and late La Tène cultures there are several groups which betray close links with cultures centred on areas further north in east Germany and Poland, for example the Kobyly and Podmokly groups of northern Bohemia.[50] These were probably Germanic in origin but were strongly influenced by Celtic technology, especially in iron-working. Later references in classical writers give names to some of the Celtic tribes situated in these regions. From Poseidonios we learn that the tribe of the Boii were settled about the Hercynian forest (probably in southern Bohemia) as early as the late second century B.C. But this had long been their seat and their lengthy association with the region is commemorated in the very name of Bohemia (*Boiohaemum* to the Romans). Further north, in northern Bohemia and Moravia, lay the Volcae Tectosages who took part in the great Celtic expedition against Greece in 279 B.C., and also in Moravia were settled the Cotini, Celtic-speakers who long remained subject to the Sarmatians and to the Germanic Quadi and who worked iron deposits for their masters.[51]

It has long been recognized that the inhabitants of Bohemia and Moravia played a major part in the development and dissemination of certain industrial techniques, especially connected with the working of iron, from the third century B.C. Extensive iron-working centres were established in at least four areas in Bohemia: around Nové Strašecí, around Prague, in the foothills of the Ore mountains and in southern Bohemia. In Moravia there were further important workings about Brno and Prostějov. Precisely who was responsible for the promotion of this unusually large-scale industry is unknown, but the Boii may well have played the crucial role. The fact stands out that when Germanic settlers, in the form of the Marcomanni of Maroboduus, entered Bohemia in force late in the first century B.C., they came into close contact with people whose skill in producing good-quality iron weapons and implements was long established. The products of the Bohemian industrial centres, and no doubt some of the craftsmen too, could thereafter be dispersed throughout the Marcomannic realms, which at this time extended northward to the lower Elbe and Mecklenburg.

La Tène colonization was also directed north-eastwards to the Lusatian culture of south-west Poland. During the third century B.C. the trickle of Celtic imports—chiefly fibulae—became a steady flow. Some scholars have been so impressed by the bulk of this La Tène material in Poland that they have argued for Celtic immigrants as the agents. The idea is inherently plausible: the rich deposits of iron in southern Poland, together with the commerce in salt and amber, will scarcely have escaped notice by the enterprising Celts of Bohemia. But it is not yet possible to assess the intensity of Celtic colonization in the upper valleys of Oder and Vistula. Celtic elements in certain river names in southern Poland have been discerned by some philologists, but the matter is still controversial. Some mixing of La Tène and Germanic elements is only to be expected.[52] The clearest example is the mixed Puchov culture, which developed in northern Slovakia and southern Poland in the first century B.C. and survived until the early third A.D.

The area of Celto–German contact to which most attention has been paid is the Rhine valley. That the Rhine has figured so prominently in the discussion is rather because the Roman writers knew most about this fringe of the Germanic world than because it was an unusually significant meeting place of Celt and German. According to Julius Caesar and later Roman writers, the Celtic world marched with the Germanic along the Rhine. This frontier between Celts to the west and Germans to the east was accepted without question by the learned world until the late nineteenth century. The first criticism of Caesar's account (since it was Caesar who first drew this cultural boundary on the map of western Europe) was voiced by Müllenhoff in 1887.[53] He held that the 'Rhine frontier' between Celts and Germans was an invention of Roman writers and that the Celts extended far to the east of the river.

Müllenhoff appears to have been the first to draw attention to the potential value of place and river names in this connection. The names of the Elbe and the Weser seemed to him undoubtedly Germanic, whereas the Rhine, Lippe, Embscher, Main and Lahn appeared equally certainly Celtic. The numerous river and stream names of north-western Germany ending in *–apa*, *–afa*, *–efa* and the like, he identified as Celtic, deriving them from a Celtic word for river, *ab* (fig. 4). In the succeeding century, the *–apa* names have been at the centre of a heated debate, being claimed now as

Celtic, now as German. Some later scholars carried the argument much further than Müllenhoff. Karsten, for instance, argued that the name of the Weser was Celtic, comparing it with the French Vézère and the British Wear and Wye.[54] Fortified by declarations of this kind, the leading French archaeologist of the earlier twentieth century, Albert Grenier, envisaged a Celtic empire which may have embraced the Elbe valley and Jutland.[55] By and large, however, there was no unanimity among philologists about the frontier between Celts and Germans. Nor is there yet. But by 1960, it was clear that Caesar's cultural frontier along the Rhine could not be upheld. The archaeological evidence, too, clearly did not support a sharp cultural division along the Rhine valley. On the contrary, such late La Tène II and III phenomena as hill-forts, coinage, brooches and wheel-made pottery indicated the closest of cultural connections between east and west (fig. 4). The archaeological evidence cannot, however, be definite on the ethnic situation to east and west of the Rhine. For that we must turn to the evidence of philology.

A major development in this field during the past fifteen years has been due to the work of Professor H. Kuhn on the river and place names of north-western Germany.[56] Not all of Kuhn's deductions have been accepted by his fellow philologists, but there is no doubt that his work has placed the entire subject of the relations between Celt and German on a new and surer footing. He argues that the northern limits of the names which are indubitably Celtic run on an east–west line from the mouth of the Somme to the Main valley. If so, this boundary should represent the northward limits of Celtic speech, though not necessarily of Celtic culture, in the first century B.C. To the east, in southern Germany, the evidence for the extent of Celtic names is much less full and it is thus far from clear where Celtic-speakers met Germans to the east of the Rhine. Kuhn suggests that the linguistic boundary lay north of the Erzgebirge, probably in Thuringia or Saxony, though the argument is not conclusive.

A still more significant and far-reaching conclusion drawn from Kuhn's recent work is the recognition that at the opening of the historical period there lay between Celts and Germans a third distinct block of people,[57] whose existence eluded ancient writers entirely. These people, according to Kuhn, spoke a language which was neither Germanic nor Celtic, or even Indo-European at all, but which had links with certain early names found in the

Mediterranean lands. The area covered by these people, as suggested by the names, reached from the river Aller in the east to the valley of the Oise in the west. At present, virtually nothing is known about this third grouping—the *Nordwestblock* as it has come to be known—apart from the fact of its existence. Before the advent of the Romans in north-western Europe, the territory of the *Nordwestblock* was being entered by German-speaking settlers. The regions east and north of the lower Rhine, and the Rhine valley itself, had certainly been settled by Germans by the second half of the first century B.C. Tribal names beginning in *Ch*–, those ending in *–varii*, and certain river names provide ample support for this. As examples of the tribal names, we may note the Chatti, Cherusci, Chamavi, Chattvarii, Angrivarii, Ampsivarii, Hasvarii. Among the river names one may pick out the German names for the Schelde (*Scaldis*) and the Waal (*Vahalis*). (The much discussed *–apa* names, and those in *–nt–*, are now classed as pre-Celtic by Kuhn, who also clearly demonstrates the zoning of these names from the Channel coast eastwards to well beyond the Rhine.) The chronology of the German advance into these regions will never be precisely outlined. The likeliest interpretation is still that the push westwards of the Suebi and their adherents in the earlier first century B.C. marked the first major penetrative movement. There are, however, grounds for thinking that as late as the Augustan campaigns at the end of that century the process of Germanization was not yet complete. The Romans may well have been aware of this change in the character of the barbarians who lay just beyond their bounds, and their concern probably helped promote the offensives of the Augustan generals.

The idea of a *Nordwestblock* between the Aller and Oise has its critics, especially among philologists, but the basic elements of Kuhn's argument deserve respect. Archaeology does not provide evidence for a separate cultural grouping which might represent the inhabitants of the *Nordwestblock*, but then there is no particular reason why it should do so. What the archaeological evidence does make clear is the cultural unity, in essentials, of the inhabitants of the Rhine valley and the region to the east in the first century B.C. This is an extremely important emendation of Caesar's text.

The region where Celto–German contact is most startlingly attested in the archaeological record is undoubtedly Denmark.[58]

Some of the finest of all the products of Celtic metalworkers have been found in Danish votive deposits, the most remarkable being the great cauldron from Brå in east Jutland (third or second century B.C.), the Gundestrup bowl (first century A.D.?), and the two handsome carts from Dejbjerg in west Jutland. The last-named are particularly interesting, for these cult objects from some Celtic workshop found their way to an area where a sacred cart is known from other evidence to have played an important role in a fertility cult. Brå and Dejbjerg demonstrate links with the western Celtic world. The celebrated silver bowl or cauldron found at Gundestrup (Himmerland) suggests another link, with the Celto–Sarmatian regions of the Carpathians and the north Pontus. This bowl has been seen as a Gaulish product, but it has closer stylistic affinities with gold and silver works from Thrace and Dacia. All these splendid objects have to do with matters of cult, and they are not the only pieces of evidence for Celtic influence on northern cults. A defended enclosure at Borremose (Jutland), dating from the later pre-Roman Iron Age, has within one corner a structure which recalls the Celtic *Viereckschanzen* of central Europe, while in central Germany there occur deep ritual shafts of a kind well known in Celtic Bavaria and France.

Denmark has produced much else to demonstrate close links with the Celtic world in the late pre-Roman and Roman Iron Age. A Celtic source is the most likely for the twenty or more mail garments in the Hjortspring votive deposit of about 200 B.C.[59] and the same may be true of the distinctive 'barley-corn' shield bosses in the same deposit. Spear-heads and short swords based on La Tène models also are recorded in the north, as are many La Tène II and III brooches and other ornaments. Traces of La Tène III influence on local pottery have been claimed, but not proved.[60]

It is difficult to explain why Celtic influence should have run so deep in Denmark. Much more appears to be involved than strong trading contacts, though this region continued to import exotic and costly goods during the earlier Roman period. More probably a major power-centre in the peninsula had established commerce at several levels, in ideas as well as in weapons and brides, with peoples to the south and west. An early stimulus to such contacts would of course be the great migration of the Cimbri. But the emphasis should be on a steadier traffic in ideas, based on diplomatic exchange and marriage alliances rather than the return of war-bands.

## Germans, Slavs and Balts

To the east of the Germans lay shadowy peoples little known to Roman writers. These were the ancestors of the medieval Slavs and Balts. As early as the fifth century B.C., Herodotos referred to a people called the Veneti, a name which recurs in the writers Pliny, Tacitus and Ptolemy. These Veneti, or Venedi, are usually considered to be proto-Slavs. In their material culture they appeared to Tacitus to be closer to the Germans than to their nomadic neighbours: in contrast to the nomads they built houses and fought on foot.[61] In the sixth-century writer Jordanes, the Venedi appear as the *Winidae* and in still later sources as *Wends*, the name generally applied to Slavs by the Germans. These early references are of little help in locating the different branches of the Slavs and they say hardly anything about early Slav culture and its relationship with that of the Germans.

The problem of Slav origins is not a field to be blithely entered by the non-specialist.[62] Some archaeologists, notably of the Polish school, advocate an original heartland between the Oder and Vistula. Others, including several earlier Russian scholars, have put forward an eastern origin, basing their argument on a series of early Slav river and place names about the middle Dniepr. To modern philologists, and to an increasing number of archaeologists, such views of a restricted area of origin appear improbable and have been abandoned in favour of an extensive region reaching from the Oder–Vistula area to the Dniepr. Others again think that the Slav homeland could not have extended east of the river Bug.

There is no greater degree of concord among archaeologists, and there is fierce debate over the archaeological cultures which might represent the earliest Slavs. About the beginning of the Christian era, the Zarubincy culture flourished in and about the Dniepr valley. To the west, between the Vistula and Oder, the equally extensive Przeworsk culture was established rather later. The latter should embrace several important Germanic peoples rather than Slavs; indeed earlier German scholars termed it the 'Vandal' culture. Modern Polish opinion sees a strong Slav element in the Przeworsk culture, but at the present time this is supported by the most slender archaeological evidence. In this book, the evidence of Tacitus and other ancient writers is followed and the peoples as far east as the Vistula are taken to be Germanic, though there may well have been an admixture of other elements, including proto-Slavs.

The Zarubincy culture has a much better claim to represent the proto-Slavs, if indeed any one archaeological culture may be singled out in this way and identified with a people. This culture was succeeded by the Černjachov, or Chernjakhovo, culture in the third century A.D. This was a mixed grouping occupying the basins of the Dniepr and Dniestr and embracing far more elements than the proto-Slav: Goth, Dacian, Sarmatian and even Black Sea Greek. The cultural unity of Černjachov was shattered by the irruption of the Huns about 375, and the period of tumult which followed did not end until after the breaking of Hun domination in the mid-fifth century. Thereafter, certain Slav cultural elements emerged in the area which had been occupied by the Černjachov culture.

Since the early Slavs are so elusive, evidence for contact between them and the Germanic peoples is difficult to isolate and interpret. Cultural borrowing presumably lies behind the considerable number of Germanic, especially Gothic, loan-words in the Slav languages. Several of the early Gothic borrowings by the Slavs include homely terms such as bread, dish, house. Others were taken from the sphere of war: sword, helmet, raid. Some of the west Germanic loan-words are also military: others are concerned with economic and administrative affairs.

Beyond the lower Vistula lay the tribes of the Balts whom Tacitus knew as the Aestii, patient cultivators and gatherers of amber on the shore of the Baltic Sea. The 'amber-island' of Pliny, *Glaesaria*,[63] most probably the Samland peninsula, was a meeting-place of Balt and German traders, and probably Romans too. These contacts with the Roman world as well as with other barbarian cultures led to a remarkable flowering of Baltic culture from the second century to the fifth. This culture, despite the trimmings lent it by exotic trade objects, was firmly based on arable farming. Tacitus' statement about the patient agriculture of the Aestii is fully borne out by the archaeological evidence.[64] Grain-storage pits are common finds in the settlements of the Balts from the second century onward, wheat, rye and millet being the common kinds of grain. Wealthier graves of the

Imperial period fill out the story, with their iron sickles, hoes, scythes, axes and even iron-tanged plough-shares.

### Germans and the nomadic peoples

At an early date, the Germanic tribes of eastern Europe encountered nomadic peoples pressing westward round the northern shore of the Black Sea. In the early Roman Iron Age the most numerous of these nomads were the various groups whom Graeco–Roman writers called the *Sarmatae*, successors of the Scythians and Cimmerians and, like them, originating on the Asiatic steppes. By 300 B.C. they had reached the Ural foothills, and in the first century B.C. one branch, the Sarmatae Iazyges, reached the valley of the Danube, eventually settling between the Danube and Theiss. Even when this more or less permanent area of settlement had been obtained, however, they continued their nomadic ways. From their new base they threatened the Roman frontier on the Danube, being joined in these enterprises by a branch of the Alans, another nomadic grouping.

The Alans were the most formidable of the Sarmatian peoples. From the Caspian steppe they had by the first century B.C. moved into the plains between the Don and the Caucasus and from there they attacked the coastlands of the Black Sea, Persia and the territories of the eastern Germanic tribes. All the steppe nomads were superlative horsemen and their numerous military successes were largely the result of their overwhelming cavalry supremacy. On more than one occasion the Romans found the Sarmatians more than a handful, and were keen to use several mounted units raised from those peoples in their own forces.

The last of the nomad peoples to sweep round the Black Sea shores were the most ferocious of all, the Huns.[65] Shortly after A.D. 370 these people descended upon the Ostrogoths settled between the Don and the Dniestr. Their neighbours to the west, the Visigoths, were the next to suffer, thousands of them fleeing to shelter in the Roman provinces south of the Danube. Sarmatians and Alans were drawn into the Hunnic train, and in the fifth century some of the eastern German tribes passed under their domination, until this was broken shortly after the death of Attila in 453. In only eighty years the Huns had come and gone.

The results of contact between the nomads and the Germans cannot yet be clarified in full detail. Socially and politically there seems to have been no symbiosis between one and the other. The most obvious and important influence lay in the sphere of fine metalworking. Nomadic art styles and metalworking techniques were transmitted to the Goths and other Germanic peoples settled in the Black Sea regions and were later spread westward during the middle and late Roman Iron Age. This was to be the most abiding legacy of the meeting of nomad and German in south-eastern Europe.

## References

1. *Germania*, 5. On this question, Jankuhn, H. (1963) and the same writer in Much, R. (1967), 109f. and Klose, O. (1966). Further, Schlüter, O. and August, O. (1958).

2. Most recently, and reasonably, by Mildenberger, G. (1972), 25. He suggests one to three million in all, but does not say to which period this figure pertains.

3. On eighteenth- and nineteenth-century views of the early Germans, W. Capelle, *Die Germanen im Frühlicht der Geschichte* (Leipzig, 1928), and K. von See, *Deutsche Germanen-Ideologie* (Frankfurt-am-Main, 1970).

4. Those views were expressed in many works over a long period. The following are only a selection: Kossinna, G. (1911), (1897), (1902) and (1936). On Kossinna's methods, Eggers, H. J. (1959), 247ff.

5. Kossinna, G. (1911), 17.

6. On these, La Baume, W. (1963), Schwantes, G. (1951).

7. Discussed by Wenskus R. (1961), 156ff. and J. de Vries, *Kelten und Germanen* (Berne, 1960), 45ff. Some scholars date the sound shifts to the early Roman Iron Age.

8. Hachmann, R. (1960), 117ff. K. Tackenberg in *Alt-Thüringen*, vi (1962–3), 403ff.

9. Conveniently in J. Neustupny, *Czechoslovakia* (London, 1961), 48, Hachmann, R. (1960), 113ff., Mähling, W. (1944), especially 222ff.

10. *de Bello Gallico* ii, 4.

11. Birkhan, H. (1970), 181ff.

12. The argument that Germanic elements had reached the lower Rhine by about 600 B.C. and that thereafter there were other thrusts into Gaul *before* the movements of the second and first centuries B.C. rested on equivocal archaeological evidence. That evidence has undergone revision and the argument can no longer be advanced.

13. *de Bello Gallico* i, 3–12.

14. Hachmann, R. *et al.* (1962), especially 29ff., 55ff. and 76ff.

15. Hachmann, R. (1970), especially 221ff.

16. Detlefsen, D. (1904–9) is basic to the subject. A useful survey of the written sources is J. O. Thomson, *History of Ancient Geography* (Cambridge, 1948), 230ff.

17 Now edited by L. Edelstein and I. G. Kidd (1972). See also Tierney, J. J. (1960).

18. Norden, E. (1959).

19. *de Bello Gallico* iv, 1–3; vi, 22, 29.

20. G. Walser, *Caesar und die Germanen* (Wiesbaden, 1956), 37ff. Hachmann, R. *et al.* 1962), 44ff.

21. H. Kuhn in Hachmann, R. *et al.* (1962), 105ff., especially 127ff. Kuhn, H. (1973).

22. Norden, E. (1959). R. Syme, *Tacitus* (Oxford, 1958), 127f. The best English edition is still that of J. G. C. Anderson (1938). An excellent German edition is Much, R. (1967), with archaeological commentary by H. Jankuhn. Convenient translation by H. Mattingly in *Tacitus, On Britain and Germany* (Harmondsworth, 1948).

23. Edited by C. Muller (1883 and 1901), with a parallel Latin translation, and by C. F. A. Nobbe (1843–5: reprinted 1966). See also Schütte, G. (1927). Map of Germania in J. O. Thomson, op. cit., 245, Fig. 32.

24 *Archaeology,* xxiv (1971), 156.

25. Ammianus Marcellinus, *Histories*, 3 vols., Ed. J. C. Rolfe, Loeb Classical Library.

26. Ausonius, 2 vols., Ed. H. G. Evelyn White, Loeb Classical Library. C. E. Stevens, *Sidonius Apollinaris and his Age* (Oxford, 1933). N. K. Chadwick, *Poetry and Letters in Early Christian Gaul* (London, 1953).

27. E. A. Thompson in *Historia,* iv (1955), 331ff. Text in *Analecta Bollandiana*, xxxi (1912), 161–300.

28. Procopius, *History of the Wars*, Ed. H. B. Dewing, Loeb Classical Library. There is no English version of the entire text of Agathias.

29. Nierhaus, R. (1966), 182ff.

30. The Augustan offensives have recently been exhaustively surveyed by Wells, C. (1972). On Roman frontiers in Germany, H. von Petriko-vits, *Das römische Rheinland* (Cologne and Opladen, 1960); Schön-berger, H. (1969).

31. Schönberger, H. (1969), 175ff.

32. On the Frankish settlement, Böhner, K. (1963); Roosens, H. (1967); Werner, J. (1958); on historical sources, C. Verlinden in *Trans. Royal Hist. Soc.*, series v, iv (1954), 1ff.

33. *Germania,* xxxiv (1956), 83ff. especially 94.

34. Jones, A. H. M. (1964), vol. ii, 619ff.

35. Waas, M. (1969); Stroheker, K. F. (1955) and (1961).

36. *de Bello Gallico* iv, 20.

37. *Germania* 41.

38. Eggers, H. J. (1951) is still basic on Roman imports. See also Majewski, K. (1960) for Poland, Sakař, V. (1970) for Bohemia.

39. Pliny, *Nat. Hist.* xxxvii, 45.

40. Nierhaus, R. (1969) on Hildesheim; La Baume, P. (1971) on finds in north-west Germany in general.

41. R. Joffroy, *L'Oppidum de Vix et la civilisation hallstattienne finale* (Paris, 1960), 142ff. S. Piggott, *Ancient Europe* (Edinburgh, 1965), 195f.

42. Laser, R. (1965).
43. Bolin, S. (1930) and (1926).
44. *Germania*, 5, 5.
45. Lüders, A. (1955).
46. Thompson, E. A. (1966), 14ff.
47. Tacitus, *Annals* iv, 72.
48. Ammianus Marcellinus xxii, 7, 8; xxxi, 5, 6.
49. Hachmann, R. *et al.* (1962); Schrickel, W. (1964); Kuhn, H. (1968); Birkhan, H. (1970).
50. Mähling, W. (1944); Hachmann, R. (1960), 113ff.
51. *Germania* 43, 2.
52. Jazdzewski, J. (1965), 135ff.
53. K. Müllenhoff, *Deutsche Altertumskunde*, ii (Berlin, 1887), 45.
54. T. E. Karsten, *Die Germanen* (Helsingfors, 1928), 89ff., cf. also G. Neckel, *Germanen und Kelten* (Heidelberg, 1929), 58.
55. A. Grenier, *Les Gaulois* (Paris, 1945), 89ff.
56. Hachmann, R. *et al.* (1962), 105ff. Kuhn, H. (1973).
57. Hachmann, R. *et al.* (1962), 127ff.
58. Klindt-Jensen, O. (1949), 41ff.
59. Rosenberg, G. (1937).
60. Klindt-Jensen, O. (1949), 53ff.
61. *Germania* 46, 1.
62. Recent general discussions are included in Vana, Z. (1970) and Gimbutas, M. (1971).
63. *Nat. Hist.* xxxvii, 42.
64. *Germania* 45, 2.
65. Thompson, E. A. (1948); Werner, J. (1956).

# 2 | The archaeological groupings

The archaeology of the early Germans, in particular the definition of the principal archaeological cultures found in their territories, is a subject of immense scope and complexity. This chapter is intended to identify the distribution areas of the various cultures and, wherever possible, the relations between them. The aim is not to equate those areas with the territories held by individual tribes or groups of tribes: this was a major goal of archaeologists in the period before about 1945 (see p. 20), but none of the identifications then confidently put forward are now widely accepted. Occasionally, in certain special circumstances, identification between a particular culture and a known tribal grouping may be near, as in the case of the March basin group which probably represents the tribe of the Quadi (see p. 78), but such cases are rare indeed. Normally archaeology will not assist us much with the mapping of tribal boundaries, or at the very best will be a halting guide. A tribal map of Germania will therefore not be established, and the positions of the major tribes in the early Roman Iron Age can be indicated only by the literary sources with all their shortcomings.[1]

In discussing the various cultures, more attention has been paid here to their pottery series than to such minor metal objects as brooches. The metalwork types, though they can make a certain contribution, appear to be of less value in delineating culture-provinces than the ubiquitous pottery. First, metalwork items could be and were transported over considerable distances, either directly by trade or indirectly by imitation, in a way in which common pottery was not. Secondly, in several areas fundamental study and publication of brooch types has not yet been carried out, whereas for most of Germania the broad outlines of the ceramic tradition are clear, although adequate type-series cannot yet be presented for all the proposed cultures.

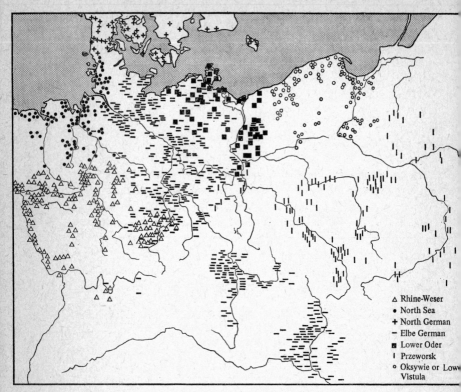

Fig. 5  Archaeological groupings of the earlier Roman Iron Age

*The Rhine–Weser region*

As was noted in Chapter 1 (see p. 46), the culture of the region
between Rhine and Weser, and the Lippe and the Main, was at
one in the first century B.C. with that of the Rhine valley and the
area to the west of that river. Between Rhine and Weser lay the
'barbarian-fringe' of the La Tène culture, as German archaeologists have none too felicitously termed it. Here there were the
same hill-forts that figured prominently in the settlement pattern
of Celtic lands, the same circulation of Celtic coinage, the same
use of currency bars, and a similar facies of wheel-made La Tène
pottery types as were current west of the Rhine. At the end of the
first century B.C. all these cultural elements vanished. The hill-
forts were almost all abandoned and not re-occupied. The
coinage rapidly went out of circulation. The wheel-made pottery

was quickly supplanted by a multiplicity of hand-made wares. The exploitation of local iron deposits, notably in the Sieg valley, abruptly ceased.[2]

There can be little doubt that these profound changes were brought about by a major migration of people into the region, and the areas from which they came fairly certainly included the Elbe basin and north-western Germany. The incoming settlers were Germanic, and they brought with them a less developed material culture than already existed in the La Tène regions east of the Rhine. They also introduced a Germanic language, which replaced the Celtic and pre-Celtic dialects spoken there. The tribal groups involved in this westward movement included the Chatti, who were not mentioned by Julius Caesar, probably the Cherusci, the Bructeri and a number of smaller peoples. There is no need to suppose that the newcomers drove out the earlier inhabitants: a peasant population is not easily uprooted in any circumstances, and on this occasion there will have been plenty of land to satisfy the intruders. Several extensive areas actually remained wholly or largely devoid of settlement throughout the Roman Iron Age, notably the higher ground between the Lippe and Ruhr, between the Main and Fulda, and the region east of the Taunus hills.

The culture which sprang from this mingling of pre-Germanic and Germanic populations extended from the Rhine valley to beyond the Weser, reaching the Hannover region in the north-east. To the south-east it reached still further, to the valley of the Saale, though it was later supplanted in this area by the Elbe German *Kreis*. A small number of find-spots lie immediately north of the Roman *limes* covering the Wetterau plain, and Germanic pottery occurs in some quantity in some of the frontier forts in this stretch (notably Zugmantel and the Saalburg) and also in the Wetterau itself. The most southerly occurrence of Rhine–Weser material is on the middle Main about Würzburg. Between the Ruhr and the Roman *limes*, scarcely any find-spots of the early Roman Iron Age have yet been mapped and even in the later stages of the Roman Iron Age this broken and wooded terrain remained largely devoid of inhabitants.

The forms of burial practised in the Rhine–Weser culture-province are similar to those of the coastal areas of north-west Germany. The common forms are the urn-grave, the *Brandgrube* and the *Brandschüttungsgrab*, invariably with very few or no

grave-goods apart from a single pot. One feature of a few ceme-
teries dating from the later pre-Roman Iron Age and the early
Roman period provides a link with funerary practices among the
La Tène cultures west of the Rhine. This was the placing of a

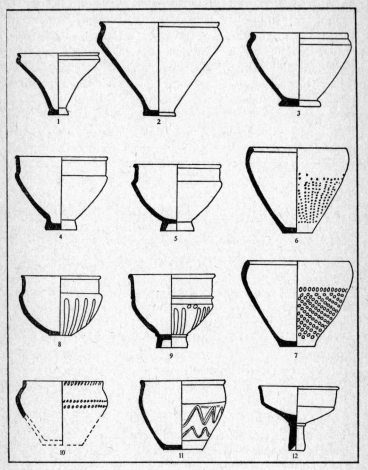

Fig. 6    Pottery types of the Rhine–Weser group

grave, or graves, within a square or rectangular ditched enclosure,
recalling the *Grabgärten* of the Eifel and other La Tène burial
enclosures in northern Gaul. Large cemeteries on the lines of those
of the coastal areas and the Elbe basin are unknown, and most of
the available material has been recovered from remarkably small

groups of graves. *Fürstengräber* are unrecorded and even moderately well furnished graves are not common.

The pottery of the Rhine–Weser *Kreis* is clearly marked off from that of the neighbouring Elbe Germans and the coastal groups by its forms and the poverty of its ornament[3] (fig. 6). Incised linear ornament and the maeander patterns popular in the Elbe basin are almost entirely missing. Vessels are frequently entirely plain and when decoration does occur it usually takes the form of finger-tipping or stabbing arranged in elementary designs. Combing, scoring and stamping are very occasionally recorded. The range of main forms is not wide. The tall, funnel-shaped pot with sharply angled shoulder is common in the early Roman period, as are several variants of a jar with inturned rim and stabbed decoration. Another characteristic form is a carinated bowl with shallow vertical grooves on the body. Some of the other bowl forms have foot-stands and even in a few cases tall pedestal feet. The vast mass of the pottery was hand-made. Wheel-made wares did appear in the third century but were never as common here as in Thuringia or southern Poland.

The later Roman Iron Age between Rhine and Weser bristles with problems, chiefly because strikingly little material has been recorded from the third and fourth centuries.[4] Many of the known cemeteries and settlements came to an end well before 250, in some cases before 200. No extensive settlements or large urnfields dating from the late period have yet been found and it looks as though the pattern of dispersed and sparse settlement which prevailed in the first and second centuries remained in being until the Migration period. The reasons for the very sparse finds of late Roman Iron Age material are obscure. There may indeed have been migration into Westphalia and, of course, into the Roman Rhineland, but this will not adequately account for the apparently empty landscape. A contributory factor may have been a change in burial rites, for if the cremated dead were being provided with still fewer grave-goods, or none at all, the cemeteries would frequently elude detection altogether.

## The North Sea coastal group

At the beginning of the Roman period, there can be distinguished a major culture-province which extended along the flat lands near the coast from Schleswig-Holstein to the Zuyder Zee, i.e. the territory where Roman writers locate the Chauki and the Frisii. Inland the culture-province extended up the valleys of the Ems and the Weser to meet the Rhine–Weser province roughly on the line Hannover–Osnabrück–Rheine. Of all the regions of Germania this has been the most thoroughly studied and both settlements and cemeteries afford an outstandingly rich amount of material for analysis. As yet, however, publication of the material from the major settlements, including Feddersen Wierde and Ezinge (see p. 98), is still pending, and therefore it is the cemeteries which must form the basis of our account.

In the earlier Roman period, the burials take the form of urn-graves and *Brandgruben*. They are invariably poorly furnished and metal objects, including weapons, are extremely rare. Urn burial with few attendant goods remained normal throughout the Roman period and into the fifth and sixth centuries, although from the later second century a small number of richer burials do appear in the record. *Fürstengräber*, however, are absent. Inhumations began to appear in the third century but were always in a minority.

The most characteristic component of the pottery[5] was the funnel-shaped urn (*Trichterurne*) with or without a foot-stand (fig. 7, 10, 11), and often bearing incised linear ornament. Carinated bowls with rather conical bodies and steeply everted rims, also with linear ornament, were also prominent. A third common form was a tall pot with narrow neck and usually with two small handles on the shoulder (Eddelak type). All these three forms, as we will see, had a long life and greatly influenced the pottery types of the early Anglo-Saxons. From the Elbe Germans the rather flat bowl known as the *Schalenurne* was taken over.

From the second century, the funnel-shaped urn gave way to a bowl with a high shouldered carination and, normally, with a flat base (*Trichterschale*) (fig. 7, 1), and the type survives until the end of the Roman period. Later versions of the form are commonly known as the Dingen type after its occurrence in the urnfield of that name. It is found not only in the coastlands but also in Schleswig-Holstein, for instance at Fuhlsbüttel and at Hodorf. Another major form which developed from early Roman Iron Age vessels was the carinated bowl on a pedestal foot (*Standfussgefäss*). Two variants may be distinguished, one with a rounded profile and everted rim, the other with a sharply angled carination and an upright rim. From the middle Elbe, its probable area of origin, this form spread into the coastlands and westwards to the Rhine valley and northern Holland. But it became most common in the area between Elbe and Weser, and was an important element in Saxon pottery of the fourth century.

The tall vessels with two handles, or occasionally three lugs, on the shoulder lived on as the Eddelak and Westerwanna types. The Eddelak pots,[6] named after a settlement in Süderdithmarschen, began in the late second century and extended into the

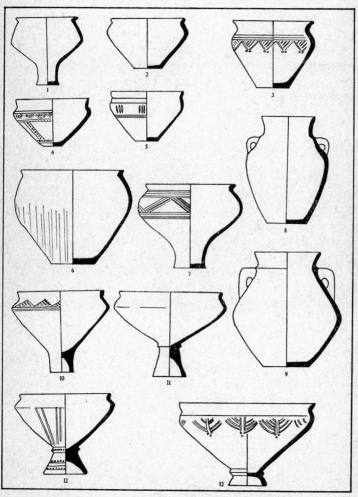

Fig. 7   Pottery types of the North Sea coastal group

third, becoming one of the main characteristic types of the pottery in use between Elbe and Eider (fig. 7, 8, 9). It was also represented further north, in central Jutland, and extended westwards as far as northern Holland. The closely related Westerwanna type,[7] which takes its name from the famous urnfield, emerged somewhat later than the Eddelak pottery, in the third century, and provided a probable model for the common Cuxhaven–Galgenberg type of the later fourth and early fifth century. This is essentially the same form but is distinguished by decoration which includes incised chevrons and *stehende Bogen* on the shoulder. The small handles of the Eddelak and Westerwanna pots by now are usually omitted. Thus three of the commonest fourth-century types can be traced back to an ancestry in the early Roman period, and those same types were to exert a further influence upon Anglo-Saxon pottery in the fifth century.

The most familiar feature of the region between Elbe and Weser is the series of huge urnfields, characterized by a monotonous uniformity in their grave-goods. A small group of cemeteries of the second to third centuries can be distinguished from the main mass of urnfields by virtue of their small size and the quality of their grave-goods.[8] This group has long been recognized and interpreted as an individual tribal grouping (for example by W. Asmus and F. Tischler) but this is made very unlikely by the wide distribution pattern. Most of these cemeteries occur in the lower valley of the Weser and between that river and the Elbe. The full list is as follows: Helzendorf (Kreis Grafschaft Hoya), Hemmoor (Kr. Land Hadeln), Osterholz (Kr. Grafschaft Hoya), Barnstorf (Kr. Diepholz), Veltheim (Kr. Minden) and Westersode (Kr. Land Hadeln).

The first distinguishing features are the relatively small number of burials, with normally less than thirty in a region where cemeteries of several hundred interments are common. Secondly, an unusually high proportion of the graves contain imported Roman bronze vessels, sometimes two to a grave, as containers for the cremation or as ancillary vessels. 'Hemmoor' buckets and bronze dishes were the most favoured types. At Hemmoor itself there were at least nineteen such vessels, at Veltheim twenty-one and at Barnstorf twenty. In contemporary cemeteries of more than 100 graves, only one or two bronzes of this quality are normally found. The date to which most of these groups of richly furnished graves must be assigned is the late second and third centuries, although the series probably begins in the early second. Not all the graves in these six cemeteries are richly furnished; in all cases cremations accompanied by only a single pottery vessel lay alongside the more elaborate burials, suggesting the interment of retainers close to their masters.

These small cemeteries call to mind the Lübsow group of rich graves in their separation from large urnfields (see p. 143). They differ from the graves of Lübsow chieftains,[9] however, in that they are not so splendidly furnished and include poor graves. Again, unlike the Lübsow group, they begin not about A.D. 1 but more than a century later. East of the Elbe and in the Danish islands the phenomenon of wealthy families burying their dead in style is familiar from the beginning of the Roman Iron Age. West of the Elbe the practice begins much later. These burials of the middle of the Roman period have no late Roman counterparts between Elbe and Weser, no parallels to Leuna and Sakrau.[10]

It has already been noted that the coastal *Kreis* extended westwards to cover the Dutch provinces of Friesland and Groningen. But this process was only completed in the early Roman Iron Age: before this time the culture of the Frisians had followed its own lines of development. In the late pre-Roman Iron Age[11] that culture is represented by the so-called *Streepband* pottery, a greyish-yellow to orange-red ware, tempered with dung. The name is derived from the two or three grooves which vessels normally bear on the shoulder. The *floruit* of *Streepband* pottery lay in the first century B.C., but it began about 200 B.C., supplanting the Ruinen–Wommels pottery which had flourished in the earlier phases of the Iron Age. By the first century A.D., *Streepband* pottery was beginning to fade out and some settlements of the early Roman period have produced no examples of the ware. Commonest in Westergo, it occurs also in the province of Groningen and a few vessels have been found as far east as Feddersen Wierde on the Weser estuary. To the south it travelled to the Rhine estuary, where it mingled with the pottery called after the La Tène site of La Panne, a ware often linked with the tribe of the Menapii.

The term *Streepband* is by no means a satisfactory one. It refers to the grooved ornament only, and this ornament can occur on a wide range of vessel forms. It may be possible to sub-divide the ware further on the basis of vessel forms when more work on the pottery from well stratified settlements has been carried out. The material from Ezinge and Tritsum, two extensively excavated *terpen*, should be of great assistance here.[12]

In the earlier Roman Iron Age, too, the pottery of Friesland reveals a certain degree of independence.[13] The funnel-shaped urns and the carinated bowls are rather rare, and the Eddelak and Westerwanna pots later make no prominent showing. Stronger links with the lower Elbe and Weser are evinced by the province of Groningen and by Drenthe. For Drenthe we now have the large series of pottery from the settlement at Wijster[14] at our disposal, and this material reveals that in the later stages of the Roman period the main ceramic characteristics of the coastal *Kreis* had been absorbed by the settlers in Drenthe.

### The middle Elbe–Saale basin

In the late first century B.C., one branch of the Elbe Germans extensively colonized the area about the confluence of the Elbe and the Saale south of Magdeburg, and the middle Saale region about Halle and Naumburg. This region forms an enclave shut in on three sides by wooded high ground and it is tempting to see it as the heartland of a major tribe, probably the Hermunduri.[15] This period of colonization saw important changes in the culture. Several cemeteries and settlements came to an end, the grave forms underwent radical change and Elbe German pottery first appeared in quantity. The graves were now normally urn-graves in flat cemeteries, occasionally in small stone cists. Another new feature is the appearance of warrior interments, normally with spears only, but now and again with swords.

For the material culture of the early Roman Iron Age, the cemetery at Grossromstedt (Kr. Apolda) near Jena—badly excavated before 1914—is still of great significance.[16] All the 582 graves recovered were those of men and in them weapon burials were very much to the fore. Only eight graves contained imported Roman bronze vessels. The mass of the grave-goods consisted only of the pottery urns, some of which were wheel-turned and beautifully finished with even burnishing over their black fabrics. The following forms were the most distinctive.

(1) A situlate vessel with sharply turned shoulder and a tapering body (*Trichterurne*). These vessels were frequently undecorated,

and when decoration was applied it was usually in the form of geometric panels on the shoulder (fig. 8, 1, 2).

(2) A tall, oval vessel with slightly everted rim, deriving from a La Tène prototype. These normally bore bands of incised decoration on the body (fig. 8, 3).

(3) A wide-mouthed jar with geometric or maeander decoration on the shoulder (fig. 8, 6–9).

(4) A wide-mouthed jar in coarse fabric, with combed decoration on the body (fig. 8, 4, 5).

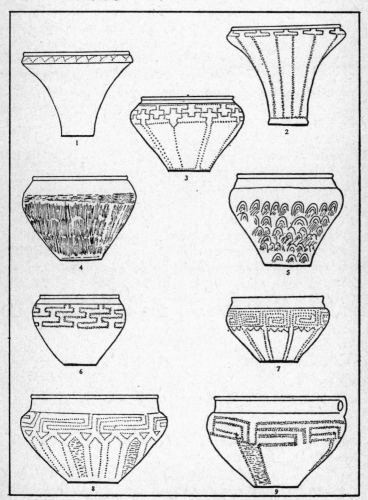

Fig. 8 Pottery types of the Middle Elbe–Saale group

Several other cemeteries provide analogous material in their series of urns, notably Prositz (Kr. Meissen), Wahlitz (Kr. Burg)[17] and Kleinzerbst (Kr. Köthen). Further afield, the cemeteries in the Havelland and Brandenburg to the north-east have produced closely similar pottery dating from the beginning of the Roman period, though this link does not seem to have been long maintained.

As the Roman period progressed, this *Kulturkreis* moved westwards into western Thuringia, there to supplant the Rhine–Weser culture, while at the same time becoming more sparsely represented between the Elbe and the Saale. This strongly suggests a slow-moving migration into better lands, the date of which should fall in the second century. There were changes in the burial rites in the same period, occasional inhumations now appearing alongside the prevalent urn burials, while the warrior graves become scarce. In the early third century, *Brandgruben* are represented for the first time and inhumations, aligned usually north–south, become steadily more common and more richly furnished. To the end of the century belong the famous groups of *Fürstengräber* at Leuna and Hassleben[18] (see p. 150 and fig. 9). These, and other contemporary burials at Flurstedt, Emersleben, Grossoerner, Leubingen and Voigtstedt, date from a limited period, probably 275 to 325, and the influx of wealth which they attest is to be related to successful assaults on the Roman frontiers. Ample opportunities for this kind of enterprise were now available since the Alamanni, quite possibly with the aid of these Saale Germans, had broken through the Upper German frontier in 259–60.

The most fully recorded of these rich burials are those from Hassleben and Leuna. In these, as in the other graves of the Saale series, imported silver and bronze vessels are prominent, and these are of types current on the Rhine and Danube frontiers at the same period. Weapons are usually absent, except for silver arrow-heads which presumably served as insignia of rank or prestige. Several of the Leuna–Hassleben chieftains and their families had been buried in large rectangular chambers lined with planks. Others lay in wooden coffins placed in narrow graves. By the side of one grave at Leuna (Grave 5) lay the relics of a horse sacrifice, in the form of the skull and foot bones, an occurrence which is paralleled in northern Europe, especially Scandinavia, at this time and later, but which carries with it an echo of practices on the steppe-lands.[19]

The Elbe–Saale *Fürstengräber* also contained among their
grave-goods wheel-made pottery of high quality, the main forms
being carinated bowls with pronounced cordons, tall beakers
with corrugated bodies, and beakers with indented sides. These
forms, so close to contemporary Roman provincial examples,
and the fine, well levigated fabrics point to the activity of craftsmen who were thoroughly familiar with Roman standards.
The vessels do not appear to have been looted from the Roman
frontiers and thus they are best explained as the work of Roman
potters whose workshops lay in central Germania. Whether
these men arrived there as captives or as voluntary immigrants
is impossible to decide.

The hand-made wares of the later Roman Iron Age reveal a
great increase in bowl forms. The *Trichterurne* and the tall jars

Fig. 9   The distribution of richly furnished graves

of the earlier Roman period have given place to wide-mouthed bowls with upright necks and, above all, to the *Schalenurne*. Decoration of these forms is usually sparse, when it is present at all. The whole range of the pottery makes it clear that Thuringia belonged firmly to the Elbe German *Kreis*, with only minor elements harking back to the influence of Rhine–Weser cultures in the earlier Roman period.[20] A small number of graves attest cultural influence from the east of Thuringia, from the area of the Przeworsk culture. One instance is a grave at Zwethau (Kr. Torgau),[21] which contained an Elbe–Saale vessel alongside a buckle and a strap-end which would be at home on the Vistula. From a burial at Döbrichau (Kr. Torgau),[22] not far from Zwethau, pottery which is clearly of the Przeworsk culture has been recorded, prompting earlier investigators to see here a relic of the westward thrust of the Burgundians. There were influences, too, from the Roman provinces, especially on the brooch types. Bow brooches and disc brooches with enamelled ornament came in from the Danube provinces and stimulated widespread imitation. From the lower Danube and the Black Sea came other types of ornamental metalwork.

Numerous Thuringian cemeteries were in continuous use until the late fourth or early fifth century, cremation being the prevalent rite,[23] but inhumation was widely practised, in some cases in the same communities. The inhuming element in Thuringia does not necessarily represent the presence of intruders. More probably the practice spread through the influence of the Leuna–Hassleben chieftains and their followers. In fact, the evidence, such as it is, of continuously used cemeteries and an undisturbed settlement pattern, indicates that the population of Thuringia in the later Roman period was stable. What that population was is not certain but there must be a strong presumption in favour of the Thuringii. These were first mentioned about A.D. 400[24] but it is not until the late fifth century that they were certainly attested in the area which bears their name. When they first emerged as a discrete unit is also unknown. Possibly the period in which the Saxons, Franks and Alamanni formed their confederacies also saw the emergence of the Thuringii as a league of smaller peoples. The element of continuity in Thuringia, dimly discernible from the later second century to at least the end of the Roman period, lends a little support to the idea.

## Brandenburg

The material culture of the early Roman period[25] in Brandenburg and the Prignitz reveals close links with that of the middle Elbe–Saale region and its general characteristics need not be reiterated. The most fully published series of pottery is provided by the two cemeteries in the Havelland west of Berlin, Fohrde

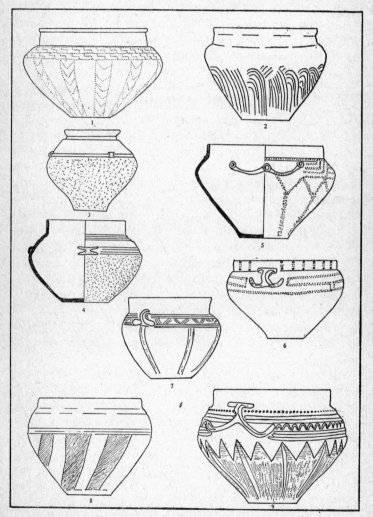

Fig. 10   Pottery types of Brandenburg and related material in Schleswig-Holstein

and Hohenferchesar and by the cemetery at Nitzahn (Kr. Rathe-now)[26] (fig. 10). All three have pottery types which are precisely paralleled in Thuringia, but they have also produced vessels which would not be out of place on the lower Elbe and in Holstein, notably a series of urns with pedestal feet. An equally striking feature of Fohrde and Hohenferchesar is the marked degree of influence, detectable in the metalwork as well as in the pottery, issuing from the Oder–Vistula region. Brandenburg, like Thuringia to some extent, lay at a cultural crossroads, where impulses from east to west met and mingled with Elbe German culture. The tribe in residence in these valleys was probably the Semnones and several smaller satellite peoples.

### Holstein and the lower Elbe

The lower valley of the Elbe about Hamburg and Holstein to the north of the river contain the most fully excavated and published cemeteries in the entire Elbe German culture-province. The major tribal grouping in this region was probably the Lango-bardi in the Hamburg area. The peoples in Holstein included the Saxons in the west, a minor grouping in the early Roman Iron Age, and the Reudigni in the east. The material culture of the early Iron Age was linked with Mecklenburg, and the middle Elbe, but its pottery displays such a degree of independence that Tischler was led to define a separate grouping north of the lower Elbe to which he gave the name Fuhlsbüttel group after a large urnfield near Hamburg. The separateness of the culture in Holstein must now be seriously questioned and the region is here treated only as the most northerly part of the Elbe German province.[27]

The classic cemeteries are Fuhlsbüttel, Darzau, Harsefeld, Rebenstorf and Tostedt-Wustenhofen on the lower Elbe, and Preetz, Hamfelde and Hornbek in Holstein,[28] the last two recently published. The urn-grave was the normal form of burial, inhumation occurring sporadically at the beginning of the Roman period and again from the third century onward. The most conspicuous feature of the cemeteries of the first and second centuries is the segregation of male and female burials in separate burial grounds: of the well recorded cemeteries, most can be shown to be either exclusively male or exclusively female. In general there is little differentiation in quality between the goods in different graves, and there are no recorded cases of outstandingly rich *Fürstengräber*, except those of the mounted warriors at Marwedel.[29] There are, however, a few instances of burials which seem to be those of an elevated social group. One instance is a little cemetery of five well furnished inhumations at Heiligenhofen in Holstein,[30] dating from the late third or early fourth century. This very unusual group of inhumations in an area where urn-burial was overwhelmingly dominant is difficult to explain, except as a family cemetery of immigrants from further north, probably Jutland or the Danish islands.

The pottery reveals an uninterrupted development from the pre-Roman to the Roman period and consists largely of tall situlate pots and necked bowls, usually in fine fabrics with a highly burnished black surface and bearing the distinctive geometric decoration found throughout almost the entire Elbe German province. Other vessel forms included shouldered bowls with upright rims and occasionally with lug handles. These may bear either incised geometric ornament (as at Hamfelde, fig. 10) or combing (as at Rebenstorf). Another common decorative feature is the use of plastic ornament, often in the form of 'moustaches', at the base of the handles or on the shoulder.

Between the early and late Roman Iron Age there is an unusually clearly marked break. Several major cemeteries, including Darzau, Fuhlsbüttel, Harsefeld, Tostedt-Wustenhofen, Hamfelde and Hornbek, came to an end shortly before or shortly after A.D. 200, and in those cemeteries which came into use about that time the range of pottery reveals many important changes. The best examined of these is the cemetery at Preetz in Holstein, an unusual case of an urnfield which has been virtually completely excavated.[31] Preetz may serve as a guide to the pottery of the period from the late second century to the late fourth. The tall vessels with fine geometric ornament have vanished and bowl forms are now prevalent, some of them showing close affinities with the pottery of Mecklenburg (for example from the cemetery at Pritzier (Kr. Hagenow)) and the middle Elbe region. The bowl with a single knobbed handle is one such widespread form. A large proportion of the Preetz urns are bowls with a rounded profile and upright or steeply everted rims. Their decoration consists of groups of shallow incised grooves and cordons in low relief on the shoulder, the latter often with slashed ornament. The most characteristic form of decoration is, however, the *stehende Bogen*, normally placed at or just below the shoulder. Bosses also occur, occasionally in combination with stamped ornament. A common variant of the main type of these bowls has been designated the Preetz type. Its distinctive feature is its decoration which consists of a group of three bosses on the shoulder, *hängende Bogen*, and above these a narrow zone of slashed ornament. The lower part of the vessel commonly bears three sets of three vertical grooves and occasionally a border of dots below the *hängende Bogen*.

During the fourth century, the pottery of the entire region about the lower Elbe, including western Mecklenburg, Schleswig-Holstein and northern Lower Saxony drew closer together into a form-series which is inevitably linked with the emerging Anglo-Saxon power.

## Mecklenburg

A large number of rather small cemeteries, most of them excavated before their importance was realized, provide us with our material evidence for Mecklenburg.[32] The tribal situation here is far from clear. The Semnones may have occupied the south, the Varini the northern plain. Pottery and grave forms indicate that from the later first century B.C. to the third century A.D. Mecklenburg firmly belonged to the Elbe German world, the connections with Holstein and the lower Elbe being particularly close. There is little uniformity within the region, however, and a number of sub-groupings can be readily distinguished, the most significant being those named after the cemeteries at Döbbersen, Körchow and Grevesmühlen. The Döbbersen group lay south of the Mecklenburg Bucht and west of the Schweriner See, the Körchow group to the south of Döbbersen on the lower Elbe, and the Grevesmühlen group to the east. The connections between the lower Elbe valley and western Mecklenburg were maintained until the end of the Roman period, leading some scholars to argue that the inhabitants of Mecklenburg were politically, as well as culturally, associated with the Saxons of the Elbe.

During the third century, there are clear signs that Mecklenburg had established contacts with parts of Scandinavia, in particular the Danish islands. A number of ornamental discs and brooches found their way here from workshops in Zealand, and a few of the more richly furnished inhumations, such as Häven and Jesendorf, contain pottery which is most closely paralleled on the same island. The spread of inhumation burial among the predominant urn-graves and *Brandgruben* may also be due to influence from Scandinavia. Elaborately equipped *Fürstengräber* are not common; the most striking instance is a grave at Grabow,[33] containing a gold arm-ring and silver spurs, which is more reminiscent of the Sakrau (Silesia) and Osztropataka (Slovakia) burials than of contemporary rich graves in north-west Germania. The Grabow warrior ought to be an intruder, perhaps from Silesia.

The pottery forms of the later Roman Iron Age are dominated by bowls, chiefly the *Schalenurne* and bowls with steep or even vertical sides. The latter are particularly common in the Pritzier (Kr. Hagenow) cemetery,[34] the best published of the larger Mecklenburg cemeteries. The *Schalenurnen* betray close similarities with those of Holstein and this western connection is again evident in the presence of the distinctive bowls with knobbed handles. Other characteristic forms include beakers and bowls, with foot-rings, narrow necked jars, and the so-called 'late Roman' cooking-pot with three small bosses on the body.

## Bohemia

At the beginning of the Christian era the robust La Tène culture which had prevailed for centuries in Bohemia came to an abrupt end, leaving relatively few traces behind it in the succeeding cultural sequence. In the place of those elements which had been particularly characteristic of the La Tène culture—large *oppida*, wheel-turned pottery, coinage—we now find a peasant culture which ignored the *oppida*, had no extensive settlements of their own, only small villages and groups of homesteads, and which had no great experience of using wheel-made pottery and handling currency. There can be no doubt that the incoming culture was carried in by the Marcomanni, induced to leave the Main valley and settle on the upper Elbe by Maroboduus at the end of the first century B.C.[35]

The earlier inhabitants of Bohemia included at least two groupings which had cultural links with the Germanic regions further north. In the middle La Tène period, the Podmokly (or Bodenbach) group in northern Bohemia reveals itself in a number of cremation cemeteries.[36] The bearers of the Podmokly culture were fairly certainly descended from the Hallstatt cultures of south-central Europe, but their pottery and metalwork types suggest that they may have included among their ranks a Germanic element, perhaps colonists who had moved up the Elbe valley as the Marcomanni were later to do. These northern connections of the settlers in Bohemia survived into late La Tène. The Kobyly (Kobil) group[37] now occupied northern Bohemia, another mixed La Tène and Germanic culture. The type cemetery, which consisted of some sixty urn-graves, reveals that the pottery of the Kobyly group was normally wheel-made, the common types being a tall beaker and a flask-like jar. Grave-goods other than pottery and brooches were not frequently provided. Weapons are particularly rare in the burials, only spears and the occasional shield-boss being represented at Kobyly itself.

The settlement area occupied by the Marcomanni after their entry into Bohemia about 6 B.C. seems to have been relatively limited, corresponding broadly with that held by the preceding inhabitants. The tribal heartland lay about the upper reaches of the Elbe—especially west of the river—and the lower stretches of the Ohre and Vltava valleys (fig. 11). The pottery of these[38] settlers of the beginning of the Roman period reveals that they shared in the widespread Elbe German tradition but it gives no clues to the precise regions from which they had set out. The upper Main valley, suggested by the literary sources, seems as likely as any. The somewhat surprising conclusion which must be drawn from recent work on the early Roman Iron Age pottery and metalwork is that the La Tène craftsmen of this region (for not all can have left Bohemia as the Marcomanni moved in) influenced the development of Marcomannic material culture scarcely at all. Indeed the incoming culture was more profoundly influenced by the Roman provinces to the south than by the largely Celtic population among whom it had lodged itself. For this there was a historical reason. Maroboduus evidently allowed, and possibly encouraged, Roman traders to establish agencies for the dissemination of their goods among the Marcomanni.[39] When Maroboduus fell from power, his successor found numbers of Roman *negotiatores* residing at the principal tribal centre and apparently plying their trade under certain privileges. The results of this policy are clear enough in the grave-finds of the period. Imported items, especially high-quality bronze vessels, of the first half of the first century A.D. are commoner here than in any other part of free Germany at any time in the

Roman period.[40] After about A.D. 50 this import trade dwindled rapidly and by the second century, a time when Bohemia lost its cultural pre-eminence, it had been almost extinguished.

Although on the face of it Bohemia is an area in which the archaeological evidence is abundant, it has not been better served than most of the other regions of free Germany. Most of the available material comes from early, poor-quality excavations,

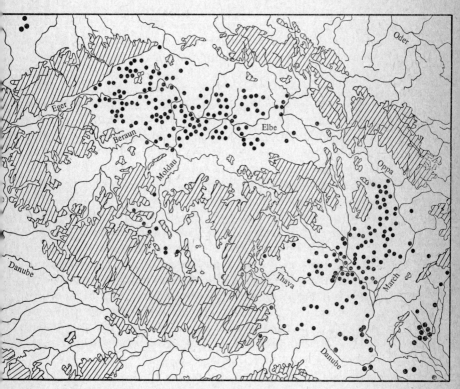

Fig. 11   Germanic settlements in Bohemia and Moravia

almost all of them on the sites of cemeteries. Not a single settlement has been extensively dug, although more than a hundred are known from chance finds and field survey. Two recent excavations of cemeteries, those at Třebušice and Plotiště, have not yet been fully published. Despite these drawbacks Bohemia in the early Roman Iron Age remains an area of unusual interest, not least because here a tribal grouping can be related with confidence to an archaeological culture. And, at least for a brief interval, historical figures like Maroboduus, Catualda and Vibilius play their part.

The pattern of burial in Bohemia during the first two centuries A.D. is much less uniform than in the adjacent regions, considerable numbers of inhumations being found alongside the more usual cremations. The cremations are themselves represented in several forms. The commonest are simple urn-graves in pits, normally containing a single pot which may be a large *Terrine* or a slender jar. Metal objects were often laid inside the vessels with the ashes after passing through the fire while large objects were bent to allow their inclusion. Richer burials used imported bronze bowls and buckets to contain the cremation and might include other bronze vessels as ancillaries. Both *Brandgruben-gräber* and *Brandschüttungsgräber* are recorded but not in great numbers. Inhumations occur fairly widely but never in numbers at a single site; normally they are found singly or in groups of up to four, and do not seem to have been placed within cremation cemeteries. A few are richly furnished but weapons never appear in their grave-goods and pottery only rarely. A proportion have stone cists or walled chambers around them. All thirty-three graves (from twenty sites) date from the early Roman period and not from the latest phases of La Tène. Their segregation from the commoner cremations and the special treatment accorded to some of them suggests that they represent a distinct element in Marcomannic society, marked off from their fellows on either social or religious grounds. Two rich graves of the Lübsow type are known from Bohemia, an inhumation from Repow (Bezirk Mladá Boleslav) and a double cremation from Zliv (Bez. Jičín).

During the second century Bohemia became more and more of a cultural backwater. Changes in the pottery types are probably to be linked with movements of population within the region and perhaps intrusion from the north. Several cemeteries and settlements went out of use towards the end of the century and were replaced by new sites. Examples of the new cemeteries are, Pňov, Plotiště, Vrutice, Dobřichov-Třebická and Libochovice. But there were others that continued in use, e.g. Lužec, Třebušice and Tvršice. At the same time richly furnished warrior graves became much commoner than earlier. The most impressive of the grave-goods are weapons and equipment looted or otherwise acquired from the Roman world. These graves occur either on their own or among the graves of less prominent individuals.

They date from the period which covers the Marcomannic Wars and continue into the early third century. Like the Leuna–Hassleben group of *Fürstengräber* of about a century later, they mark a period when the military initiative began to swing towards the Germans.

Since the publication of a famous study by Oscar Almgren in 1913,[41] it has been widely accepted that Bohemia and Moravia, both areas rich in iron deposits, played an important role in the development and dissemination of industrial techniques, especially those connected with the working of iron. The Boii, it was argued, transmitted their skills to the immigrant Germans early in the Roman period, and the confederacy of Maroboduus helped to spread La Tène technology widely throughout central Europe. The view has its superficial attractions. There were extensive iron-working centres in at least four areas in Bohemia: around Nové Strašecí, near Prague, in the Ore foothills and in southern Bohemia. There were further important iron fields about the Moravian towns of Prostějov and Brno. But the case for a Bohemian supremacy in technological matters has been overstated. It is becoming clearer that there were several other parts of Germania where iron-working was making great strides during the early Roman Iron Age, e.g. south Poland and Schleswig-Holstein (see p. 144). It is now equally clear that earlier claims for intensive manufacture of bronze objects, notably brooches, in Bohemia at this time were much too ambitious. The survival and continued vigour of La Tène bronze-working after the beginning of the Roman period owes at least as much to craftsmen working in central Germany and in the 'barbarian fringe' between Rhine and Weser as to a Boian remnant in Bohemia.

## Moravia

Early settlement in Moravia was closely trammelled by the topography of the region. To north, west and east, the broad basin of the river March (Morava) and its tributaries is shut in by high ground, none of which was particularly attractive to settlers owing to a predominance of podsols. Roman Iron Age settlement was concentrated in the March basin, and especially between the March and the Svratka, on alluvial land and on the fertile *Schwarzerde* soils immediately adjacent to it. Not surprisingly, this enclave in the hills of central Czechoslovakia produced a distinctive archaeological culture within the Elbe German *Kreis*, to which term 'March basin group' may be applied. Other archaeological groupings make no prominent showing in Moravia. The upper Silesian branch of the Przeworsk culture (see p. 86) extends across the northern border around the town of Opava, and the Puchov group of south Poland and Slovakia had outliers near the Moravian gates. The dominant culture, however, was the March basin group. The bearers of this culture were most probably the Quadi, a people which maintained close and friendly relations with the Roman Empire for much of the first century A.D., later becoming one of its most feared enemies. From their base in the March valley, the Quadi extended their influence eastwards into Slovakia in the early Roman Iron Age, a move which may be reflected in the archaeological record.

Work since 1945 has considerably extended our knowledge of the Iron Age in this region, and many modifications are now necessary to the pioneer work of Beninger and Freising.[42] The number of well excavated cemeteries is still small, however, and the type series of pottery offered as yet cannot be relied upon as presenting anything like a complete picture. Two large cemeteries of the later Roman period have been extensively dug: Kostelec na Hané (437 graves) and Šaratice (163 graves). For the earlier Iron Age the unpublished cemetery at Šitbořice is of great importance. The other sites present an unsatisfactory face: in all the graves of the Roman Iron Age amount only to between 700 and 800, the great majority dating from the third and fourth centuries. Extensive work on settlements is yet to take place, although useful information is forthcoming from Vícemilice and Křepice.

Urn-burial was the normal rite throughout the early Roman Iron Age, and it remained the commonest form of burial until at least the end of the fourth century. The early inhumations known in Bohemia are wholly absent here so far, and even at the end of the Roman Iron Age inhumations are much rarer here than in adjacent cultures. *Fürstengräber* of any date are unknown and warrior-graves are rare. Roman imports are only to be expected as the southern gate of Moravia lies open to the Danube valley, but they are markedly less common than in Bohemia.

The main pottery forms reveal several close links with the Bohemian series, but wider connections are also apparent, particularly with the middle Elbe. The commonest form of the early Roman period was an urn with an S-shaped profile (*Terri-nenschüssel*), which has seemed to some to originate in a La Tène form. Other major forms of the early Iron Age include wide-mouthed bowls with angular shoulders, footed bowls and beakers, flat bowls with plain or slightly inturned rims, and jars with free use of finger-tipping on the body and rim. Certain of these forms, especially the footed vessels, flat bowls and the jars, are also found in Bohemia, as are the common Elbe German decorative patterns of geometric maeander and scoring.

## The Poieneşti group

In the later pre-Roman Iron Age, a distinctive grouping with well-defined Germanic cultural characteristics in its material equipment can be discerned in Moldavia and Bessarabia. It is usually termed the Poieneşti group, after the type cemetery, discovered and excavated in 1949.[43] The general characteristics of this culture—its graves, pottery types and dress ornaments—are much closer to those of the Germanic cultures of central Europe than to the Daco-Getic cultures of Romania and there can be little doubt that we are here dealing with a Germanic grouping. Apart from the material from Poieneşti itself, together with twenty graves from Lukaschew,[44] material evidence for the culture is still slight. Its main features are as follows. The pottery is invariably hand-made and the range of its forms is narrow. The commonest vessel form is a handled jar with pear-shaped body and a stumpy, often faceted rim. Other forms include egg-shaped vessels with slightly conical necks and flat platters. Decoration is very rare. The metalwork is similarly limited in range: only three fibula types are known as yet. There is, too, a relentless monotony about the other grave-goods, and apart from the occasionally dagger or knife, weapons are not found with the dead.

The archaeological origins of this small group are to be sought much further to the west than Romania, but a precise location of its source is far from easy. Vulpe suggests that the Poieneşti group originated somewhere in eastern Germany and Poland, probably from a wide area between the Oder and the Vistula. Hachmann[45] has formulated the bold thesis that the group was derived from southern Brandenburg, and it is true that there are striking ceramic parallels to the Poieneşti and Lukaschew material in that region. But it is still too soon to claim that this is proven beyond all question. There has, of course, been speculation about the identity of the people represented by Poieneşti. Though several scholars have tried to link them with the shadowy Bastarnae, this is subject to the usual uncertainties which surround such identifications. The Bastarnae and their adherents were not the only Germanic grouping which penetrated so far to the southeast in the late pre-Roman Iron Age.

## Jutland and the Danish islands

The pre-Roman Iron Age of Jutland[46] comprises several local cultural groups, three of them of particular interest since they influenced the cultural development of Jutland in the Roman period (fig. 12). One such group was distributed over south Jutland and northern Schleswig. It is characterized by large urn-cemeteries (e.g. Uldal and Aarre) and by certain distinctive metalwork types, including roll-headed pins, large belt-rings and triangular belt-fasteners. A second grouping occupied central Jutland and is characterized by small urnfields and by single graves. Another striking feature of this group is the number of peat-bog votive deposits containing bronze rings, some of them with up to 500 objects. Further north, a north Jutland group may in due course emerge, but there are as yet only faint signs of it. The region has produced scarcely enough material for a satisfactory analysis. As far as can be seen at present, the Roman Iron Age cultures kept to the same or broadly similar bounds as those of the pre-Roman period. An overall study, however, is still lacking and is unlikely to appear until the material from the cemeteries begins to match the fine series recovered from settlements. The group which mainly concerns us here is the so-called Oberjersdal group of central Jutland and the island of Fyn.[47] The tribal pattern in the peninsula is one of numerous small units, most of them no more than names to us: Charudes, Aviones, Eudoses, Huitones. But the Cimbri and Teutones appear to have returned to Jutland after their wanderings across western Europe, and in the south, and on Fyn there were the Anglii, whose later migrations were to have such profound effects far beyond Jutland.

The Oberjersdal group takes its name from a cemetery in Amt Haderslev (properly Over Jerstal in Danish, but the German form of the name is commonly used), excavated before 1914.

The group has links with neighbouring Angeln, Schleswig and east Holstein; its influence extended over the northern part of Fyn.[48] In the north the group extended from a line drawn between Vejle and Oksböl to a line from Aabenraa to the island of Römö. From the beginning of the Roman period, Oberjersdal cemeteries

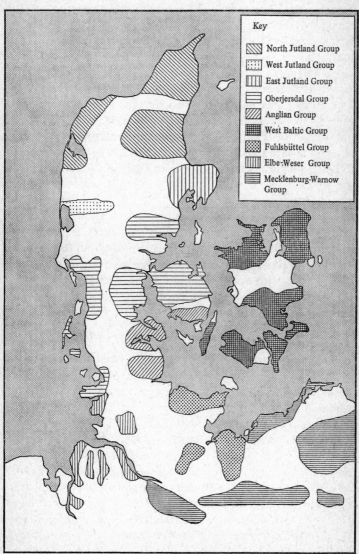

Fig. 12 Settlement cells in Jutland and Holstein

contain various kinds of grave, urn-graves, *Brandgruben* and inhumations. The last-named gradually became more common, but the process was far less rapid than in northern Jutland, where inhumation in large stone-lined chambers was widespread. There is no evidence of a segregation of male and female burials in separate burial grounds as in the Fuhlsbüttel group to the south. Secondary burial in barrows of the Bronze and earlier Iron Ages is fairly frequently attested. The pattern of burial rites on the island of Fyn was broadly similar, except that the individual cemeteries were much smaller, very few of them containing more than about twenty graves. Inhumations, unknown in the pre-Roman Iron Age, steadily increased in the early Roman period, making up 18 per cent of the total number of burials known. The great majority of graves were in-urned cremations or *Brandgruben* in flat cemeteries, or very occasionally in barrows.

The main pottery types of the Oberjersdal *Kreis*, including Fyn, are globular vessels with wide mouths, often ornamented on the shoulder with incised chevrons, tall jars and flasks with everted rims and lug handles, small one-handled cups and flattish handled dishes (fig. 13). The small cups with handles are particularly common on Fyn. The pottery from northern Jutland reveals certain connections with the Oberjersdal group, especially evident in the flasks with everted rim, the handled bowls with chevron ornament, and the ubiquitous lug handles.

### Southern Sweden and the islands of Gotland and Bornholm

The southern parts of Sweden and the adjacent islands[49] shared much with Jutland during the Roman Iron Age. In certain important respects the islands were more advanced than the Swedish peninsula. They were more receptive of influences from the continental mainland, imported more goods from the Roman Empire, and were more densely settled. The tribes of these northern regions are shadowy in our sources. The Dauciones may have held Skåne at the southern tip of Sweden. Further north lay the Gautae, the Sitones and the Suiones. The last-named should be the ancestors, however remote, of the early medieval Svea of Uppland province. The Heruli, too, appear to have originated in the western Baltic lands, probably in the Danish islands and in Skåne.

The evidence for the rather sparse settlement of Skåne comes

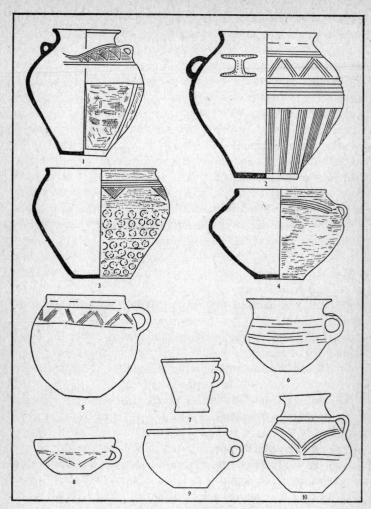

Fig. 13 Pottery types of Jutland

almost entirely from cemeteries, the most fully examined being that at Simris[50] in the south-eastern corner of the peninsula. Burials of the late pre-Roman Iron Age were normally cremations. The early Roman Iron Age introduced inhumation burial, a rite which thereafter steadily became commoner. The early inhumations were very poorly furnished, containing usually no more than a pot, or knife, or brooch, or occasionally a spearhead. Rough stone cists were often provided, frequently with a low cairn over

them. Once established, these burial forms persisted for long
after the end of the Roman period. Coffins of planks or hollowed-
out tree-trunks also occur. Often the inhumations lie among
cremation graves; others occur in isolation or in small groups.
There is no cultural distinction between the two rites: the equipment accorded to the cremated dead is broadly the same as that
found with the inhumations. This, together with the fact that the
replacement of cremation by inhumation was a very gradual
process, must indicate that the spread of inhumation was not due
to the intrusion of new settlers. By the third century, inhumation
had become so predominant that some cemeteries of that date
consisted entirely of such burials, although the rite of cremation
lingered on elsewhere until about 300.

Among the pottery from Skåne four forms are outstandingly
prominent, all with analogues in Jutland.

(1) Handled beakers, often with linear decoration in the upper
zone. This is by far the commonest form.

(2) Tall, one-handled jugs, often bearing incised linear ornament.

(3) Tall beakers, frequently decorated with cordons, grooves
and knobs of clay.

(4) Miniature cups, with or without handles.

The pottery from sites further north, although not abundant,
suggests that different ceramic traditions existed there. Material
of the early Roman Iron Age is extremely scanty, but the site of
Helgö on Lake Mälaren provides some information for the later
period. To the fourth century belongs a series of fine wares, their
most striking representatives being highly polished black vessels
with delicate stamped ornament, often including running scrolls
and rosettes. Similar vessels are known on Gotland, though the
schemes of decoration are not exactly matched on that island.
The fabric, too, is different, and the Helgö vessels, which continued into the fifth century at least, are most probably products
of the Mälaren region itself and not imports.

Pottery and decorated metalwork from Östergötland is also
meagre. The most notable feature of the cemeteries here is the
prominence of warrior-burials, both cremations and inhumations,
often containing swords and shields alongside the more usual
spears.

As in Skåne, so on Gotland the bulk of the archaeological material comes from graves rather than settlements. The rites of burial on Gotland and on Öland parallel those of Skåne, inhumations being introduced in some numbers in the early Roman period and gradually supplanting cremation. Again, as in Skåne, the bodies were laid in cists over which cairns or barrows might be erected. A north–south alignment of the graves was normal. Warrior-burials, often containing swords were fairly common, recalling similar graves in Östergötland.

For Gotland the most informative settlement is the famous site of Vallhagar,[52] one of the most extensively excavated villages of the Roman and Migration periods in northern Europe. The material from Professor Stenberger's excavations can stand for the island as a whole. No other part of the Baltic regions produced pottery of such high quality as Gotland in the late Roman Iron Age and early Migration period. The commoner forms in the fine wares are *biconi* and shallow carinated bowls resembling *Schalenurnen*. The most distinctive feature of the wares is the boldly executed stamped ornament, which occurs in a variety of schemes. Rouletting also figures in the ornament, this being produced by a toothed wooden wheel. The coarse wares are much more difficult to classify, and their dating is a matter of great difficulty: there appears to be little noticeable development from the early Roman Iron Age to the fifth century. The commonest coarse ware form is a squat vessel with a flat base and a simple outbent rim over a hollow neck. The variation in size is great, from large storage jars to small cooking-pots. Their fabric is usually yellowish-brown or grey, occasionally black. Ornament, apart from burnishing, is very rare. Another common form is a butt-shaped pot, rather taller than its girth in similar fabrics to the squat cooking-pots. An interesting and specialized type of vessel is the strainer, presumably used in the production of cheese.

The stamp-ornamented vessels begin in the middle of the Roman period, but their *floruit* was clearly the fourth and fifth centuries. The origins of the ornament have been much discussed, some scholars favouring Pomerania as a source, since that region is the nearest part of continental Germania to possess stamped ornament which is at all similar. But the development of stamping was proceeding apace all over the north in the late Roman Iron Age: other parts of Sweden can demonstrate the fact. Probably the stamped vessels on Gotland represent a 'school' of Gotland potters following a line of their own.

The island of Bornholm is much less rich in material of the Roman period than of the fifth and sixth centuries, although both settlements and cemeteries of the Roman Iron Age are known. Several of the recorded cemeteries begin in the Roman period and continue until the sixth century without break, and a few, e.g. St Kannikegård[53] with 800 graves, are very large in consequence. The pottery of the period is conservative in the extreme, the main types echoing those of Gotland and Skåne. The links with Skåne are particularly evident. The handled beakers and the *biconi* are once again to the fore, the latter being often decorated with applied strips of clay and lightly incised linear ornament. The commonest coarse ware form is a large storage jar with a tall upright neck, and the cheese-strainers familiar from Vallhagar are again in evidence here.

The history of burial rites on Bornholm follows the pattern already observed in Skåne and on Gotland. Inhumation appeared in the first century A.D. and had become the prevailing rite by the early fourth century. The best recorded cemeteries are St Kanni-kegård, Kobbeå, Lousgård and Slamrebjerg. Of the settlements, the most informative are Dalshøj and, for the Migration period, Sorte Muld.

### The Przeworsk culture-province

Towards the end of the second century B.C. there emerged in the Vistula basin and between Vistula and Oder a large culture group, the roots of which lay in the Jastorf culture and the Pomeranian Face-urn culture east of the river Rega. The new grouping owed something to external forces, chiefly to impulses from the La Tène culture which had now reached southern Poland, but in essence it was derived from well-established elements in the Oder–Vistula region. Earlier German scholars referred to this grouping as the Vandal culture—a very optimistic identification, as the *Stammsitz* of the Vandals[54] in the late pre-Roman Iron Age is entirely unknown. More recently, it has been dubbed the Oder-Warthe group by German investigators and, in Poland, the Prze-worsk culture, a name which is now gaining general acceptance.[55]

The Przeworsk group is really an amalgam of several local cultures with close mutual links. The heart of the culture-province

lay in central and southern Poland, Kuyavia and Masovia. To
the north, about the lower Vistula lay a grouping, the Oksywie
culture, whose grave forms were closely related to those of
Przeworsk but whose somewhat rarer pottery belonged to a
different tradition (see p. 90). Whether these cultural groupings
were Germanic or Slav, or a mixture of the two, is still hotly
disputed.[56] The issues are too complex (and not always strictly

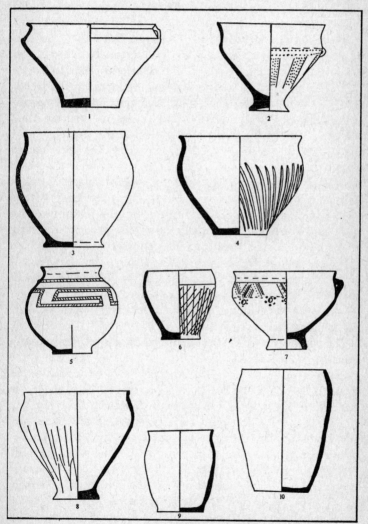

Fig. 14 Pottery types of the Przeworsk culture

archaeological) to treat here at length, but since it is clear that the Przeworsk culture had close links with undoubted Germanic groupings further west, and since Roman writers agree among themselves that the inhabitants of these regions were Germanic, it is reasonable to accept that Przeworsk represents a predominantly, if not wholly, Germanic population. If the testimony of ancient writers is entirely ignored, it is doubtful if the quality of the evidence so far published, philological as well as archaeological, is good enough to permit a final decision on the ethnic issue.

The material evidence for the Przeworsk culture—virtually all of which comes from cemeteries—is abundant but not yet well published. The more important large cemeteries include Chorula (*powiat* Krapkowice), Zadowice (pow. Kalisz), Opatów (pow. Kłobuck) and Tarnów (pow. Opole).[57] Cremation was the prevalent burial rite, with sporadic occurrences of inhumation in Silesia and Kuyavia, *Brandgruben* rather than urn-graves being the normal way of disposing of the remains. The grave-goods, which were frequently much richer than those of the Elbe German *Kreis* and other cultures in the west, were commonly broken or bent before being placed in the grave pits. Warrior-graves are fairly common and they include an unusually high number with spurs and horse-gear. Very richly furnished graves of the early Roman Iron Age include a significant number of the Lübsow group: Gosławice, Dembe, Łęg Piekarski and Kosin. No *Fürstengräber* are recorded from the middle of the Roman period, but they are again in evidence in the late third and fourth century, for instance the famous Sakrau (Zakrzów) group in Silesia,[58] Białęcin and Pielgrzymowo.

The chronology of Przeworsk pottery is not yet firmly based, the main basis being the horizontal stratigraphy of a few of the better recorded cemeteries, notably Opatów and Chorula, rather than a widely distributed series of dated graves. Throughout, the range of forms is varied. In the late pre-Roman Iron Age, tall vase-shaped vessels with small handles at the neck are particularly prominent (fig. 14, 1). These pots have a rather square profile, almost vertical sides and a wide mouth. Characteristic of the early Roman period are jars with a rounded profile. Occasionally their sides tend to adopt an angular profile, recalling the *Terrinen* of the Elbe basin. The geometric ornament (fig. 14, 5) which they often bear also points to the Elbe German province as a likely origin of this form. The coarser vessels occasionally have rough impressed decoration or combing (fig. 14, 4, 6). Other forms current in the first and second centuries include handled beakers and cups, and round-bottomed bowls, some of them with omphalos bases.

From the later third century onward, there was a noticeable increase in the number of pedestal-urns, the pedestals themselves being frequently more than a third of the total height of the vessel. The decoration of these normally consists of a single zone of grooves or cross-hatching. Small applied lug-handles occur near the rim. Shallow bowls with omphalos bases continue into the late Roman period, as do the rounded coarse ware vessels (fig. 14, 9–10) and the handled beakers. There was no clear hiatus between early and later Roman Iron Age in the pottery. In the later fourth century, the range of vessel forms became still wider. Situlate pots now appeared, alongside shallow bowls which seem to have been derived from the *Schalenurnen* of cultures to the west. On some vessels elaborate stamped and incised ornament now made its first appearance.

Wheel-made pottery is found from about the middle of the third century, but at this time it made no prominent showing and the vessels were mostly small. The chronology of the wheel-made series, like the mass of the hand-made wares, is still shaky for want of adequately published grave-groups. From the end of the third century a major factory situated somewhere in southern Poland[59] began to produce considerable quantities of wheel-turned pottery, a development which was accompanied by a marked impoverishment in the forms and ornament of the hand-made wares (see p. 151).

From the late second century, the Przeworsk culture began to extend its influence to the south-east, into the Ukraine and the Carpathian basin, and thus the region between Vistula and Oder may have suffered a measure of depopulation. Later in the Roman period, the grave-goods in many cemeteries here were poor in comparison with those of the first and second centuries. Urn-less graves become common in certain areas, and the slow spread of inhumation accelerated. The Dobrodzien series of cemeteries, found in Upper Silesia and south-west Poland, date from this same period.[60] In these the remains of the cremated dead and the grave-goods were scattered over a wide area instead of being laid in separate graves. Excavation thus reveals a layer of cremated bone and objects representing many burials.

## The Lusatian group

To the west of the Przeworsk culture, in eastern Saxony and south-east Brandenburg, there emerged a small grouping at the beginning of the late Roman Iron Age.[61] The area which it occupied was previously partly devoid of settlement, partly within the sphere of the Elbe German province. Earlier termed the 'Burgundian culture', it is now known as the Lusatian or Lubusz-Lusatian group. Most of the relevant cemeteries were excavated in the nineteenth and early twentieth centuries and thus type-series of the pottery cannot be assembled. The links, however, were plainly with the lower Oder area and the Silesian region of Przeworsk. As in the Przeworsk culture, *Brandgruben* were far more common than urn-graves. Inhumations were rare before the fourth century. Several *Fürstengräber* have been recorded, the most significant being Lubusz and Görlsdorf, which belong to the same series of wealthy burials as Sakrau, thus providing another link with Silesia.

## The lower Oder valley

A distinctive but not fully studied grouping occupied the lower valley of the Oder, western Pomerania and the island of Rügen, thus overlapping with the easternmost Elbe German finds. This Oder estuary grouping can be clearly distinguished in the pre-Roman Iron Age but representative finds of the Roman period are rather scarce.[62] Study of this region has been severely hindered by the fact that there has been no large-scale publication of the cemeteries, and by the tragic circumstances of the Second World War in which several of the major museums and all their contents were destroyed. Illustrations of the earlier finds from the lower Oder valley and Pomerania indicate close links with the culture of eastern Scandinavia, notably with Bornholm and southern Sweden, and with the west Baltic islands, thus foreshadowing the later closeness of these areas in the Viking period.

## Lower Vistula and Pomerania

An important grouping which occupied the lower valley of the Vistula and the eastern part of Pomerania[63] is now generally known as the Oksywie group (in German *Oxhöfter Gruppe*). Its relations with the Przeworsk culture to the south were close, but its somewhat scarce pottery series displays a degree of independence. Like the Przeworsk culture and the lower Oder grouping, the Oksywie group can be first distinguished in the later pre-Roman Iron Age. The typical burial rites of the early phase were *Brandgruben* and, less commonly, *Brandschüttungsgräber*; urn-burial was rare. Weapons were frequently placed in the male burials, and the women's graves contained an unusual amount of personal ornaments and pottery. At the end of the first century B.C. there were major changes in these burial forms. Inhumations now appeared alongside the cremations. Pottery vessels became rare in the series of grave-goods and their forms altered. The ornaments in the female graves were also replaced by new forms. Weapon burials vanished completely.

These profound changes in the material culture of the lower Vistula basin were interpreted by Kossinna, Schindler, Oxens-tierna and others as marking the arrival there of the Goths from Scandinavia. While the Goths must have been somewhere in these regions by the early Roman Iron Age—Ptolemy places them east of the Vistula—no close link between the archaeological culture of the lower Vistula valley and Sweden, or Gotland, has yet been established, despite several determined attempts. As it appears at present, such links are conspicuous by their absence, and this applies to grave forms as well as pottery and metalwork. If the Goths *did* cross the Baltic, as their own traditions asserted, then they did so without leaving any detectable archaeological traces on the southern shore. Much more probably the changes which prompted all the speculation were due to internal causes which we cannot hope to fathom. It is worth note that at the time when they occurred, at the beginning of the Roman Iron Age, cultural change was proceeding on all sides in eastern Germania, possibly stimulated by the changing cultural scene in central Europe and by movements of peoples eastward from the Elbe and Oder basins.

The development of the Oksywie group during the Roman Iron Age awaits investigation and the accumulation of much more published evidence. The pottery of the early Roman period is remarkably rare, and it is not until the fourth century that the situation changes. But by then it appears that extensive areas about the lower Vistula were becoming depopulated, perhaps because of migrations to the south-east. Some scholars have placed the Burgundii as far to the east as Pomerania and argue that the disappearance of the population may be explained by the westward movement of that people in the late third century. The meagre evidence at our command does not allow us to arbitrate between these views.

## References

1. The tribal map of Germania in the early Roman Iron Age has been discussed so often that repetition here is unnecessary. The map (fig. 2) of the major peoples of the period draws mainly upon the evidence of Tacitus, Pliny and Ptolemy.
2. Hachmann *et al.* (1962), 87ff.
3. Above all, von Uslar, R. (1938) and in *Germania*, xlii (1964), 51ff. See also, Behaghel, H. (1943), Uenze, O. (1953), Nierhaus, R. (1966), K. W. Kaiser in *Mitt. des hist. Vereins der Pfalz*, lviii (1960), 35ff.
4. Schirnig, H. (1969); Beck, H. (1970).
5. On the pottery of the pre-Roman and Roman Iron Age, Schmid, P. (1957), (1965) and (1969a).
6. Tischler, F. (1939).
7. Plettke, A. (1921), type B1.
8. Weidemann, K. in *JRGZM*, xii (1965), 84ff.
9. Eggers, H. J. (1950).
10. Grempler, W. (1887–8), Schulz, W. (1953).
11. Waterbolk, H. T. (1962) and (1966).
12. Ezinge: van Giffen, A. E. (1936); Tritsum: Waterbolk, H. T. (1961).
13. Van Es, W. A. (1966), 46ff.
14. Van Es, W. A. (1967), 158ff.
15. On their eastern flank lay the federation of the Semnones.
16. Eichhorn, G. (1927), with discussion by Hachmann, R. (1951) and (1960), 102ff.
17. Prositz: Coblenz, W. (1955); Wahlitz: Schmidt-Thierlbeer, E. (1967).
18. Leuna: Schulz, W. (1953); Hassleben: Schulz, W. and Zahn, R. (1933). On both, J. Werner in *Marburger Studien* (1938), 259ff.
19. Shulz, W. (1953), 30f. On the practice, S. Piggott in *Antiquity*, xxxvi (1962), 110, O. Klindt-Jensen in *Kuml*, 1967, 143.
20. Kuchenbuch, F. (1938), Guthjahr, R. (1934), Voigt, T. (1940), Laser, R. (1965), Mildenberger, G. (1970), especially 37ff., Capelle, T. (1971), B. Schmidt in *Jahresbericht für mitteldeutsche Vorgeschichte*, xliv (1960), 252ff.
21. E. Meyer in *Ausgrabungen und Funde*, xi (1966), 83.
22. ibid.
23. Mildenberger, G. (1970), 17ff.
24. Vegetius, *Mulomedicina* iii, 6, 3.
25. In general, von Müller, A. (1957); Schach-Dörges, H. (1969).

26. Fohrde and Hohenferchesar: von Müller, A. (1962); Nitzahn: von Müller, A. (1956). For the Prignitz, the large (and mainly unpublished) cemetery of Kuhbier, containing a fine series of silver brooches, is of great importance. The pottery from Kuhbier reveals close links with the Brandenburg material.

27. This region has been well served by publication and only a short selection of the recent major studies is noted here. Tischler, F. (1937) and (1954); Klose, O. (1966); Hachmanm, R. (1960), 127ff.; Capelle, T. (1971); H. Keiling in *Zeitschr. für Archäologie*, ii (1968), 161ff.

28. Fuhlsbüttel: Tischler, F. (1937) and (1954); Darzau: C. Hostmann, *Der Urnenfriedhof bei Darzau* (Brunswick, 1874); Harsefeld: Wegewitz, W. (1937); Rebenstorf: Körner, G. (1939); Tostedt-Wustenhofen: Wegewitz, W. (1944); Preetz: Brandt, J. (1960); Hamfelde: Bantelmann, N. (1971); Hornbek: Rangs-Borchling, A. (1963).

29. Krüger, F. (1928).

30. K. Raddatz in *Offa*, xix (1962), 91ff.

31. Brandt, J. (1960), 11ff.

32. Schach-Dörges, H. (1970) for the later Roman period; Asmus, W. D. (1938) for the earlier.

33. *Mecklenburg Jahrb.*, xxxv (1870), 99ff.; Eggers, H. J. (1951), 113, no. 866.

34. Schuldt, E. (1955).

35. Conveniently in *Cambridge Ancient History*, x (1934), 364ff.

36. Mähling, W. (1944), 222ff.

37. Hachmann, R. (1960), 113ff.

38. Important recent studies are Motykova-Sneidrova, K. (1963), (1965) and (1967). Good general account in Mildenberger, G. (1966).

39. Tacitus, *Annals* ii, 62.

40. Sakař, V. (1970).

41. 'Zur Bedeutung des Markomannenreichs in Böhmen für die Entwicklung der germanischen Industrie in der frühen Kaiserzeit', *Mannus*, v, 265ff.

42. Beninger, E. and Freising, H. (1933). Recent work is summarized by R. M. Pernička in *Sborník prací filosofické fakulty brněnské university*, xiii (1964), 53ff. and by Zeman, J. (1961). On pottery, Pernička, R. M. (1966).

43. Vulpe, R. (1953); Hachmann, R. (1960), 117ff.

44. K. Tackenberg in *Alt-Thüringen*, vi (1962–3), 403ff.

45. Hachmann, op. cit. 117ff.

46. Becker, C. J. (1961); Brøndsted, J. (1960), 13ff.

47. Tischler, F. (1955).

48. Albrechtsen, E. (1956), Band 2, especially 143ff.

49. Stenberger, M. (1964) is basic. Short account in English by the same author in *Sweden* (London, 1965), 123ff. Almgren, O. and Nerman, B. (1914–23) for Gotland. Stenberger, M. (1933) and (1948) for Öland. Roman Iron Age material from Bornholm is not extensive: collected in O. Klindt-Jensen, *Bornholm i folkevanderingstiden* (Copenhagen, 1957). For connections with Germany, Mackeprang, M.B. (1943).

50. Stjernqvist, B. (1955).

51. W. Holmqvist, *Excavations at Helgö*, I (Stockholm, 1961), 182ff.; II (1964), 143ff.; III (1970), 81ff.

52. Stenberger, M. and Klindt-Jensen, O. (1955), especially vol. 2, 1113ff.

53. O. Klindt-Jensen, *Bornholm i Folkevandringstiden* (Copenhagen, 1957), 58ff.

54. Somewhere in this immense region lay the territory of the Burgundians, at least in the earlier Roman Iron Age.

55. Godłowski, K. (1968) and (1970), 10ff.

56. Vana, Z. (1970), 27ff, expecially 36ff.

57. Godłowski, K. (1970), 10ff. and (1962).

58. Grempler, W. (1887–8).

59. L. Gajewski in *Arch. Polski*, iii (1959), 101ff.

60. Godłowski, K. (1970), 26f.

61. op. cit. 28ff.

62. Schubart, H. (1955).

63. Schindler, R. (1940); Oxenstierna, O. (1945); Kmiecinski, J. (1962); and especially Hachmann, R. (1970), 221ff.

# 3 | Settlements and agriculture

Long before the Germanic peoples entered the historical period, the main elements in the pattern of their settlement and the principal kinds of settlement had been established. Relatively few settlement sites of what might be termed the middle phase of barbarian Europe, from Urnfield times to the *floruit* of the early La Tène culture, have yet been extensively excavated, but those which are known include villages of stable and fairly large social units, alongside the *Einzelhöfe* of single families. The nucleated settlements, considerably smaller than the Neolithic settlements of the Danube basin of 3000 years earlier, are known from the middle Bronze Age onward (*c.* 1200–750 B.C.).

One of the most remarkable of the Urnfield settlements is that on an island in the Federsee, Buchau, in south Germany, usually called the Wasserburg.[1] In the earlier of its two phases this consisted of thirty-eight small, rectangular, log-built houses protected by a palisade. Later, these dwellings were replaced by nine larger houses with a distinctive winged plan, together with ancillary cattle-stalls or barns. Sizeable Urnfield villages existed in eastern Germany also, as the Perleberg site testifies.[2] This consisted of five large houses, probably representing five component families, and a further eleven substantial timber structures housing stock, fodder and food supplies. The excavation of the Urnfield settlement at Elp in Drenthe has helped to illumine the situation in the west in the late Bronze Age.[3] Here, a settlement of the period *c.* 1280–800 B.C. comprised a single farmstead, the buildings of which were renewed time after time on the same site over a lengthy period. These structures at Elp are of great interest for they were to become the norm in northern European settlements from the late Bronze Age down to the early Middle Ages and beyond. The dwellings were the familiar aisled long-houses with living quarters at the one end and animal stalls at the other.[4] Subsidiary farm buildings included small sheds and grain-stores supported on piles.

The single homestead represented by Elp, and by another site at Angelsgo, continued for centuries in the north. A steading of the sixth century B.C. at Jemgum on the lower Ems echoes the late Bronze Age sites, except that there is no trace here of animal stalls or granaries.[5] Small villages are also in evidence, such as that at Boomborg-Hatzum,[6] dating from the end of the Bronze Age. Certain settlements stand out in this pattern of small villages and *Einzelhöfe*. One of the most striking of these is the fortified peninsular settlement at Biskupin (pow Znin) in Poland[7]. This has an extraordinarily regular internal planning of timber corduroy streets, separating narrow blocks of nearly identical houses, 102–6 in number. The total population may have been in the order of 1000–1200, a remarkable concentration in a barbarian society. Biskupin can only be explained as a developed form of settlement representing a specific social unit, presumably under the control of a powerful local chieftain. Another strong

Fig. 15 Major settlements mentioned in the text

1a. Part of the settlement at Feddersen Wierde,
showing excavated long-houses

1b. Iron-smelting furnaces at Stara Słupia, Lysa Gora,
Poland

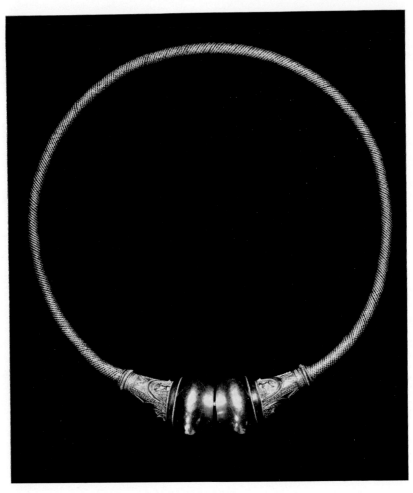

2. Gold torc from Havor, Gotland

hint of the influence of such local figures comes from the Hallstatt C settlement at the Goldberg near Nördlingen in south Germany.[8] Here, a group of some twelve large timber buildings, including some aisled long-houses, recalls the much earlier Urnfield settlements. One significant difference lies in the presence in one corner of the Goldberg site of two buildings with massive uprights, marked off from the other structures by palisades. This looks remarkably like the headman's quarters, and it has at least one parallel in the later Iron Age (see p. 104).

## The North Sea coastal region

It is logical to begin this inquiry in the coastal regions of northern Holland and Germany, from the Zuyder Zee to Schleswig-Holstein. This region has for long been the scene of extensive and highly skilled excavation of Iron Age settlement sites, notably under the auspices of the Dutch *Vereeniging voor Terpenonderzoek* and the more recently established *Landestelle für Marschen und Wurtenforschung* in Wilhelmshaven. The coastal lands thus provide by far the fullest picture of the history of settlement from the early Iron Age to the Migration period and beyond.

In the coastal claylands of Friesland many ancient settlement sites reveal themselves as mounds, standing above the flat countryside around them.[9] In many cases, modern villages still occupy the tops of the mounds, which may rise to a height of up to twenty feet. The great majority are lower than this and many are now all but invisible, particularly those with a small diameter. The name given to these dwelling-mounds in Holland is *terpen*: in Germany they are more usually termed *Wurten*, less commonly *Warften* or *Wierden*. They caught the eye of the Elder Pliny during his visit to the north between A.D. 40 and 50, for the *tumuli alti* (high mounds) and *tribunalia manibus exstructa* (platforms raised by the hand of man) must surely be *terpen*.[10] The building of the mounds has been shown to be partly due to the natural accumulation of debris and animal dung on a restricted occupation site, and partly to the deliberate piling up of thick layers of clay to provide a building platform for dwellings and other structures, clear of the land which was vulnerable to marine flooding. The modern history of the *terpen* has not been happy. The rich organic deposits sealed inside the mounds have long been prized as fertilizer and thus many of the larger *terpen*, particularly

D

in Friesland and Groningen, have been literally quarried away, leaving behind in some cases only a sad remnant topped by a medieval church.

The *terpen* did not all begin in the same period of time. There are in fact several 'generations' of them. The earliest of them appear to belong to the sixth or seventh century B.C., when settlers moved into the drying parts of the claylands from Drenthe. To this generation belong the earliest phases of the *terpen* Ezinge and Tritsum and, further east, of the settlement of Boomborg-Hatzum near the mouth of the Ems. Another series, probably including many of the well known Frisian sites, began about the start of the Christian era in a period of renewed colonization. Others appear not to have begun their development until after the Migration period, some still later in the Middle Ages.

The sixth-century B.C. colonization of the marshland seems to have been set in motion by settlers moving into the drying parts of the marsh from the sandy areas of Drenthe and from the valley of the Ems. The reason for their emigration, Professor Waterbolk argues,[11] was a sharp decline in the agricultural productivity of their land as a result of extensive sand-drifting. The areas into which these settlers penetrated included Westergo, Oostergo, the banks of the river Hunze and about the lower Ems. The evidence for the last-named area comes from the two sites Jemgum and Boomborg-Hatzum, the latter a small village of long-houses and raised granaries, the former a single farmstead. Both were occupied for a relatively brief period, the marsh about the Ems estuary—and indeed between the Ems and the Elbe also—remaining subject to marine inundation until the first century B.C. Beyond the Elbe in Schleswig-Holstein, enduring settlement on the coastal marshland was not possible until the following century.[12]

The earliest phase of the Dutch *terpen*, as revealed by the most fully excavated examples at Ezinge and Tritsum, took the form of settlements on the flat surface of the marsh (*Flachsiedlung*). The phases represented in the Ezinge settlement, not yet published in detail, are of the greatest interest.[13]

(1) *Flachsiedlung* of the sixth century B.C., incorporating at least two long-houses and a large granary set within a roughly rectangular palisaded enclosure. It is possible that more structures existed than those excavated.

(2) In the fifth century B.C. a small *terp* was erected, a low mound on which stood three houses and a byre. One of the houses was later replaced by a large house-cum-byre.

(3) During the middle and later pre-Roman Iron Age, the settlement consisted of a number of long-houses, probably between twelve and fifteen, arranged on a radial plan about a central space. In this phase the *terp* measured about 150m in diameter and stood 2·8m high.

(4) The radially planned village continued down to the end of the Roman Iron Age, its houses being frequently rebuilt on the same site. About 400, the settlement was radically re-planned. The long-houses vanished and were replaced by a large number of *Grubenhäuser*. It is just possible that long-houses did exist in this phase, but if so all trace of them has been removed by later ploughing. The excavator of Ezinge attributed the replacement of long-houses by *Grubenhäuser* to the arrival of Anglo-Saxon invaders from the east, but this is not a necessary postulate.

The slight evidence from other *terpen* suggests that many, if not most, of those founded in the sixth century and those which began in the early Roman Iron Age originated in *Flachsiedlungen*. A considerable number of sites did not pass beyond the *Flachsiedlung* stage or the stage of primary *terp* building which followed upon it. Most of these settlements appear to belong to the Roman Iron Age. Good examples are the sites recently excavated at Paddepoel, near Groningen.[14] Here, some five or six dwellings existed in the same general period of time, but separate from their neighbours. They date from the first century A.D. and seem to have been abandoned at the primary *terp* stage. Other *terpen* were abandoned during the third century A.D., apparently as a result of marine inundation. This marks the beginning of the late Roman marine transgression, the effects of which were felt along the entire coast from the Zuyder Zee to Jutland. The Roman period settlements abandoned at this time include many which lay at the inner margin of the salt-marshes, at the junction with the clay and the peat.

The history of the settlement of the sand regions of Drenthe is very different from that of the coastal marshlands. From the pre- and early Roman Iron Age in Drenthe date a number of rectangular palisaded settlements consisting of small groups of long-, houses. The most striking of these is Zeijen (near Vries), where in all, five periods of occupation are in evidence, beginning in the early pre-Roman Iron Age.[15] In the early Roman period, the village consisted of eight substantial houses, together with their associated granaries. The houses were sited immediately inside the stout timber palisade. The central area was left largely open, there being only one house at the heart of the settlement. A similar settlement lay nearby at Rhee. Here, however, the long-houses were situated side by side in the centre of the defended area.

Single farmsteads existed side by side with developed villages during the Roman Iron Age in Drenthe, as the evidence from the site at Fochteloo reveals (fig. 16a).[16] Here a substantial long-house, originally 19m long by 8m wide, and lying amid small closes marked off by wattle fences, was situated only 500m from a small contemporary hamlet, which comprised three houses, together with small huts and granaries. It is difficult to interpret the isolated long-house as anything other than the dwelling of the local landowner or chieftain, and the group of smaller farmsteads as the homes of his adherents or tenants. This is the clearest case of such tenurial relationship expressed in actual settlements yet recorded in western Germania. Early in the first century A.D. we hear of Cruptorix a Frisian who had served in the Roman army, owning a villa in the area of the wood of Baduhenna. About A.D. 70 the Batavian leader Civilis owned a villa on the tribal territory. The evidence of Tacitus and of the site of Fochteloo thus hang together. During the first century A.D. important distinctions were becoming marked between men of property and those of lesser means. The latter were increasingly drawn into the following of men like Cruptorix or the owner of Fochteloo, or still more important members of their tribe. Both Civilis and Cruptorix had served with the Roman army and their view of the private ownership of land may well have been coloured by this experience.

North-western Drenthe had in any case close connections with the coastal marshlands, and it is apparent that there was no intensive colonization of the Drenthe sands otherwise during the first 150 years of the Roman period. Only a few settlements of the first century A.D. are known in this region of sandy soils and small peat-fens, and most of these did not survive after about 200. The start of a major colonization was made during the second century, probably at the hands of settlers from the clay regions

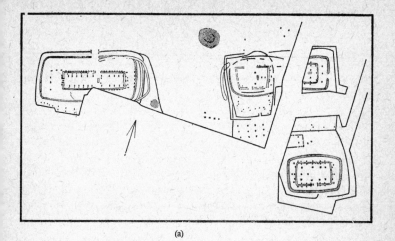

(a)

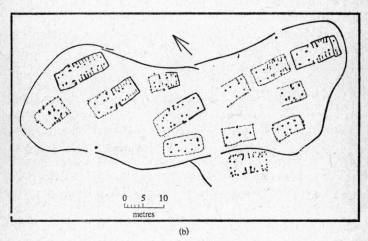

0  5  10
metres

(b)

Fig. 16 Settlements: Fochteloo and Grøntoft

on the coastal fringe, if the pottery types are secure guides to the settlers' origins.

By far the most informative site for the region is the large settlement at Wijster (fig. 17) in the centre of the province.[17] From humble origins as a single farmstead, this settlement developed into an extensive planned village by the fourth century. Its history is complicated and can best be understood when studied in three main chronological periods.

*Period I* (Second century–*c.*225). The earliest occupation took the form of a single substantial homestead, successively rebuilt at least three times on a slightly different site and growing steadily in size with each rebuilding. By the end of the period there were probably three dwellings, suggesting tenure by an extended family rather than a single farmstead.

*Period II* (A.D. 225–300). Early in this period, the small hamlet continued but with new buildings replacing those of Period I. Shortly, however, the settlement was greatly enlarged, now taking the form of houses and their outbuildings roughly ordered in two east-west rows and one running north-south. Towards the end of the period a new east-west row was added, after some of the earlier dwellings had gone out of use.

*Period III* (A.D. 300–425). Early in the fourth century the settlement may have declined somewhat. At this time five or six families made up the Wijster community. Most of the buildings at this time lay within a rectilinear palisaded enclosure reminiscent of Zeijen and Rhee.

Thereafter, the village greatly increased in size and was radically replanned. It was now laid out in a number of rectangular blocks marked off by palisades, with streets or driveways between them; the central block was the large enclosure surviving from earlier in this period. This remarkable planned layout survived, with only minor modifications, until the later stages of the history of the site, the end coming with a total abandonment about 425. In all, more than twelve, and probably fourteen or fifteen long-houses existed at one time when the settlement was at its height. If each long-house represents one family and the average family numbered at least sixteen persons, in its third period Wijster held at least 200 inhabitants. Since it is certain that only a part of the fourth-century settlement has been excavated, the total population at its peak may have been between 400 and 500.

The subsidiary buildings add much of interest. As elsewhere, 2-, 4- and 6-post *Grubenhäuser* were associated with the long-houses in all three periods. Four- and six-post granaries are found from Period I onward, again associated with individual dwellings. In Period III two twelve-post granaries occur. Storage pits lined with wood or basketwork, and ovens are generally present, as are the graves of animals, mostly cows and horses, probably representing foundation burials. As in the *terpen*, cattle formed the dominant element in the economy, the other animals represented being horses and pigs. Oddly, there are no certain traces of sheep or goats. The overall picture is of a very stable and thriving farming community, raising cattle, growing grain, and probably cultivating certain vegetable crops.

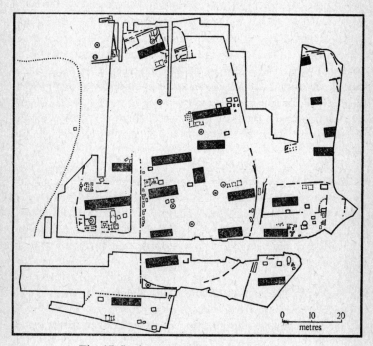

Fig. 17 Settlements: Wijster: third century

The coastal marsh between the Weser and the Elbe contains the most intensively studied of all northern settlements, Feddersen Wierde (pl. 1a).[18] This is a large *Wurt* among several on the right bank of the Weser estuary near Bremerhaven and 3·5km from the edge of the *Geest*. Full publication of the massive excavation carried out here since 1955 by Professor Haarnagel still lies in the future but the accounts already issued make it clear that this will be a major source of information for the development of a large settlement over several centuries, as well as for the entire culture sequence of the Roman Iron Age in this region. The

*Wurt* was occupied from the first century B.C. to the fifth century A.D., its main phases being as follows.

*Phase I.* In the late first century B.C., the marshland here first became amenable to settlement. Arable farming is revealed in plough marks in the natural soil at this time, but the area was still vulnerable to flooding; this ploughed land was covered by a layer of sand, 2–3cm thick, a relic of flooding. No traces of buildings have been recovered from the beginnings of this phase. Near its end, however, two substantial houses and a granary were constructed, and by the beginning of the first century A.D., seven or eight dwellings, of which four were substantial long-houses, and their attendant granaries had appeared. All but one of these were aligned in the same east–west direction. At this stage, the settlement was made up of a number of farms, each occupying its own low mound. Coalescence into a developed *Wurt* was to follow.

*Phase II.* During the first century A.D., the settlement steadily grew in size, developing a radial planning similar to that seen at Ezinge and elsewhere in Friesland. Only a segment of the site has been excavated but the density of houses in it indicates that even at this early time the village was a large one, including at least thirty dwellings.

*Phase III.* The early second-century phase has a considerable overlap with Phase II, but there was a striking new development on the south-eastern edge of the settlement. A large house, marked off from the others by a palisade and ditch, now dominated this part of the village (fig. 18). Around it lay a concentration of buildings which housed craftsmen working in wood, leather, antler and bone. Also within the palisade lay other houses, these being equipped with stalling, a building which may have served as a meeting-place or banqueting hall, and a number of granaries. The total number of dwellings in existence at this time is difficult to estimate, but fifty is probably not an exaggeration. They varied greatly in size, from 30m in length to about 10m.

During the third and fourth centuries, the settlement continued to number about fifty houses and the *Herrenhof* at the south-east end still dominated its plan. Bronze- and iron-working were

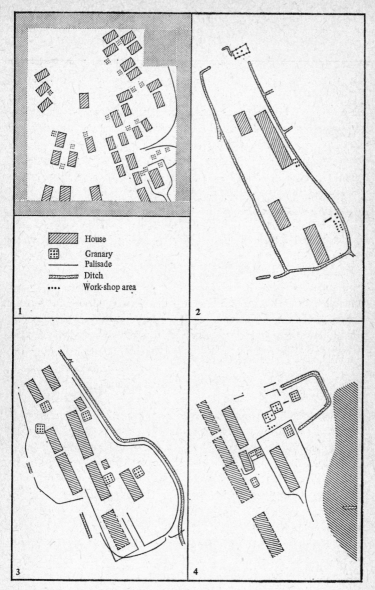

Fig. 18 Settlements: Feddersen Wierde

added to the crafts practised in its environs. Apparently the internal organization established about A.D. 100 had undergone no change. The final phase of Feddersen Wierde extended into the fifth century, the abandonment coming about or shortly before 450.[19]

The main interest of this village centres upon the information it provides about the enclosed *Herrenhof* on the edge of the settlement. It is notoriously dangerous to make deductions about social organization from purely archaeological evidence, but the information provided by Feddersen Wierde tempts us to draw a threefold conclusion. First, about A.D. 100 an individual or a family group raised himself in status and wealth above his fellows and reserved for himself and his adherents an area on the edge of the village. Secondly, the successors of this man, whether his own family or another is impossible to know, maintained their position in the *Wurt* community until the fourth century, if not until the end of the settlement in the mid fifth. Thirdly, the economic activities of the village headman included not only stock rearing and arable farming, but also a number of crafts. Conceivably, some of the products of these crafts were dispersed for profit to other communities, although evidence for this traffic is impossible to identify.

There is little doubt that one of the principal factors influencing this long-lived predominance of a single family group was the stability of the settlement, and this was itself conditioned by the local environment. The social differentiation so clearly defined at Feddersen Wierde may be expected elsewhere in the marshland, but it need not be regarded as 'normal' throughout northern Germania. In the amorphous and shifting villages on the *Geest*, for example Hamburg-Farmsen and Gristeder Esch,[20] it may well have been much more difficult for one family to maintain a dominant role. Even here, however, there are suggestions of the existence of unusually large houses surrounded by granaries and other ancillary buildings, for instance at Hamburg-Bramfeld.[21]

Alongside large villages like Feddersen Wierde and Tofting, a large, partially excavated *Wurt* at the mouth of the Eider,[22] there were many much smaller communities settled in the marshland. The most completely known is a little hamlet at Ostermoor, near Brunsbüttel on the Elbe estuary, dating from the earlier Roman period.[23] Here, five long-houses lay on the bank of a creek, their gable ends towards the stream. One building was much smaller than the others and may have been a store or a workshop. A community of three or four families seems therefore indicated. Behind the houses, away from the creek, lay ditched arable fields, identifiable by traces of plough furrows in the subsoil.

The accelerating colonization of the marshland after about A.D. 100 is a striking phenomenon, as remarkable in its own sphere as the draining of the eastern Fenlands of England under Roman tutelage at about the same time. No doubt before the marshes were actually settled they had been used for fishing, the catching of game, and perhaps as pasture grounds for cattle, but the determined onslaught upon them in the early Roman period was clearly made by settlers seeking new land and not by men who were merely developing activities already in progress there. The most probable reason was an increase of population on the neighbouring *Geest* of Schleswig-Holstein and Lower Saxony, for from the second century onward the increased size of urnfield cemeteries suggests that communities were growing more rapidly than in the period 100 B.C. to A.D. 100. The development of large villages as at Wijster at the same time points towards the same conclusion. The colonization of the marshland may then be an early indication that the land suitable for agriculture in these parts of Germania would one day prove to be inadequate for the needs of its population. Later, under the additional constraint of the late Roman marine transgression, this circumstance was to have far-reaching effects on the history of western Europe.

## The Jutland peninsula

Knowledge of the Iron Age settlements in Jutland has greatly improved in the past twenty years. The fieldwork of Hatt before and after the Second World War laid the essential foundation, showing that much could be expected of the sites, both in terms of building plans and of vital information about the relation of the settlements to their fields. In more recent years there have been major advances in the study of the late Bronze Age and the various phases of the pre-Roman Iron Age. Until very recently, extensive plans of pre-Roman Iron Age settlements had not been recovered. An important contribution towards closing that gap is Professor Becker's extensive and productive excavation at Grøntoft (fig. 16, 6).[24] The earliest known settlement here dates from the Jastorf phase of the Iron Age, i.e. probably from the fourth century B.C. The plans of nine long-houses with cattle-stalls were recovered, together with four long-houses without stalling and five smaller store buildings. The structures all lay on the same east–west alignment, apparently arranged in three or four rows, and the phases of construction are evident on some of the buildings. At some distance from the dwellings lay a cemetery of low barrows, apparently associated with them. Immediately south of this settlement lay another of a somewhat later date. This probably had a short life during the third century B.C., suffering in that brief period one or more extensive confla-grations. This second settlement consisted of twelve major buildings, five of them long-houses with stalling for up to eighteen beasts. There were also long-houses with stalls for only three to five cattle and the remaining structures were houses without any provision for animals at all. All twelve dwellings, which were surrounded by a timber palisade on a roughly oval plan, together with one other outside the palisade, appear to have been standing at the same period. The houses and the palisade went through two or three phases of rebuilding, but the village remained on the same site (fig. 16.6).

Three further villages, or rather successive stages in the history of the same village, have now been discovered nearby, these dating from the period between the two settlements already described. This does not exhaust the tale; in the same locality there are still further traces of Iron Age occupation sites as yet unexamined. The overriding importance of these settlements at Grøntoft is that they have pushed back to at least the beginning of the Iron Age the origins of the Jutland village. For Grøntoft differs in no notable way from the villages of the Roman period and of the early Middle Ages. Before these excavations began, the origins of such settlements were believed to lie in the middle of the pre-Roman Iron Age, a period which followed a marked interruption in the cultural sequence. Now these origins must be sought still further back, at least at the beginning of the Iron Age, and quite probably earlier.

Grøntoft has so far produced no evidence of occupation during the Roman period, but many other Jutland settlements were either continuously occupied into the Roman Iron Age, or later reoccupied. A good example of the latter class is the site at Borremose (Himmerland).[25] In the early pre-Roman Iron Age, an island in the peat-bog of Borremose, measuring about 150m by 100m, was provided with a rampart and ditch. Buildings associated with this phase were not identified in the excavation and the precise character of this defended enclosure is not clear. It stands almost alone in this part of north-west Europe at this time. The enclosure was abandoned and lay empty for an interval, before being reoccupied in the late pre-Roman Iron Age. The defences now lost their function and the ditch was used as a refuse dump. The new settlement was linked to dry ground at the edge of the bog by a stone-paved causeway, 3m broad, resembling those of Krogsbølle (Fyn) and Tibirke (Zealand) and the later example at Broskov (Zealand). Occupation was maintained until well on into the Roman period, the settlement amounting in all to twenty long-houses and three smaller structures. Not all, however, were standing at the same time, and the village was made up of twelve to fifteen dwellings at a time. The pollen spectrum reveals that the area about the bog had been fairly intensively cultivated in the later phase of the settlement. The grain-pollens sharply increase after the period of abandonment came to an end and remain high until the end of the occupation in the later Roman period.

A settlement of a very different kind was that at Nørre Fjand, which lay on sandy ground close to the coast of west Jutland.[26] In all some sixty houses and other buildings were excavated here by Hatt, about half of these being dated by him to the later pre-Roman Iron Age, and the remainder being of the Roman period. Among all the houses, there are very few which seem to be true long-houses of the type encountered elsewhere in Jutland. Only three seem to belong to that group. Of the others, many have internal subdivisions but these do not mark off the customary animal stalls and other houses have no subdivisions at all. At the heart of the settlement stood one of the large dwellings with stalling for cattle: up to seventeen or eighteen beasts could have been housed here. The prominent position of this house, which was maintained for a lengthy period, seems to mark it out as the dwelling of a wealthier family in the community, possibly that of the village headman. The large number of other dwellings without stalling present a problem to which the economy of the village appears to supply the solution. Large number of weights for fishing nets indicate the importance of fishing to the community. The scarcity of dwellings with stalling may thus be taken to mean that this community was primarily composed of fishermen, but that the leading element was a family, or small group of families, who possessed a small herd of cattle.

Two further settlements in Jutland may be selected out of many to give substance to the outline already sketched. At Mariesminde, the Iron Age settlement appears to resemble a street-village, two rows of houses running parallel to each other on either side of a roadway.[27] Only a fragment of the site has been excavated, including five houses in the southern row. These are rather small, square or rectangular huts: typical dimensions are 6m by 4m and 4·5m by 3·5m. One larger dwelling has been recorded but it does not appear to have been a long-house. This settlement raises several interesting questions, answers to which are frustrated by its incomplete examination. Were there long-houses in the vicinity, with which the humble dwellings were associated? Were the inhabitants of the five simple huts the dependants of wealthier peasants living in such long-houses, or were they an independent community? Only large-scale excavation will provide the answers.

A very large settlement, occupied during the first three centuries of the Roman Iron Age, lay at Ginderup.[28] On a deeply stratified site, more than thirty houses were excavated in a sequence of seven levels. The total area covered by the Iron Age occupation measures at least 500m by 100m of which a minute part has been dug. As at Grøntoft and Mariesminde small houses without stalling were present alongside long-houses, some with, some without, stalls. Large-scale fieldwork may reveal here as complex a picture of a shifting settlement as has been obtained at Grøntoft.

In summary, the evidence of the Jutland settlements reveals a notable continuity in the essential character of agricultural settlement from the beginning of the Iron Age to the later Roman period and probably beyond. Throughout the Iron Age, settlement forms included single farmsteads, small groups of farms, in which long-houses and smaller dwellings may be represented, and much more extensive settlements for which the term 'village' does not seem too ambitious. The Grøntoft excavations have revealed that such developed villages already existed in the early pre-Roman Iron Age. In settlements of all dates, shifts in the siting of long-lived villages (e.g. Grøntoft, Nørre Fjand, Ginderup) mean that the total area occupied during the late Iron Age may be very extensive: 18 000 sq.m at Mariesminde,

15 000 sq.m at Borremose, 50 000 sq.m at Ginderup, and possibly 100 000 sq.m at Østerbølle. Finally, several settlements, and especially the larger instances, have produced evidence of some differentiation in the size of dwellings and in the number of cattle stalled within them. From this it is an unexceptionable deduction that within such communities there were differing degrees of wealth, and thus of social position.

## Sweden and the Baltic islands

The islands of Gotland and Öland are rich in sites occupied during the Roman Iron Age and the Migration period, and since many of their constituent houses were large and substantially built, large numbers of them have survived. As well as the remains of houses, the walls which bounded paddocks and fields survive in many localities, giving an unusually full picture of Iron Age agricultural economy. Some 1400 such settlements, dating from the first six centuries A.D., are recorded on Gotland and about 900 on Öland, most of them in the centre and the north of the island. The excavated examples date mainly from the Migration period, but it is certain that settlements of this type were being built in the Roman Iron Age. It is permissible, then, to use the evidence of the most informative of the sites, Vallhagar (dating mainly from the late fourth, fifth and sixth centuries A.D.), to illumine economic conditions in the Roman period.

The twenty-four buildings excavated at Vallhagar,[29] amid the remains of abandoned field-walls or *västär*, indicate a community of five or six farmsteads. The social unit was probably a group of interrelated families, each living on its own steading but combining for certain major agricultural activities, such as ploughing, harvesting and ground-clearance, under the supervision of the leading figure in the community. The economy of the place was based firmly on mixed farming, with stock rearing playing a somewhat more important part than arable cultivation. Cattle and sheep were the mainstays, and the Gotland farmers did what they could with the herds of semi-wild russ horses, rounding them up periodically and adding their meat to the diet. A wide range of grain crops was raised: *Einkorn*, emmer, rye, spelt and above all barley, for bread and beer. Various kinds of wild grains too were gathered, and flax and cameline cultivated for their seed-oil. Vallhagar provides us with our clearest view of peasant economy in the western Baltic regions, its inhabitants taking full advantage of the fertile limestone soils and rich meadows to produce a rounded and well-balanced economy.

A striking phenomenon of the western Baltic, and one unmatched in other parts of Germania, is the large number of ring-forts crowning hill-tops on Gotland, Öland, and in the area between the Baltic and the central Swedish lakes. Similar sites are known in Norwegian Rogaland. Some of the Swedish examples are well preserved but few are closely dated; only one, Eketorp's Borg on Öland, has so far been completely excavated.[30] There is evidence from a number, however, that they were being erected during the Roman Iron Age, even though their *floruit* was undoubtedly the Migration and Viking periods. A few were still being used as refuges as late as the seventeenth century.

The largest is Graborg on Öland, which measures 210m in diameter and has a defensive wall still standing 9m high. Most of the forts are much smaller than this. Ismantorp, also on Öland, is 125m in diameter and has no less than nine gates in its massive walls. The interior has been meticulously planned, about eighty-eight stone rectangular buildings being arranged in four quarters with streets between. The place was not occupied for long, despite the care lavished on its elaborate planning, and thus few finds have been made here. The buildings date from well after the Roman period. The most completely examined of the forts, Eketorp's Borg, was first occupied in the fifth century and thereafter sporadically used until the Middle Ages. In its period of most intensive occupation, between 450 and 700, the interior of this fort was ordered on strikingly regular lines. Radial walls projecting from the rear of the ramparts defined a ring of buildings, including houses, byres and store buildings, completely encircling the site. The roughly circular space in the centre was occupied by a further fourteen buildings which may be interpreted as three or four separate farms. These ring-forts clearly lie outside the normal range of Germanic settlements, being evidently places of refuge rather than settled villages; they lie also outside the limits of our period, and we must return to the Roman Iron Age.

### The Rhineland

An area which has so far produced relatively little information about the character of Iron Age settlements is, surprisingly, the

Rhineland and the regions adjoining it: surprisingly because this is an area where archaeological survey and fieldwork of high quality has long been active. The major reason lies in the soil conditions of the Rhine valley. The alluvium deposited by the river during the period when it was unconfined by artificial banks has covered many sites of pre-medieval date to a considerable depth, thus making their detection by field survey or aerial reconnaissance unlikely if not impossible, in normal conditions. The settlements that have been recorded have thus tended to lie away from the river alluvium.

From the pre-Roman Iron Age, the settlement at Weeze-Baal (Kr. Geldern) near Xanten may be selected, as a recently and extensively examined site.[31] Unfortunately, the dwellings of this settlement were not found in the excavation, although an extraordinary complex of granaries and store buildings came to light. Their plans were very various, the structures being framed on four, six, eight or nine large timbers thrust deep into the subsoil. Some twenty such structures were identified altogether, including successive rebuildings of the same granary. Occupation was continued down to the early Roman period, abandonment of the site being possibly connected with a reordering of rural settlement under Roman supervision on the *Territorium* of the legionary fortress at Xanten.

One of the most extensively excavated of the Rhineland settlements of the Roman period is that at Haldern (Kr. Rees), near Wesel, on the right bank of the Rhine.[32] Though only partially excavated, it is the central area that received attention. A settlement consisting mainly of *Grubenhäuser* was revealed, but with two or possibly three larger rectangular structures dominating the plan. One of these measured 9m by 6m—an unusual set of dimensions. Though it clearly was not an aisled long-house, the complex of post-holes in the centre give no certain evidence as to how the roof was supported. The second of the two certain rectangular buildings was a substantial hall measuring 20m by 7m. This too lacked the double row of uprights of the aisled long-houses, the only apparent roof supports being rows of large uprights set close to the walls along the longer axis—a strong suggestion of cruck construction. If the greater part of the Haldern settlement was excavated (which is not entirely certain) it may be argued that this community comprised two or three family groups, represented by the large halls, and their dependent peasants, who lived in the smaller huts. On the whole, however, it seems safer to suspend final judgement on this community, since sand extraction has robbed us of the opportunity to determine the limits of the settlement. The life of the known occupied area was confined to the first and second centuries A.D.

Extensively excavated settlements are much rarer in the eastern territories than in the west. This lack is regrettable for there are strong suggestions of influence upon these territories from the Black Sea hinterland, the lower Danube and the Ukraine; it would be worth knowing whether this influence extended to social organizations and settlements. Between the Oder and the Elbe, the settlement which provides the clearest picture of its layout is the compactly planned village of the Bärhorst near Nauen, some 48km west of Berlin.[33] This was a fenced settlement of about 40 000 sq.m, the perimeter being formed by a palisade on a roughly square plan. The dating evidence has never been published, but the excavator argues that the place reached its peak of development in the third century. Within the palisade the houses lay closely packed about an open space near the centre, most of them on the same east–west alignment. The thirty or so dwellings, most of which are said to have been standing at one time, included several types of long-houses, relatively few *Grubenhäuser* being present for a settlement of this size. None of the houses stand out as a *Herrensitz*, either by virtue of size or the number of stall divisions. The excavator saw the Bärhorst as an unusual case of westward-moving Germans settling down in one place for a lengthy period, but as more large-scale excavations are carried through, settled villages like Wijster, Haldern and the Bärhorst are seen to be normal. It was from such settlements that the medieval villages of northern Europe derived their ancestry.

Broadly contemporary with the Bärhorst was the group of settlements excavated in 1937–42 at Kablow, 32km south-east of Berlin.[34] These began in the first century B.C. with two rows of houses, two dwellings in one and three in the other. By the third century more than sixty buildings made up the settlement, mainly aisled halls-cum-byres and large oval *Grubenhäuser*. At the north-east end of the village lay a particularly large house with a row of granaries close by, quite probably the seat of the local headman. During the later third century this large village dwindled in size and was replaced by another extensive village immediately to the north. Tragically, the finds from Kablow were destroyed in the Second World War and records alone survive.

Hill-forts or other defended refuges played no prominent part in the pattern of settlement during the Roman Iron Age. A brief phase of hill-fort building did occur in the later period of the pre-Roman Iron Age, possibly under the influence of La Tène fortifications in central Europe, but none of these forts seem to have been occupied after the first century A.D. The Alteburg near Arnstadt, a promontory fort,[35] was indeed abandoned before the Roman period began. The Weser basin contains a large number of hill-forts, but few of them have been examined so that their Iron Age date is far from certain. The Babilonie near Lübbecke and the Grotenburg in the Teutoburg forest, however, certainly belong to the Iron Age and are larger than most. In other regions the recorded fortifications stand in isolation amid their landscapes. In Denmark the only known instance is the pre-Roman period fort on an island in the marsh of Borre-mose in Himmerland. In the coastal lands, there is the Heiden-schanze, a bivallate work near Wesermünde, situated on a sand knoll clear of the marshland.[36] This was a settlement and not merely a refuge, founded about 50 B.C. and occupied for about a century.

The literary sources add little to this meagre list. When Tacitus mentions a *castellum* of Maroboduus (*Annales* ii, 62) and the stronghold of *Mattium*, *chef-lieu* of the Chatti (*Annales* i, 56), he refers to forts in areas where La Tène culture was, or had been flourishing. The forts are simply being re-used by new Germanic masters. The most interesting cases of reoccupation of earlier hill-forts come from that part of south-western Germania held by the Alamanni in the late third and fourth centuries. These forts lie on both sides of the artificial Roman frontier, destroyed by 260. Two forts, the Glauberg near the Roman *limes* fort of Altenstadt and the Gelbe Burg,[37] were certainly occupied by barbarians, as abundant finds of pottery and metalwork testify, but unfortunately only the Glauberg has been competently examined. This was originally an Urnfield stronghold, later occupied by La Tène settlers. In the fourth century A.D. a dry-stone wall was added to the crest of the prehistoric ramparts and stone houses were erected inside. The datable artifacts can be assigned to the fourth and fifth centuries and no later. Other small hill-forts in the area close to the *limes* may have been reoccupied at about the same time, but this awaits confirmation. What excavation might reveal about the social units which were established in these forts can only be guessed at, but the *reges* and *regales* recorded by Ammianus Marcellinus as the leading elements among the Alamanni are the most likely masters of these hill-top strongholds. We may not be very far away from the social order of Urnfield times here.

Ammianus tells us other interesting things about the Alamannic settlement of the old *agri decumates*. In 357, the emperor Julian's army came across 'villas rich in livestock and crops' and 'homes carefully built in Roman fashion'. (Amm. Marc. xvii, 1, 7). Abandoned Roman villas, set in cultivated farmlands, must surely have attracted the attention of the newcomers. A little archaeological testimony is brought forward by the site of the Roman villa of Praunheim[38] in the suburbs of Frankfurt-am-Main and near to the Roman town of Heddernheim-*Nida*. This villa had been destroyed in the third-century disturbances, but was later restored by barbarian settlers (perhaps with help from surviving provincials?), dry-stone walling being added to the ruinous Roman structure.

To sum up this survey, the types of settlement which existed in Germania during our period included the isoated farmstead, the hamlet or group of two or three farms, and the larger agglomeration of farmsteads to which the term 'village' may unhesitatingly be applied. The overriding impression conveyed by the excavated sites is of stable and enduring communities, some occupying the same sites for many decades or even centuries, others shifting their dwellings without moving far beyond their original confines. A few, such as Wijster and the Bärhorst, display a degree of planning which is comparable with that of peasant villages within the Roman Empire and which would have surprised a Roman observer. Occasionally, as at Feddersen Wierde and Fochteloo, there is clear evidence of social differentiation, but the territorial power of leaders was only rarely expressed by the building of hill-forts or other defended strongholds—in striking contrast to the Celtic realms—and there was no development of the town-like *oppidum* on the Celtic model. In the Migration period and beyond, at sites like Warendorf, there can be found village communities akin to Wijster and Feddersen.

Thus in the early Germanic settlements are the very roots of medieval European villages. A distinguished ancient historian has recently written:

The latter [i.e. the Germans] were illiterate, organised in loose tribal federations rather than in more advanced political systems, and constantly on the move, both because their relatively primitive agricultural techniques exhausted the soil rapidly and because from time to time they were driven by invaders, such as the later Huns, who swept across the eastern and central European plains.[39]

This view of the Germans as a semi-nomadic people is still surprisingly widespread among historians of the ancient world. The archaeological evidence discussed above tells a very different story.

Having reviewed the evidence for settlement types, it is fitting to consider now the main preoccupation of their inhabitants, subsistence agriculture.

## Livestock

The ancient literary sources have little to report about the domesticated animals of northern Europe and, as yet, fully published studies of the animal bone assemblages from excavations are not abundant. Several major sites, for instance Feddersen Wierde, will greatly increase the store of information when they are published in full, but at present we must depend upon the evidence from only about half a dozen settlements. A further limitation lies in the fact that where the evidence is available it is concentrated in north-western Germany, Holland and parts of Scandinavia—a fairly small part of all Germania and unusual in that it contains a high proportion of marshland, especially in Friesland and Schleswig-Holstein. Thus, although it is possible to give a reasonably detailed account of the domesticated animals in these areas, it cannot be assumed that circumstances were exactly similar in east and central Germania.

The animals of the pre-Roman Iron Age have not yet been adequately studied but enough is known to indicate that in all regions cattle were of the greatest importance, both as draught animals and as producers of meat and milk. As a source of meat, pigs came next, followed by sheep and goats. On present evidence sheep and goats appear to have been of much less significance than the other animals. At Hallstatt they accounted for only 20 per cent of the total animal bone, and at the Heuneburg only

11 per cent. These figures apply strictly to those settlements alone but similar proportions for sheep and goats have been recorded from later Iron Age settlements of humbler status. One of the largest series of animal bones yet obtained is that from the Celtic *oppidum* of Manching in Bavaria. These firmly based statistics for the animals reared are unfortunately not yet matched for a Germanic settlement of this period.

PROPORTIONS OF ANIMAL BONES FOUND AT MANCHING

| Type of animal | Percentage of total finds |
| --- | --- |
| Cattle | 43 |
| Pig | 32 |
| Sheep/Goat | 19 |
| Horse | 4 |
| Dog | 0·9 |
| Fowl | 0·03 |

*Note:* The figures are for excavations to 1955.

The slight evidence for breeds suggests that the cattle of the pre-Roman Iron Age, like those of the Bronze Age, were small and short-horned. At Hallstatt, a settlement in contact with the north Italian world, larger beasts were being bred, probably with the aid of imported strains. The pigs were descended from native wild animals and were rather small, scrawny and long-legged. Horses, too, were small, although at least one strain resembled the modern Arab horse and another was a still larger animal. They were used mainly for draught and riding, though some sites have produced evidence that they were eaten.

This information about animal breeds accords closely with the data so far recovered for the animals of the Roman Iron Age. For these, the work of Nobis on the bones from Tofting and other *Wurten* provides a most valuable source.[40] Like those of earlier periods the cattle from the marshland settlements were small, slender and short-horned. Nobis calculates that at the shoulder they measured on average no more than 1·10m. Earlier writers held that the breed derived from small, wild cattle, *Bos brachyceros Adametz*, but it is now generally agreed that it was descended from *Bos primigenius Boianus* and that its small size was due to a continuous process of non-selective breeding from the Neolithic period onward. There is no sign of any change in the size or breed of cattle in the marshland settlements during the Roman period. Since the *Wurten* enjoyed commercial contacts with the Roman provinces it might be expected that larger Roman breeds might have been introduced into the north but there is no indication that this occurred. After the end of the Roman period, too, no change in the cattle breed has been detected at any *Wurt*, except at Hessens where larger beasts were introduced from some unknown source in the early medieval centuries.

The horses also were short and stocky, measuring approximately 1·35m at the shoulder. The animals were probably not much shorter than many in the Roman provinces, but were broader and less graceful. Once again, there is no evidence of imported breeds: larger and heavier animals are first apparent from the later Migration period. The pigs display all the characteristics of a dwarf breed, even though their remote ancestors seem to have been the large wild *Sus scrofa antiquus*. This marked diminution in size, as in the cattle and horses, was the direct result of breeding from the same stock over a lengthy period. The process continued into the medieval period and the pigs at Hedeby and Alt-Lübeck were even smaller than those of the Roman Iron Age.

Sheep, on the other hand, compare fairly closely in size with several modern breeds. Only one breed has been noted, and this is derived from the wild Moufflon. There is no apparent influence from the Roman world. Marked differences in the size of bones and horns are probably due to sexual dimorphism within the one breed. Although their wool was highly prized, most sheep will have been kept for their milk as well as their fleeces. For the quality and colour of the latter no evidence is available.

The relative proportions of farm animals reared on marshland sites is made clear by the following table.

PROPORTIONS OF ANIMAL BONES FOUND AT MARSHLAND SETTLEMENTS IN NORTH-WEST GERMANY

| Settlement | Percentage of total finds | | | | | | |
|---|---|---|---|---|---|---|---|
| | Cattle | Sheep/Goat | Pig | Horse | Fowl | Dog | Cat |
| Einswarden | 54·3 | 23·9 | 10·4 | 10 | 0·1 | 1·3 | — |
| Tofting | 66·1 | 22·9 | 6 | 3·8 | 0·5 | 0·2 | 0·5 |
| Hessens | 66·3 | 19·8 | 6·6 | 7·2 | 0·1 | — | — |
| Barnkrug | 59 | 5·8 | 12·1 | 20·7 | — | 2·4 | — |
| Hodorf | 64·4 | 10·2 | 17 | 6·7 | — | 1·7 | — |
| Wulfshof | 68·1 | 17·8 | 6·9 | 6·7 | — | 0·5 | — |

*Note:* The figures are taken from G. Nobis in Bantelmann, A. (1955).

Cattle were everywhere the most important stock, ranging from 54 per cent at Einswarden to 68 per cent at Wulfshof. The greatest variation occurs in the figures for sheep/goat and pig. In the coastal marshland (i.e. at Einswarden, Tofting and Hessens) where there were extensive pastures but no trees, sheep rearing followed that of cattle. The riverine marshes (Barnkrug and Hodorf) lay closer to the *Geest* where there was mixed woodland providing ample mast for pigs, so that here swine husbandry took precedence over sheep rearing. Horses make no prominent showing, except at Barnkrug where they outnumber sheep and pig put together. The reason for this is obscure.

The data for Jutland are not so extensive or detailed as for the marshland: on the whole the proportions of the different animals are similar.

TYPES OF ANIMAL BONES FOUND IN JUTLAND

| Settlement | Cattle | Bone types Sheep/Goat | Pig | Horse |
|---|---|---|---|---|
| Degnegaard | * | * | – | * |
| Nørre Fjand | * | * | * | *(?) |
| Ginderup | * | * | * | – |
| Solbjerg | * | – | – | * |
| Engelstrup | * | * | * | – |
| Tolstrup | * | *(?) | – | – |
| Holmsland | * | * | – | – |

*Note:* Finds are indicated by * and lack of finds by – ; percentages are not available.[41]

The outstanding importance of cattle in the coastal regions is also apparent in a few settlements inland. The most impressive amount of evidence comes from the excavation of the Roman Iron Age hamlet of Seinstedt which lay on loess at the edge of the Mittelgebirge. The animal breeds represented here correspond closely to those of the marshlands: small, short-horned cattle, small horses, pigs and sheep. Cattle made up the bulk of the stock, followed by pigs with horses and sheep much less prominent. The great majority of the swine had been slaughtered between the ages of eighteen months and three years, the sheep at less than two years, clearly for their succulent meat. The horses and cattle, by contrast, had been kept well beyond their maturity as in the *Wurten*.

Another source which underlines the dominance of cattle in the northern regions is provided by the plans of long-houses with stall divisions occupying a substantial proportion of their length. At the Ezinge *Terp* in the pre-Roman Iron Age as many as forty or fifty mature cattle might have been housed in the largest of the byre-houses (House E), though this was clearly exceptional. The majority of the houses at Feddersen Wierde had stalling for some fifteen to twenty-five beasts and similar figures may be suggested for Wijster. In the drier areas of Jutland the figures are not so large and a higher proportion of dwellings had no stalls at all. Normally, between twelve and twenty cattle could have been housed in the Jutland long-houses.

CATTLE-STALLS IN JUTLAND HOUSES

| Settlement | House no. | Head of cattle |
|---|---|---|
| Nørre Fjand | XIV | 17 |
| Nørre Fjand | XVIII | 16 |
| Skørbaek Hede | F | 10 |
| Sjaelborg | II | 12 |
| Østerbølle | A | 12 |
| Gording Hede | II | 6 |

*Note:* The figures are taken from M. Müller-Wille (1965), 97, Table 24.

*Crops*

A wide range of evidence gives a clear and full picture of the food plants grown during the Roman Iron Age, although once again the fullest body of information comes from northern Germany and Denmark. This evidence includes the results of pollen analysis, samples of actual or carbonized grain from occupation sites, the stomach-contents of corpses found in peat-bogs, and impressions of grains and other seeds preserved on pottery sherds.

Significant changes were wrought on the kinds of crops grown in northern Europe by the change to a damper, cooler climate in the later second millennium B.C. The various kinds of wheat, especially emmer and *Einkorn*, which had been the staple crops from the Neolithic period, now began to give way to other grains, particularly to barley. This was probably the commonest grain crop throughout the Iron Age, naked barley being prevalent in the pre-Roman Iron Age, the hulled variety in the Roman period. Oats, apparently originally collected as a weed, gradually became more important from the Bronze Age onward, until in the Roman period they were the second commonest grain crop. Rye was also first gathered as a weed, but its cultivation does not seem to have been intensive in the Iron Age. Millet had been grown since the Neolithic period but declined in importance during the earlier Iron Age. In some settlements in central Europe, however, for instance Kablow in Brandenburg, there are reports of large quantities of millet being found. In addition to these well known grains, the seeds of various kinds of weeds were harvested. 'Harvested' rather than 'collected' seems to be the appropriate term, for weed seeds occur not only in the internal organs of bog corpses but also in pits and storage vessels on settlement sites.

The following table gives some idea of the relative proportions of the different grain crops. The figures are drawn from sites in Denmark but they are likely to be applicable to the adjacent areas of north Germany as well.

GRAIN-SAMPLES AND GRAIN-IMPRESSIONS FROM SITES IN DENMARK

| Grain | pre-Roman I.A. | early Roman I.A. | late Roman I.A. |
|---|---|---|---|
| Wheat | 13 | 1 | 2 |
| Spelt | — | 1 | 1 |
| Barley (naked) | 68 | 33 | 18 |
| Barley (hulled) | 12 | 46 | 66 |
| Oats | 1 | 15 | 6 |
| Millet | 6 | — | — |
| Rye | — | 4 | 7 |

Other food crops included flax, prized for its oil-bearing seeds, beans and peas. Particularly large amounts of bean-straw were recorded at Feddersen Wierde. Other vegetables are attested, although it is rarely possible to be sure that they are cultivated and not wild forms. These vegetables are carrots, cabbage, rape, radish, asparagus and a form of lettuce. Various herbs were also available, but it is not clear to what extent they were used in cuisine. These included coriander, dill, garlic, parsley and carroway.

Surprisingly, the rich palynological evidence from the *Terpen* and other marshland settlements includes very little information about fruit growing or collecting. The apple had been known since *Bandkeramik* times and the pear is occasionally attested from the end of the Neolithic period. Plums and wild cherries have been recorded from Schwäbisch-Hall in the pre-Roman Iron Age, and morello cherries and sloes are known elsewhere in the Roman period. The apricot and the peach were known in southern Germania, and even the grape was grown in places, again in the south and in the Alpine Foreland. Various wild fruits, such as strawberry, raspberry, bilberry, blackberry and elderberry, may have been collected. As well as supplementing the diet, some of these might have been used in the making of fermented drinks like that borne into the grave by a woman at Juellinge in Denmark.

## Fields

Traces of settled agriculture in the form of fields with fixed boundaries are abundant in certain areas of northern Europe, pre-eminently in north and west Jutland, Schleswig-Holstein, northern Holland and parts of southern Sweden.[42] Published evidence on field systems from the north German plain and from eastern Europe is still slight in quantity. In Jutland, Schleswig-Holstein and Holland the ancient fields have survived largely on soils which lay outside the bounds of cultivation in more recent times, especially on sterile, sandy heaths, and although the condition of some of the field-remains is very striking, scarcely any field systems survive on the richer lands, which were certainly cultivated in the Roman Iron Age as they were in later periods. No conclusions can therefore be drawn about the extent of settled agriculture from the present-day distribution of Iron Age field systems. Indeed, it must be considered likely that the areas in which ancient fields can still be examined were, in antiquity as now, mainly areas of marginal land.

The surviving Iron Age fields are commonly represented by terraces or lynchets on sloping ground, or as plots of varying size defined by low banks of earth and stones. In many cases these banks seem to be no more than the result of a piling up of stones on the balks at the field margins during tillage, but at least some of the field-banks existed from the start of cultivation, especially in areas of sandy soil where there could be marked 'drifting' of the topsoil in dry weather. In excavation of some

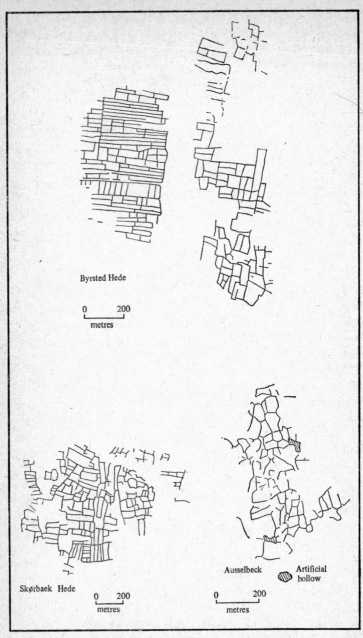

Byrsted Hede

0    200
metres

Skørbaek Hede

0    200
metres

Ausselbeck    Artificial hollow

0    200
metres

Fig. 19 Field systems in northern Germania

field boundaries, small gullies or ditches have been located beneath the banks, the original use of these being to mark out the plots. Gradually they were choked and obliterated with dumped stones and drifted soil.

Thanks to the careful work of Professor Jankuhn and Dr Müller-Wille, we are in possession of reliable figures for the size of surviving field systems and their component plots. The systems range, in their present state, from 20 000 sq.m to about 1 000 000 sq.m. The larger systems now occur in Jutland. In Angeln and in northern Holland, the largest groups of fields measure less than 300 000 sq.m. In all those areas recently surveyed by Müller-Wille, 75 per cent of the recorded field groups measure less than 200 000 sq.m and 35 per cent less than 50 000 sq.m. There are certain limitations to the use of these figures in any comparative study. First, there is no way of knowing how much of the field systems had vanished before the first records were made. Secondly, it cannot be assumed that the whole of a surviving group of fields is homogeneous in date, or that it was originally associated with a single homestead or settlement. In a few cases, however, it is possible to calculate approximately the size of a field system associated with an individual settlement. At Skørbaek Hede in Jutland a hamlet of four farmsteads lay on the edge of a field system of about 600 000 sq.m (fig. 19).[43] If, as is likely, this area of fields was associated with this settlement alone, then each steading would have the rather generous allotment of some 150 000 sq.m each. This extensive amount of ground presumably included pasture, and perhaps hay meadows, and the arable land may have amounted to no more than 30–40 000 sq.m to each farm. This is the figure which can be deduced from historical sources for farmsteads in north-west Germany in the early medieval period. A settlement of 3 or 4 steadings would require on this reckoning about 100–160 000 sq.m of arable and, indeed, in Jutland, where there are numerous examples of such hamlets, several of the field groups do cover between 100–200 000 sq.m.

Few of the field systems have been examined archaeologically and thus, while something can be said about their morphology, their development and date are generally obscure. One of the most impressive of the surviving field groups is that already referred to at Skørbaek Hede, which covers in all some 1 sq.km. Out of 134 identifiable plots, 45 are irregular in shape and 89 regular, mostly squarish or rectangular. Most of the fields are less than 10 000 sq.m in area and a third of the total are between 10–20 000 sq.m. Another extensive system, now completely obliterated lay at Byrsted Hede also in Jutland (fig. 19). This was divided into two by a flat, sandy trough, which was probably never cultivated. Of 175 fields, more than half measured between 10–20 000 sq.m and most of the remainder were less than 10 000 sq.m. Unlike the Skørbaek Hede fields, only a very small proportion, about 10 per cent, were irregularly shaped. The most striking feature of the Byrsted Hede fields is a series of regularly planned and sized narrow fields on the western side. Such regularity is encountered rarely in Iron Age fields, the closest analogy being Braendsgaard Hede, again in Jutland.

Of the field systems in northern Holland, that at Noordse Veld, Zeijen, dating from the Roman Iron Age, is the best example of its class.[44] 131 fields are known, covering at least 270 000 sq.m, and more than half of them are between 10–20 000 sq.m, as is common in Jutland. An unusually high proportion, however, almost a third, are between 30–40 000 sq.m. Most tend to the square or rectangular. Another group with similarly shaped fields is that at Balloer Veld. Here, too, the field size is comparable with instances in Jutland, most of the units measuring less than 20 000 sq.m.

Numerous groups of Iron Age fields can be traced in wooded areas of Angeln and Schleswig.[45] In only a few cases can they be related to dated settlements and thus their precise dating remains unknown. The great majority, however, will ultimately prove to belong to the late pre-Roman and Roman Iron Age. Three main types of field system have been distinguished in Angeln, the commonest form by far being an irregularly planned system of rectilinear fields, usually polygonal or quadrilateral. In size the individual plots vary between 625m and 3500m square.

An excellent instance of this kind of field system is the large group of fields at Ausselbek, Ülsby, near Schleswig (fig. 19), which covers an area more than 750m by 400m in sum. On the rising ground the fields are terraced and bounded by low earth walls running across the line of the contours. Where the ground is flat, the field boundaries are earth walls alone. Near the centre of the surviving block of fields, the units tend to be smaller and polygonal, but on the periphery, especially on the south-west and western edges, there is a greater tendency to the rectangular, suggesting that there have been planned additions to a haphazard early growth. One of the most striking features of the Ausselbek fields is also the most puzzling. A number of irregular, shallow delves are in evidence in several places, notably about the centre of the system, some of them with ramps leading down into them. These ramps are often large enough to afford access to the hollows for a cart. These features are plainly not the result of natural agencies and excavation has demonstrated that they are broadly contemporary with the life of the field system. Their function is not easy to divine. An agricultural purpose seems to be more appropriate than a connection with industry, and the most plausible explanation for them is that they are the result of excavation for clay which was used to 'marl' the fields. If so, this would be useful evidence that marling was practised so far north. The only other fragment of evidence on the subject is the statement of the Elder Pliny that the Ubii of the Rhineland practised marling.[46]

Systems of strictly rectangular fields are much rarer in Angeln, although they are well known in northern Holland and Jutland. The only certain instance yet recorded in Angeln is that at Klappholz, near Schleswig, where a planned series of fairly precise rectangles is defined by a system of low walls and terraces. The whole group of plots covers at least 450m by 200m. Unfortunately, the field boundaries are poorly preserved and some have vanished beneath modern ploughing so that the size of individual fields can be determined in very few cases. One plot measured 70m by 50m, another 50m square.

Narrow terraced fields which follow the contours put in an occasional appearance in Angeln and on the North Frisian islands, though they appear to be unknown in Jutland. In form they are remarkably similar to the familiar strip lynchets of southern Britain. A site at Wittkiel (Kr. Flensburg) has a group of terraces which vary in width from 15–36m and measure up to 150m in length, dimensions which make them longer and narrower than the other terraced fields of Angeln. A hundred metres to the south lay a group of irregular polygonal fields whose chronological relationship with the terraces cannot be determined. It would be worth knowing whether or not the irregularly shaped plots were replaced or added to by the terraces, but as yet there is no evidence of date for either.

The distribution of surviving field systems of the Iron Age

in relation to the prevailing soil types is very revealing. Very few are known on light sandy soils, a few more on areas of mixed loam and sand. The great majority lie on the intermediate loams and light clays which cover most of Angeln. The heavier land in the east seems to have been studiously avoided by the Iron Age settlers.

## Implements

The implements used in cultivation in the northern Iron Age, particularly the ploughs, are much better known than those of any other period of European prehistory, a circumstance primarily due to the recovery of a number of complete ploughs and a series of plough-parts from bog deposits, notably in Jutland.[47] Around these finds a considerable literature has accumulated and thus only their more important features need be touched on here. The circumstances of discovery of these implements rarely allow close dates to be assigned to them, and where dates are available it is clear that few extant ploughs or their components actually date from the Roman Iron Age. This is fortunately not disastrous, for it can be demonstrated beyond doubt that some types of plough were in use from at least the late Bronze Age to the end of the Roman period, while other types were equally certainly current from the Roman period to relatively modern times.

Two main kinds of plough can be distinguished among the Iron Age implements. The first type has a symmetrically placed share which cut a groove in the earth and pushed the soil to both sides of it. The only part of this implement which operated on the soil was the share itself. This instrument is usually termed an *ard*, following Scandinavian terminology. The second form is a fully fledged plough (Danish *plov*, German *Pflug*) and this had an asymmetrically set share which could turn the sod to one side only and thus create more clearly defined furrows. It might be further equipped with a mould-board to assist in turning the sod and a coulter to cut a slice in advance of the share. But neither mould-board nor coulter has yet been certainly attested among the plough parts found in free Germany. Iron plough-shares, however, were in use from at least the first century B.C. in certain areas; probably they had been introduced from the Celtic parts of central Europe.

In all, the ards can be classified in three groups (fig. 20). The

3. Wooden idol from
Rude Eskilstrup,
Zealand, Denmark

4a. Spur with silver inlay
from Hörninge, Köping,
Öland

4b. Shield from Thorsbjerg

first is known in England as the crook-ard or sole-ard, and on the Continent as the ard of Walle type, after the find-spot of an example in Schleswig-Holstein.[48] In the Walle type the beam, sole and share were made from a single piece of wood, usually oak, the only necessary addition being an upright stake carrying the hand-grip. Six ards of this type have so far been recovered from bog deposits, all of them apparently of late Bronze Age or

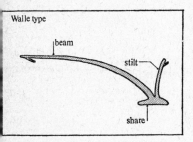

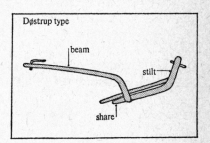

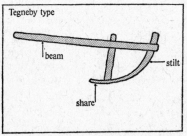

Fig. 20 Plough types

pre-Roman Iron Age date: Walle (Kr. Aurich); Dabergotz (Kr. Neuruppin); Hvorslev (Viborg); Nysum (Aalborg); Sejbaek (Viborg); Vebbestrup (Aalborg). The type continued in use into the Roman period and long afterwards. Simple ards with only slight modifications to the Walle type were still being employed in parts of Europe into modern times.

The second ard type is named after a complete specimen found at Døstrup (Aalborg).[49] The Døstrup type, usually called the bow-, beam- or spade-ard in England, is a much more complex piece of carpentry, formed out of several separate parts, the share and the stilt being inserted through a hole near the base of the beam. The share could be more elaborate than that of the Walle type, in that its shape was a more pronounced arrow-head and over it occasionally was a narrow fore-share. In all,

E

seven such ards have been found, six of them in Jutland: Svarvabo (Uppland); Donnerupland (Veijle); Døstrup (Aalborg); Trollerup (Veijle); Nørre Smedeby (two examples: Aabenraa); Hendriks Mose (Viborg). Two further examples are known from the Roman Iron Age in south-west Scotland. The extraordinary care taken over the construction of such an important piece of equipment is demonstrated by the use of four different kinds of wood in the Døstrup ard, hard alder in the beam, softer lime in the stilt, and hazel and elder for the other parts.

The third type is represented not by actual examples but by rock pictures in the Bohuslän region of Sweden. After one of these ploughing scenes the ard is given the name Tegneby type (English stave- or three-sided ard).[50] This has a curved stilt forming one piece with the sole. The beam is fixed to the stilt at one end and linked to the sole by a cross-member. Like the first two ard types, the Tegneby ard survived in use down to recent times in certain areas of the north.

Remains of ploughs, as opposed to ards, are far less prominent in the archaeological record and not one can yet be confidently dated to the pre-Roman or Roman Iron Age. Even the occasional finds of asymmetrical shares have not been shown to be earlier than the medieval centuries. Nevertheless, it is certain that ploughs with asymmetrical shares were known in the Roman Iron Age if not earlier. Observations of plough furrows which can only have been produced by an asymmetrical share have been made on several sites in the coastal marshland: at Feddersen Wierde, Ostermoor, Barward and Uttum. But the introduction of the plough did not make the ard redundant. From the same regions at the same time clear traces of ard furrows have also been reported.

Information about how these implements were used is naturally very scanty. The Bronze Age rock pictures show both horses and oxen being used for traction. On sloping or rocky ground human energy might have supplied the power. There is a little evidence to indicate that some ards had been used to produce furrows which aped those made by a plough with an asymmetrical share. The state of wear on the right-hand side of the sole on the ards from Donnerupland, Hvorslev and Sejbaek suggests that they had been held obliquely during ploughing so as to throw the earth over to one side. Possibly the same furrows were ploughed twice when the ard was used in this way, once with the implement upright to open up the ground, and once with it sloping to deepen the furrow and direct the soil to one side. There are many indications that cross-ploughing was practised, in the Iron Age, as earlier. It was first demonstrated by Hatt at the pre-Roman settlement of Alrum in Jutland but subsequent observation has added many examples, one of the most striking being that beneath the Nørre Fjand settlement.[51]

The other agricultural tools attested are of uncomplicated types. Iron sickles for harvesting and leaf knives for cutting winter fodder came in during the pre-Roman Iron Age in Scandinavia and probably elsewhere.[52] The leaf knives were single-edged instruments ending usually in a flat, unsharpened hook which bent inward towards the blade. The sickles were simple crescentic knives with long wooden handles. Short-bladed scythes for reaping grain cops are known from the early Roman period onward. They had a broad, crescentic blade and a handle set at an obtuse angle to it. A well preserved example from Vimose is 31·5cm long and 7·7cm broad at its widest point. Other scythe-blades, for instance from Illemose (Odense), are narrower and straighter. The long-handled wooden rake was known, a complete specimen being found at Thorsbjerg. Its use was probably for harrowing as well as raking out weeds after the ard had done its work. From the Frisian *terpen* come pairs of antler tines converted into small rake-heads. Farm carts were well known, oxen being most probably used in their traction. The yoking together of oxen is attested by a completely preserved yoke found at Peters-fehn in Oldenburg.

Unlike many other aspects of early German affairs, there is scarcely any evidence of Roman influence upon their agricultural practice. It is also true that there is little indication of changes brought about by internal forces. At the end of our period subsistence agriculture was much the same as it had been in the pre-Roman Iron Age. Without the assistance of an advancing technology, and without any external motors of change, it is difficult to see how major innovations could have been wrought. It is clear all the same that the early German economy was well adapted to its environment and able to support fairly large communities. In this respect, as well as in its general character, that economy was probably essentially similar to peasant agriculture within the western Roman provinces. When the barbarians settled in those provinces, they found there in current practice ways of making a living which were familiar to them, or to which they could easily adapt themselves.

## References

1. H. Reinerth, *Das Federseemoor als Siedlungsland des Vorzeit-menschen* (Augsburg, 1929).
2. H. Schubart in *Ausgrabungen und Funde*, iii (1958), 210ff.
3. Waterbolk, H. T. (1964).
4. Very little is yet known about the house types of the early and middle Bronze Age. It cannot, therefore, be assumed that the aisled long-house did not develop before the late Bronze Age.
5. Haarnagel, W. (1957).
6. Haarnagel, W. (1965).
7. Rajewski, Z. (1959).
8. Plan in Piggott, S. (1965), 200, Fig. 112.
9. Halbertsma, H. (1963).
10. *Nat. Hist.* xvi, 1, 3.
11. Waterbolk, H. T. (1962).
12. Bantelmann, A. (1955), 77ff.
13. Van Giffen, A. E. (1936). A final report is in preparation.
14. W. A. van Es in *Palaeohistoria*, xiv (1968), 187ff.
15. Van Giffen, A. E. (1958), 47ff.
16. op. cit. 51ff.
17. Van Es, W. A. (1967).
18. Haarnagel, W. (1956), (1957), (1961) and (1963).
19. Schmid, P. (1969b).
20. Schindler, R. (1955); D. Zoller in *Neue Ausgrabungen und Forschungen in Niedersachsen*, i (1963), 132ff.
21. Schindler, R. (1958).
22. Bantelmann, A. (1955).
23. A. Bantelmann in *Offa*, xvi (1957–8), 53ff.
24. Becker, C. J. (1965), (1968) and (1971).
25. Conveniently in Brøndsted, J. (1960), 60f.
26. Hatt, G. (1957).
27. G. Hatt in *Antiquity*, xi (1937), 166, and *Acta Arch.* (Copenhagen), vii (1936), 331.
28. *Acta Arch.* (Copenhagen), vi (1935), 278ff.
29. Stenberger, M. and Klindt-Jensen, O. (1955).
30. M. Stenberger in *Nachrichten Akad. Wissen Göttingen*, 1969, 101ff.
31. M. Müller-Wille in *Bonner Jahrb.*, clxvi (1966), 379ff.
32. R. von Uslar in *Bonner Jahrb.*, cxlix (1949), 105ff.
33. Doppelfeld, O. and Behm, G. (1938).
34. Behm-Blancke, G. (1956).
35. Behrend, R. (1969).
36. Haarnagel, W. (1965b).

37. Werner, J. (1965).
38. op. cit., 444 Abb. 1.
39. M. I. Finley, *Aspects of Antiquity* (London, 1968), 212.
40. in Bantelmann, A. (1955), 114ff.
41. Müller-Wille, M. (1965), 97 n. 30.
42. op. cit., *passim*. H. Jankuhn in *Bericht Röm. Germ. Kommission*, xxxvii–viii (1956–7), 148ff.
43. Hatt, G. (1949), Pl. I; Müller-Wille, M. (1965), 160ff.
44. Müller-Wille, M. (1965), 206ff.
45. H. Jankuhn, op. cit.
46. *Nat. Hist.* xvii, 4, 47.
47. On the whole subject, Glob, P.V. (1951).
48. op. cit. 14ff.
49. op. cit. 29ff.
50. op. cit. 54ff.
51. Hatt, G. (1957), Pl. XX; Becker, C. J. (1961), 112.
52. A. Steensberg, *Ancient Harvesting Implements* (Copenhagen, 1943), 100ff.

# 4 | Technology and crafts

The technical attainments and modes of artistic expression of the Germanic peoples in the pre-Roman Iron Age were on the whole very modest. In metal technology in particular, they lagged far behind the craftsmen of Hallstatt and La Tène Europe. The import into the north of Celtic objects in bronze and iron seems not to have triggered off any notable response among Germanic smiths, and it was not until after the beginning of the Roman Iron Age that appreciable advances were made. The most far-reaching of these advances lay in the working of gold and silver, and with this we may fitly begin.

## Gold-work

The Germans of the fifth and sixth centuries have for long enjoyed a high reputation as workers in gold and silver. Migration period gold ornaments, in particular those which were further enhanced by precious and semi-precious stones, are the most impressive items in the rather limited Germanic contribution to western European art and craftmanship. Attention is too commonly focused upon only the finest products of the Migration period craftsmen: the gold collars of Sweden, the Frankish and Ostrogothic brooches, the gold of Vendel. These high peaks of technical expertise were reached only after a long period of development. Indeed, recent finds demonstrate that that period was very much longer than had been realized. It is fitting, then, that we should begin this examination of early German craftsmanship by surveying what must be regarded as the formative period of their finest craft, a craft which was to produce some of the most marvellous objects ever made in Europe.

The pre-Roman Iron Age in the north has yielded extremely few objects of gold. There were no native resources of gold so that any chieftain who wanted to possess such ornaments had to acquire the metal from the Celts or the Roman world. The evidence is that this did not often happen and gold was clearly reaching Germania in only minute quantities before the Roman period. The earliest gold objects which may be regarded as of Germanic manufacture date from the end of the first century B.C. or the very beginning of the first century A.D., and these are no more ambitious than finger-rings and gold filigree-work on silver brooches.[1] The most striking gold object of the early Roman period is also one of the finest pieces of gold-work from northern Europe, and the fact that it is a recent find is a warning that there is still much to learn about work in the finer metals.

This object is a magnificent torc, found in a hoard at the fort of Havor on the island of Gotland (Pl. 2).[2] The hoard was contained in a Roman bucket and it included in all six imported bronze vessels which date from the first century A.D. At the latest, therefore, the burial of the Havor hoard must be dated to the first half of the second century and it may be as early as A.D. 100. The torc is a large specimen of its type, measuring 24cm in diameter. The ring is made up of a number of gold wires of rectangular section twisted together. The torc terminals are smooth, hollow bulbs of gold, ornamented with a single cable of filigree. The richest ornament was reserved for the cone-shaped elements which linked the terminals with the ring proper. This ornament consists of three symmetrically arranged half-moons of plain metal bordered by cables of filigree, each half-moon forming a frame for a steer's head. Around and inside these curved panels the ornament takes the form of narrow strips bordered by more filigree cables and containing numerous figure-of-eight motifs also rendered in filigree. The handling of a combination of curved and straight motifs is so confident and the technique so mature that it is all but incredible that the Havor torc stands near the beginning of an artistic tradition and not at its peak.

Although there is no exact analogue to the Havor torc, it is plainly related to a small group of similar objects. One other member of this group has been found in Scandinavia, a smaller torc from a peat-bog at Dronninglund (Vendsyssel) in Denmark.[3] This, too, has hollow bulbous terminals and richly decorated conical elements linking them to the ring proper. The decoration on the cones has similar narrow panels to those of the Havor torc and all of them also contain figures-of-eight in filigree.

Three other gold torcs of the same type are known, all found in south Russia; one at Olbia on the Black Sea coast and the other two in a hoard from Smjela near Kiev.[4] Once again there is a combination of plain hollow terminals and cones elaborately ornamented with filigree.

The presence of Scandinavian gold-work related to the Havor and Dronninglund torcs in technique and decoration is worth note. A number of small pendants and beads have been recorded in the western Baltic region, especially on Gotland, and these bear remarkably similar filigree ornament to the torcs. To select two out of several examples, a biconical bead from Bo on Öland has the figure-of-eight motif in filigree, while another bead from Hede (Västmanland) bears half-moons like those on the Havor torc.[5] Both these objects probably date from the very beginning of the Roman Iron Age. The torcs, therefore, cannot be regarded as freakish. They can be related to other gold-work of the period in Scandinavia (and in south Russia), but not so far in other parts of Germania. The problem of the origin of this northern gold-work now presents itself.

An older school of archaeologists, including Sophus Müller and Gustav Kossinna, was deeply impressed with the notion of cultural and technical impulses spreading to northern Europe from south Russia, especially after the Gothic migration thither in the second century. And there can be no doubt that inter-mittently from the Bronze Age onward men and ideas did follow that road. Such technical impulses can, however, move in both directions and the evidence at present available is not exten-sive enough to allow us to choose between a northward or a south-ward movement. The small objects, the beads and the pendants, are more likely to have been produced by Scandinavian craftsmen than by anyone else, and their stylistic and technical links with the torcs are as close as they can be. On balance, present evidence favours Scandinavia as the origin of these fine gold pieces, but it will be remembered that there has been no large-scale examina-tion and publication of Iron Age gold-work from south Russia, where the related torcs from Olbia and Smjela lie in a decidedly unlikely isolation. When that survey is carried out, it may be found that the Havor and Dronninglund torcs were products of craftsmen who found their way to Scandinavia from the Black Sea regions, there to found a brilliant local tradition of gold-working. But the evidence will support equally well the idea that the western Baltic was the birthplace of an original and gifted school of goldsmiths whose speciality was filigree work.

No doubt the few craftsmen working in gold in the early Roman Iron Age were producing exclusively for a few wealthy chieftains, for outside the richer burials gold objects are extremely rare. During the second century, gold ornaments are almost as rare as they were in the first, but after the Marcomannic Wars there was a marked increase in the amount of gold entering Germania and in the desire of native chiefs to possess fine ornaments. Most of these were produced by Germanic craftsmen and there is little evidence of import from the Roman world.

From about 200, too, there were evident advances in the technique of gold-working and particularly in the use of gold in combination with other materials, notably various kinds of stone and silver. The use of semi-precious stones, especially garnets, and glass paste on gold objects brought a new dimension to the craft and these third-century innovations first opened the way towards the brilliant attainments of Frankish and Kentish jewellers. Precisely where the new style of ornament came from and who carried it into central and western Europe are questions which have long provoked debate and which still have not been satisfactorily answered. It is widely agreed that the broad area of south Russia and Rumania in the hinterland of the Black Sea, an area which saw an extraordinary mingling of cultures, including steppe nomad, Dacian, Germanic and Graeco-Roman, must have been the ultimate origin of what was to become the 'polychrome' style of jewelled ornament, even though the agents of its transmission westwards remain unknown.[6] Earlier archaeologists found no difficulty in explaining this westward movement. It was, they claimed, due to the 'Gothic culture-stream', by which was meant a dissemination to north and west of cultural impulses from the Pontus region by Gothic leaders and craftsmen. Although on *a priori* grounds the Goths are likely to have played their part in the spreading of the new style, far too much has been attributed to the agency of the Gothic culture-stream, and not enough to inventive craftsmen whose racial origin is unknown (and immaterial) and who cared little whether they worked for a Goth or a Vandal or a Sarmatian.

Among the earliest gold jewellery with inset garnets are brooches from wealthy burials of the later third century. The combination of garnets with rich filigree and granulation is well exemplified by a fine brooch from the *Fürstengrab* at Aarslev (Fyn).[7] This has a large oval garnet covering the bow like a shield, a circular garnet inset in the foot, and six small stones inset elsewhere on the flat surfaces. The Aarslev brooch is of unusual interest in that the form is clearly copied from a Roman original (indeed a Roman silver brooch which could have served as the model lay in the same grave), while the ornamental idiom is thoroughly barbarian. The Hassleben graves, also of the later third century, contained examples of the early use of garnets, notably a gold and two silver brooches with the stones *en cabochon*.[8] The earliest occurrence of the new style jewellery in the richest graves of the period underlines once more the enormous importance of chieftainly patronage to the craft and its exponents. The craftsmen whose work is revealed at Aarslev, Hassleben and elsewhere, were drawn to the rustic courts of Germanic leaders, who wanted to display their rapidly growing wealth on their own persons.

Another of the notable features in fine metalwork of the third century and later is the increasing use of gold and silver-gilt foils, on objects such as brooches, ornamental discs, belt-mounts and, occasionally, weapons. Commonly the foils were laid over chased or repoussé work. The origins of the technique are to be sought in the work of Roman provincial craftsmen, particularly the Hemmoor bucket type with its frieze of animals, caskets decorated with bronze and silver mountings, and perhaps also certain painted glass vessels. Some of the earlier objects which bear foils over repoussé designs are mounts from military belts which imitated the Roman *cingulum*. These mounts or discs were commonly of bronze and their decoration often consisted of an animal or animals shown in a running or leaping posture. Thorsbjerg provides us with a fine example, as does the votive deposit at Skedemosse (Öland) and one of the rich graves at Stráže in Slovakia (Stráže II). Most striking of all are the discs from Häven in Mecklenburg, with their wild boar and bird of prey motifs.[9]

Two of the most outstanding of all early Germanic art objects are decorated with foils, namely the two discs or *phalerae* from the Thorsbjerg deposit. These discs are of bronze covered with richly ornamented gilded silver foil. One is very well preserved, measuring a little over 13cm in diameter, and has its decoration divided into an inner and an outer zone. The inner zone has nine roundels arranged in a circle about a central disc, each roundel bearing a male mask viewed from the front. The outer zone is more complex. Four large discs are spaced out with an equal interval between them and each of the four intervals is occupied by a seated figure of Mars, depicted in classical style. To this outer zone there have been additions in the form of a number of

Fig. 21 Reconstruction drawing of the fragmentary Thorsbjerg phalera

animal figures in a purely Germanic mode, similar to those on the Häven discs and the belt-mounts already mentioned. Following Werner's detailed study of the two *phalerae* published in 1941,[10] it has usually been argued that in its original form this disc was a product of a Roman provincial workshop, possibly on the lower Rhine in the Cologne area, and that the animal figures were added much later, after the object had come into the hands of a German craftsman. Granted that the animals were additions, is the disc necessarily an import from the Roman world? Its classicizing style would not be beyond a competent imitator and certain features, such as the masks and the running border (to say nothing of the foil technique itself), are more reminiscent of free Germany than of the Roman provinces. A barbarian craftsman who had learnt his trade from a Roman provincial, or who had spent some time in the Roman provinces, could well have been responsible for the first Thorsbjerg *phalera*. Much less survives of the second disc (fig. 21). This too was arranged with an inner and an outer zone, with a similar series of nine masks decorating the inner. The outer zone, clearly the work of a German artist, bears a lively frieze of beasts, in which pairs of deer alternate with sea monsters, northern versions of the classical capricorn. The date of the two *phalerae* should be within the earlier part of the third century, and thus their animal figures, along with others on certain silver beakers (see p. 143), must be among the earliest examples of such motifs in Germanic art.

The minor decorative elements found on the Thorsbjerg discs can be discerned on other metal objects overlaid with foil. Among the most striking are a series of large brooches, normally in silver with a covering of gilded silver foil, which occur in the western Baltic lands with outliers in Norway and near the Black Sea. most of them have been found in female graves of the third century. A fine example is the brooch from Vaerlose[11] in Denmark, which is adorned with large rosettes on the bow and the spring. A particularly interesting feature of these so-called 'monstrous' brooches is the fact that of the none-too-common runic inscriptions of the third century, no less than four occur on these objects, always in positions where they would not be seen when the brooch was being worn.

Characteristic gold ornaments of the third and fourth centuries include certain kinds of arm-rings and torcs. The commonest form of arm-ring, copied from Roman models, is the snake-headed ring which took two forms, one spiral, the other a single ring with overlapping terminals. These are found most commonly in eastern Sweden and on the islands of Bornholm and Gotland, though they are also recorded in Denmark and northern Germany. There is thus a strong presumption in favour of their manufacture in west Baltic, possibly island, workshops. Their typology was long ago outlined by Hildebrand,[12] who distinguished three main forms: *A* with more or less naturalistic heads, *B* with elongated and flattened terminals and stylized heads, and *C* with bulbous terminal knobs at the end of cylindrical 'necks'. The rocked tracer or tremolier ornament on the body of the Type *C* rings, the commonest group, is more elementary than that of the others. Discussion of the typological seriation of these handsome ornaments has long bedevilled their study. The evidence of a development from *A* to *C*, or *vice versa* (both have been championed) seems to be exiguous and worth no more ink. Indeed, the evidence of a late Roman Iron Age grave at Tuna in Badelunda (Sweden) is that *A* and *C* at least were contemporary.[13]

The relationship of the snake-headed rings to other late Roman Iron Age metalwork is not yet clear. Their ultimate origin has been sought in south Russia but the hypothesis rests on no more than general similarities between the Scandinavian rings and animal-headed ornaments from the Black Sea lands. There is another group of snake-headed rings, found in the Elbe valley, but these do not seem to extend into the late Roman period, so that in consequence a direct connection is unlikely. A later group of rings is represented in the Thorsbjerg find,[14] for which a Zealand origin has been suggested, and their date is later third century, thus possibly overlapping with the earliest Swedish examples.

Torcs of gold, and less commonly of silver, are also prominent among the later work in the precious metals. Their forms are extremely varied, ranging from plain rings of gold, solidly cast, to hollow tubes covered in the richest filigree and applied ornament. The entire series of torcs is too wide for detailed discussion and the examples noted here are picked out merely to display the wealth of ornament and technical skill evident in the finest objects. A distinct group of torcs is found in eastern Holland and Westphalia. The finest representatives are those in the hoards from Rhenen and Velp in Holland.[15] These torcs were fastened at the back and were distinguished by a pronounced bulge in the centre of the decorated zone at the front. The decoration was usually a close-set mass of stamped and punched impressions.

At the very end of the Roman Iron Age, a group of elaborately constructed torcs was produced in the western Baltic. These were tubes of gold, on to which a number of 'collars' had been soldered, thereby giving the impression of a massive and weighty object. In addition to the 'collars', the surface of the tube was decorated in a variety of ways. The torc from Hjallese (Fyn) has

various stamped ornaments on the flat surfaces between the
'collars', while that from Hannenov (Falster) has splendid
reversed-S designs in filigree on the actual 'collars' and also
flattened animal figures clinging to the two 'collars' nearest the
fastening.[16] These creatures have many analogues, for instance
on the Gallehus horns, at Sösdala[17] and in the second treasure
of Szilagy-Somlyo, and their date must be about 400. The decoration of the Hjallese and Hannenov torcs is laboured and unsubtle
but it points the way forward to the pinnacle of barbarian gold-
working in northern Europe achieved by the superb collars of
Ålleberg and Färjestaden.[18]

The use of animal, human and mythological figures soldered
on to torcs, brooches and other objects is a distinctive feature of
Scandinavian work in gold and silver from about 400 onwards.
Among the brooches so treated special mention belongs to a
rectangular-headed series covered with silver leaf, the animals
being here used in combination with delicate punched ornament.[19]
The most celebrated applied figures, however, are those on the
two gold horns from Gallehus in north Schleswig, where they are
employed with punched ornament in the form of animals, fishes
and star-shaped motifs. The appliqué figures include anthropomorphic and animal shapes in a mythological setting which still
defies wholly convincing interpretation after two centuries of
endeavour. The divine and semi-divine figures are plainly taking
part in certain rituals and sacrifices, but the significance of these
rites remains obscure. Here a three-headed figure holding an axe
draws a goat towards him. There a man with a curved instrument
holds a horse by the rein. Northern myth meets southern as a
centaur-like being prances alongside the world-tree. The meanings
of the picture-language of the Gallehus horns remain effectively
hidden, although a succession of seasonal festivals, as suggested
by Oxenstierna,[20] may underlie the sequence of mysterious scenes.

### Silver-work

The partiality of the Germans for Roman silver vessels is a clear
fact which confounds the statement of Tacitus that they thought
little of such things.[21] The merchant who was peddling the
objects now known as the Hildesheim treasure round Lower
Saxony knew otherwise and so did many German chieftains.
Imported silver vessels passed into barbarian hands with such

frequency that it is scarcely surprising that they stimulated the production of similar vessels by Germanic craftsmen. The few surviving examples of such products reveal the activity of strictly localized workshops or individual craftsmen, no doubt in the service of a chief or wealthy warrior. The earliest dated instances of silver table vessels certainly made by a barbarian craftsman are two drinking-cups from one of the princely graves at Lübsow in Pomerania.[22] These are tolerably close copies of a kind of Italian silver cup, two examples of which came to light in another of the Lübsow graves. They might well have served as the models for the first pair.

The most interesting group of silver drinking vessels dates from the later Roman Iron Age. The group is unusually homogeneous, and all five representatives have been found in a single locality, the Stevns peninsula of the island of Zealand. Two come from a rich grave at Vallöby, two from a similar context at Himlinghøje, and the fifth from Nordrup.[23] In style the five are closely related and all stem from the same circle of craftsmen. The most richly ornamented are the two from Himlinghøje, both of which have more elaborately designed gold foil friezes than the others (frontispiece). All the vessels in the group are distinguished by friezes in gold foil immediately below the rim. The Himlinghøje cups have friezes with galloping animals and men holding daggers, conceivably representing some cult act. The simpler animal friezes of the vessels from Nordrup and Vallöby stamp them as earlier works of the Zealand silversmiths. The models for the friezes were Roman, the most likely prototypes being the animal friezes on buckets of the Hemmoor type.

Silver inlays are first found on a wide range of small objects in the late first and earlier second century A.D. Their introduction was inspired by imported Roman metalwork but in the hands of barbarian craftsmen the technique was turned to purposes not foreseen in the Roman Empire. The technique is essentially simple. A wire of silver (or bronze or copper) was hammered into a groove cut by an engraving tool in the surface which was to receive the decoration. The edges of the groove inclined towards each other at the top so that when the inlay was hammered into place, it was firmly held beneath the overhang. Among the finest of the early inlaid objects is the buckle from Munkehøjgaard on Laaland. This piece has a rectangular buckle-plate edged with close-set inlaid silver wires. Within this frame the flat surface of the plate is decorated with silver filigree. The date of the buckle is not certain. The second century is usually quoted, but it might belong to the late first.[24]

The most outstanding examples of early inlay-work, however, are a series of prick-spurs found in Scandinavia and north Germany. The finest of these are the twin spurs from Hörninge, Köping (Öland). Their flat surfaces are covered in rich filigree, while a delicate and precise mesh of silver inlay covers the pricks. Similarly decorated spurs have been recorded in graves dating from the second century and the beginning of the third.[25]

## Iron-mining and smelting

The most important of Germanic crafts to the Germans themselves was that of iron-working. This is not a field in which the early Germans have enjoyed any repute in the past, since until quite recently Tacitus' statement that there was no abundance of iron in Germania was generally accepted.[26] This statement must be treated with a degree of reserve. It is no doubt true that German armament, among other things, in the pre-Roman and early Roman Iron Age suffered from a scarcity of iron, but it should not be assumed that things did not change after the time in which Tacitus was writing. It is true that the natural iron resources of Germania were not as systematically or as extensively exploited as those of Noricum and Gaul, but this does not mean that *all* the northern barbarians were acutely short of the metal. Some modern writers have gone further than Tacitus and have argued that barbarian methods of producing iron were vastly inferior to those practised in the Roman Empire. No ancient writer was so extreme and, as we will see, the contention conflicts with the archaeological evidence.[27]

Evidence for the large-scale manufacture of iron comes from several parts of Germania, chiefly Schleswig-Holstein, the Ruhr and Lippe valleys, Bohemia, Moravia, Slovakia, Silesia and the Łysa Gora area of Poland between the towns Opatów and Stara Chowice (fig. 22). In all these areas either ironstone or bog-iron is present in considerable quantity, and in at least one case, that of Łysa Gora, the iron-ore deposits were abundant. Germania, in fact, was not so short of iron deposits as Tacitus believed, but the resources were localized and in some areas, for instance Schleswig-Holstein, they comprised the poorer quality bog-iron.

Smelting installations and other remains of iron-production are particularly prominent in Bohemia and this is an appropriate area in which to begin the inquiry. Smelting furnaces of a fairly advanced type were in use here in the La Tène period and the Celtic craftsmen who operated them evidently played a major role in the establishment and early development of manufacture in the Roman period. Several different types of furnace have been

Fig. 22  Main centres of iron-working

distinguished, shaft and domed furnaces being the most prominent, with bowl-hearths making an occasional appearance.[28] The shaft furnace, in particular, played an important role in the iron industry in Germania and a few words on its essential features and mode of operation are necessary before the various sub-types are examined.

The shaft furnace had normally a cylindrical clay superstructure which stood either above ground or was built into a bank. A large number of furnaces found in Czechoslovakia and Poland, especially in the Łysa Gora area, differ from those further west in having a large proportion of their working volume sited beneath the ground surface, a feature which restricted their period of use. The shaft furnace commonly had one aperture to admit the necessary draught of air and another for tapping the slag, but in some examples a single aperture served both functions. Experiments with replicas of Roman period furnaces suggest that forced draught produced by blowing with bellows was essential, though one investigator has claimed that forced draught was required only in the opening stages of firing, the natural draught induced by the tall cylindrical shaft thereafter being sufficient to complete the process of smelting. This particular type of furnace has considerable advantages over the related domed furnace, and is clearly vastly superior to the bowl-hearth. It had provision for continuous charging of ore and charcoal and for tapping of the slag, so that relatively large quantities of ore could be smelted in one period of working.[29] These Iron Age installations are every bit as advanced and as efficient as the shaft furnaces known within the Roman Empire and, indeed, they probably derive from the same Celtic tradition.

To return to Bohemia, one of the earliest attested forms of the shaft furnace is the so-called Tuklaty type, named after a find-spot near Český Brod. The distinctive characteristic of this form is the fact that it was set against the side of a shallow pit. Commonly, two or more furnaces are found to occupy the same pit, though as many as four or five have been recorded. The furnaces comprise a rather small, clay-lined shaft 20–30cm in diameter, the bottom of which penetrated the floor of the pit to a depth of 25cm. The overall height of the shaft is not easily determined but may be estimated at about 50cm from the better preserved examples. A recently excavated example at Křepice in Moravia reveals a variation on the basic form.[30] Here, two large furnaces lay near the centre of a *Grubenhaus*. Their upper parts have not survived but the circumstances of the find suggest that they were probably movable clay or pottery shafts of a kind well known in Schleswig-Holstein. The date of the Křepice furnaces is rather late in the series of installations set in pits, being placed in the second century A.D. The others, where dated, have been shown to belong to the first century B.C. and the first A.D.

As early as the first century A.D., shaft furnaces were being constructed as free-standing structures on the ground surface over sunken hearths. Furnaces of this kind are named after a site at Prague-Podbaba, where numerous examples have been excavated and shown to occur in small, regularly planned batteries, in irregular groups and as isolated instances.[31] A closely related form is named after a site at Loděnice.[32] These furnaces consist of a tall, free-standing shaft up to 70cm high with no sunken hearth beneath. Dated examples of this, the most advanced type yet known, are very rare. Loděnice itself and Tuchlovice belong to the late Roman Iron Age, but earlier instances may yet emerge.

A fourth type, named from Slaný,[33] presents the oldest installations yet discovered. These furnaces take the form of conical clay-lined pits, about 40–50cm deep and 50–70cm in diameter at the base. The best preserved instances suggest that virtually the entire furnace lay underground. The Slaný type is much closer to the bowl-hearth than to the shaft and domed furnaces and like the bowl-hearth was probably capable of producing only fairly soft iron.

So far as they are known at present, the Bohemian smelting workshops were small. The usual number of furnaces on individual sites is one or two, rarely more than three. The largest group of installations so far recorded here is that at Tuchlovice, near the town of Kladno, which included eight smelting furnaces and four roasting ovens, all of the fourth century. Tuchlovice is so far the only Bohemian site which can be regarded as a truly industrial centre as opposed to sites where a few craftsmen produced metal for the needs of a single village community. Taken all in all, the scale of production on individual sites was small and the only area where larger, more centralized workshops might be expected is around Prague where there were accessible deposits of high-grade iron ore.

The next area to be considered, the Łysa Gora hills (Góry Świętokrzyskie) in southern Poland, did contain large centralized workshops of a kind which have not emerged elsewhere in Germania. Between the Łysa Gora ridge and the river Kamienna, about the modern towns of Starachowice, Ostrowiec and Opatów, a region measuring about 24km by 19km contains an enormous number of sites from which slag and furnace debris has been recovered in vast quantity.[34] In some areas the material lies so thick upon the ground that nineteenth-century peasants pursued a lively industry in its collection and re-smelting. The ore deposits were in many places accessible to open-cast working, but the local miners were aware of deeper deposits which they could reach only by mining. At Rudki there has been found the only mine yet known in Germania.[35] The ore at this site, soft and easy to extract, lay at a depth of about 18m and to that depth there had been dug a timber-boarded shaft, roughly 1·75m by 1·10m, from which led a number of galleries and adits. These yielded a number of wooden implements, shovels, wedges and the like, together with pottery of the late Roman period.

The furnace sites in the Łysa Gora region are astounding in their number and their size. Some fifty separate sites and many hundreds of furnaces have now been recorded. A few sites have produced huge numbers of furnaces: for example Jeleniów with 56 and Stara Słupia with 149. On sites with a dense concentration of furnaces, the installations were frequently laid out in close-set rows or batteries. In many cases there is so little space between the furnaces that it is clear that they could not all have been operated at the same time (Pl. 1b). When these close-set groups of furnaces are discovered, their lower parts are normally filled with a solid mass of slag. There had clearly been no attempt to remove this residue by tapping the furnace, and the iron bloom must have been removed by breaking open the body of the shaft. This type of furnace, without tap-hole, can thus have been used only for a single smelting operation, hence the large number of furnaces set so close together, whereas the more conventional shaft-furnace with provision for tapping away the slag while it was still fluid could be used over and over again.

Roman Iron Age settlements have been located in the Łysa Gora industrial area—for this term can justly be used—but as yet excavation has not elucidated the relations of the iron-smelters to them. The dating evidence of the workshops, too, is not absolutely clear. They appear to begin in the late pre-Roman Iron Age, but relatively few groups of furnaces have been firmly dated before the late Roman period. The fourth century and perhaps the later third saw the most intensive production of Łysa Gora iron. So intensive was manufacture then that export into neighbouring regions seems certain, and it is not beyond the bounds of possibility that Łysa Gora iron found its way into the Roman provinces on the Danube.

On the *Geest* and sands of Schleswig-Holstein, bog-iron was found in many localities, especially in the west of the peninsula and about the lower Elbe.[36] These deposits, although easily accessible, were not individually extensive and in consequence working of them was localized and small-scale. The furnace types were in general related to those of Bohemia and Moravia, their usual covering being a clay dome, but movable pottery shafts, like the fine example from Scharmbeck (Kr. Harburg)[37] of the earlier Roman period, were also in use. Some sunken hearths have been interpreted as cementation or carburizing ovens, in which wrought iron was covered with carbon and converted into steel. This process could have been carried out in such installations, but it has not yet been proven by finds of carburized metal in this region. Serious difficulties would have been presented to craftsmen aiming at producing steel by the high phosphorus content of bog-iron.

'Not even iron is abundant' now appears as a far from adequate statement of the facts, whether Tacitus was referring to natural deposits or to smelted iron. This view was actually already out of date by the late first century A.D.; later developments were to leave it still further behind. In the early Roman Iron Age the methods of smelting iron practised in Germania were as advanced, or, more accurately, broadly the same, as those of the Romans. The great differences between the Roman iron industry and that of the barbarians lay elsewhere. One difference was the vastly superior organization which the more advanced society could bring to the workshops and to the distribution of metal supplies and finished objects. Łysa Gora apart, the production of iron in Germania remained in essentials a village industry. Secondly, the Romans were more expert in the manufacture of iron objects, especially tools and weapons. Even at the end of the Roman Iron Age, Germanic smiths had not made much advance in this aspect of their trade, although their tools were basically similar to those used in the Empire.

## Salt

Another extractive industry of more than local importance was the production of salt, used mainly as a preservative. This was so desirable a commodity that the possession of a salt bed on their borders formed a *casus belli* for the Chatti and Hermunduri in A.D. 58,[38] and other salt wars ensued in later centuries. One might guess that those who controlled such springs aimed at making a profit by selling salt to others and not merely at supplying their own needs. The Romans knew how necessary salt was to the barbarian economy and tried to bar its export from the Empire.[39]

Scarcely anything is known about the sites of salt production. The La Tène period workings at Bad Nauheim, Halle and Schwäbisch Hall all appear to have ceased operation by the first century B.C. and the situation of the salt-springs over which the Hermunduri and Chatti came to blows is unknown. Salt-springs are not rare in Germany and it is probable that there were a large number of small centres. The production of salt from sea-water may have been carried out but is not directly attested.

## Pottery

The production of wheel-made pottery in free Germany has often been underestimated in the past. It is true that during the early Roman Iron Age the great mass of domestic and funerary pottery was hand-made, but from the third century onward wheel-made wares—in some cases produced in some quantity by centralized workshops—were on the increase. The earliest wheel-made vessels actually occur in the late pre-Roman Iron Age in central Germany, without question under Celtic stimulus, but these vanish towards the end of the first century B.C.[40] In the next two centuries, native wheel-turned pottery remained extremely rare, although the hand-made vessels in several regions reveal that the potter's craft was pursued to very high standards in fabrics, decoration and firing. The glossy black vessels with geometric ornament of the Elbe basin are by any standards fine products of the potter's art.

The potter's wheel was reintroduced, apparently rather suddenly, in the middle decades of the third century, and wheel-turned pots of new types are first attested in the third century graves of the Leuna and Hassleben chieftains, and in humbler surroundings in several other parts of central Germania, including the Harz, Brandenburg, Silesia, the middle Oder and upper Weser valleys.[41] Though not outstandingly common, the vessels were not confined to the richer circles of Germanic society. The commoner forms represented were carinated bowls with shoulder cordons, beakers with pedestal feet, and indented beakers, all of which are modelled on contemporary Roman types. The high-quality firing and the fabrics also point to the Roman provinces, in particular the upper Rhine and Danube, though whether the Roman provincials who brought in the craft did so as prisoners or voluntary immigrants is uncertain.

Another centre of wheel-made pottery production was established towards the end of the third century in the Cracow region of southern Poland,[42] and once again Roman craftsmen appear to have been involved in its early operation, coming this time from the lower Danube or the Black Sea coast. They brought with them kilns of Roman type, as well as Roman pottery forms, and the industry they founded produced more pottery than the Cracow region could absorb. A significant amount was exported to the area of the Przeworsk culture between the upper Oder and Vistula. The peak of manufacture was attained in the fourth century, and its end came suddenly in the earlier fifth, when this area was disturbed by migrations southwards and westwards.

## Wood-working

Finds of large wooden vessels, containers of various kinds and other objects reveal a high standard of wood-working and cooperage in minature. The use of the lathe is well attested by finely tuned, thin walled vessels from Hjortspring and Vimose,[43] those from the earlier deposit being outstanding. The carpenters' workshops have not been identified, except at Feddersen Wierde, where rubbish from the lathes has enabled their position to be traced.[44] The tools employed can be enumerated by assembling examples from many find-spots. Apart from the lathe, there are represented the mallet, hammer, axe, adze, awl, auger, chisel, various kinds of knife, rasp and plane. When these were introduced is quite unknown, but one may guess that the wider contacts established in the earlier Roman period led to major developments in this craft.

The making of large objects such as furniture and other house fittings can be safely assumed but actual specimens are extremely rare and fragmentary. Techniques of skilled carpentry employed on a larger scale are evident in the construction of timber-lined wells, water cisterns, funerary chambers, ships and, above all, houses. Remains of the superstructure of houses are unfortunately too rare to teach us much about building methods, but the size of many of the aisled long-houses is ample testimony to the ambition of their builders.[45] When parts of timber structures have been preserved, for instance at Ezinge, Feddersen Wierde and Tofting, the constructional details are of a high standard. Several kinds of jointing, for example, were employed, including the scarf joint, tongue-and-groove, and the mortice-and-tenon. The activity of specialist craftsmen may be suspected, but cannot of course be proved.

The skilled carpentry necessary for the building of large timber houses had been developing since the late Bronze Age at least, so that the craftsmen of the Roman Iron Age drew upon a vigorous and experienced tradition in this field, in another craft, that of the shipwright, the Roman period was one in which considerable advances were made. Plank boats, replacing log boats and dug-outs, may have first appeared in the Bronze Age but the earliest complete clinker-built vessel yet recorded is the craft from the Hjortspring votive deposit. This measured 19m in length and probably carried a crew of about twenty men. It was constructed out of five broad planks, two on each side and another forming the keel. These planks had been sewn together with cord and the holes caulked with resin. A framework for the hull was provided by thin branches of hazelwood lashed to the side planks and the structure was made more rigid by the insertion of timber cross-struts at intervals amidships. No iron nails or other metal parts were employed. There was no mast, propulsion being entirely by means of unfixed oars or paddles. Finally, there were steering oars at both bow and stern. It is unlikely that the Hjortspring boat handled well in heavy seas and swells, but its builders succeeded in making a fairly light vessel, well suited to the coastal waters of the almost tideless Baltic.

No vessels of the early Roman Iron Age have yet been recovered in anything like a complete form. A boat found at Halsnøy in Norway, dating from about A.D. 200, is closely akin to that from Hjortspring in that its strakes, or side planks, are sewn together with root fibres, and the timber framework is lashed to cleats in the sides. The main advance over Hjortspring is the fact that the Halsnøy boat has rowlocks in its topmost strake so that the vessel could be rowed rather than paddled. By the end of the Roman Iron Age, however, there had been more significant moves towards the construction of dependable seaworthy craft, as the ship from Nydam (A.D. 350–400) makes clear. This is a vessel 23m long and 3m wide amidships, and made from eleven large oak planks, five to each side over a massive keel plank. An important new feature is the use of iron nails to hold together the overlapping strakes. There was no provision for a sail, the craft being propelled by a crew of thirty oarsmen.

Like the Hjortspring vessel, the Nydam ship was a ship of war. Though it had no sail, no proper keel and would have been difficult to manoeuvre compared with later Viking ships, it represents an important stage in the development of shipbuilding in the north, falling rather more than half-way between the earliest plank-built boats and the Viking masterpieces of Gokstad and Tune. But, though it was a sea-going craft, it was better adapted to coasting about the Baltic inlets than crossing the open sea. It is difficult to imagine Anglo-Saxon migrants crossing the North Sea in a vessel of this kind, although the feat is well within the bounds of possibility. Perhaps, after all, the Nydam ship was not the most advanced vessel known about 400 and other types await discovery. It would not be incredible if the idea of the sail had been carried to the north by that date, but for this there is no evidence at all.

The building of wheeled vehicles was another specialized task. The spoked wheel, known in central Europe from the middle of the second millennuium B.C., seems not to have been made in the north until the early Roman Iron Age. An example from Paddepoel near Groningen dates from the first or second century A.D. and at Feddersen Wierde, occupied from the first century B.C. to the fifth century, parts of spoked wheels only have been recovered. The tripartite disc wheel of the pre-Roman Iron Age appears, then, to have been ousted in the earlier Roman period. The two carts from Dejbjerg in Jutland,[46] each with four spoked wheels, provide the best preserved examples of the wheelwright's craft, but the general view is that these were made by a Celtic craftsman, possibly in Gaul, about 100 B.C. or later. The sophistication of the construction of their wheels, with their wooden roller-bearings in the hubs, iron tyres, the single-piece felloes of ash, spokes (twelve or fourteen) of hornbeam and hubs of oak, is fully in accord with that view, and it is impossible to follow Brøndsted and attribute the carts to a craftsman working 'in the Celtic tradition' in Denmark. None of the later wheels so far known in Germania were nearly so ambitious and the Dejbjerg carts should not mislead us into thinking that Germanic wheelwrights were working in the most advanced tradition of their day.

But aristocratic vehicles such as those from Dejbjerg, and the wagons from graves at Langå (Fyn) and Kraghede (Vendsyssel), may well have spread the use of the spoked wheel in the north and perhaps stimulated other refinements to wheeled vehicles.

We have no information as to how widely wheeled traffic was used, but that it was used at all implies the construction or preparation of roads or trackways to allow passage through difficult terrain. Apart from ridgeways, followed from a remote period, relatively little is known about the making of roads. Stretches of paved road, for instance across the peat-bog to the island refuge of Borremose, are recorded from the pre-Roman Iron Age onward but were clearly rare. Rather commoner, and certainly better recorded, are the so-called *Bohlenwege* of northern Germania, timber or corduroy trackways laid across peat-bogs and marshy areas.[47] These trackways were constructed from the Neolithic to the Middle Ages and few can be fixed with certainty in the Roman Iron Age. They range in sophistication from the crudest rafts of logs and brushwood to skilfully constructed plank causeways, often running for many hundreds of yards across wet ground. Two examples which were built across a marsh near Oldenburg in the late pre-Roman Iron Age were both more than three kilometres in length.

The constructional details of one of these tracks in the Wittemoor (*Landkreis* Wesermarsch) will give some impression of a well built *Bohlenweg*.[48] Three parallel lines of poles were first of all laid out on the surface of the marsh, with an interval of about a metre between each pair of poles. Across these were laid a series of flat planks about 2·5m long, forming the foundation raft of the roadway proper. The ends of the planks were bored so that they could be tamped into the marsh and held firm by means of horizontal bars, each of which covered the ends of five or six planks. The exposed surface of the trackway was of turf blocks, the whole measuring about 4m wide and thus usable for carts and animals as well as foot travellers. Some such trackway across the marsh may have given rise to the report of 'long bridges' which reached Tacitus. Whether timber bridges were actually built across marshes or streams is not certain, though a bridge of the first century B.C. has been claimed near Fulda.

## Textiles[49]

The foundations of the craft of textile manufacture were also laid long before the Roman Iron Age; indeed already by the late Bronze Age the craft had been developed to a high pitch of skill. No doubt Iron Age textiles were mainly produced by individual craftsmen for their immediate domestic circle, but the recovery from peat-bogs of a few garments of outstandingly high quality indicates that the topmost levels of society were served by specialist weavers. The loom most commonly used was the upright warp-weighted loom, although the two-beam loom was also known from an early date in Scandinavia if not elsewhere. Both these loom types had developed in the Bronze Age and both were widely used in the Roman Empire as well as in the Germanic north. Tablet weaving was also practised, especially in the making of borders for garments. Sheep's wool was, of course, the most favoured material, sometimes with animal hair being added. Linen[50] was also known, as was hemp and nettle fibre.

The textile garments preserved in peat-bogs are almost our only source for the products of this craft. They reveal the predominance, in the better quality items at least, of twilled cloth over plain weaves. Two-over-two twill, in which each weft thread passes over and then under two warp threads, is particularly common in the pre-Roman Iron Age, there being several forms of it, including herringbone, chevron and diamond twills. The popularity of twilled cloth may have been due to the scope it afforded to the design of checked and other geometric patterns so beloved in the north. The simpler plain weave, in which each weft thread passed over and then under warp thread, was, of course, ubiquitous.

Men's clothing in the Roman Iron Age consisted of a cloak, sometimes hooded, trousers and a jacket or smock. Less is known about the dress of the women, but both a skirt and a full-length garment reaching to the ankles were known. Linen undergarments may have been worn, but have not survived in the peat. The quality of the finest garments is astonishingly high. The supreme example is a woollen cloak from the Thorsbjerg bog, surviving only in fragments.[51] This was a rectangular garment, 2·36m by 1·68m, of twilled cloth with tablet-woven borders. The fineness and evenness of the threads, both in the body of the cloak and in its borders, are oustanding. The quality of the finishing, too, is high, several shades of blue (probably indigo) being employed to produce a checked pattern. The whole impression given is of a garment endowed with a special function, connected perhaps with ceremonial or rank. Other fine, large cloaks are known from Vehnemoor[52] and Hunteburg. The great size of these *Prachtmantel* (as German scholars call them), up to 3m in length, suggests that they were worn folded double. The Hunteburg cloak further reveals that they were fastened at the right shoulder by a brooch. The technical expertise displayed by these textiles, and others of humbler quality, make it plain that the Germanic weavers had developed their craft virtually as far as their non-mechanical equipment would permit, and had nothing to learn from contemporary craftsmen in the Roman world.

## Leather

The importance of leather and hides in the barbarian economy for garments, capes, belts, shoes and the like, scabbards and perhaps shields, is too easily overlooked. Workers in leather were among the craftsmen who clustered near the headman's house at Feddersen Wierde, and most other large communities must have had similar specialists in the same trade. The only tool which can be specifically linked with the working of leather is the half-moon knife, a tool recorded from many parts of free Germany, as from other parts of Europe. A fine series of them have been found in Scandinavia, particularly in southern Sweden and the Baltic islands. In one cemetery on Öland, that at Sörby-Störlinge, no less than eleven graves—all of them the graves of women—contained one of these distinctive tools, clear proof that here at any rate leather-working was a female craft.[49] Some of the Sörny-Störlinge burials also included awls and needles which were probably used in the making of leather garments and other goods. At Friskeby in Östergötland, as many as twenty female graves were found to include a half-moon knife among their grave-goods.[50] Elsewhere in Germania this tool is much less prominent in the record, but there is no doubt that leather-working was everywhere of considerable importance.

It is clear that during the Roman Iron Age, and particularly from the second century onward, Germanic technology made progress on all sides after a long period of relative stagnation. Iron became more abundant in most areas and many new types of tools, weapons and utensils appeared, the majority originating in the Roman world. Bronze-working and the decorative uses of gold and silver were developed apace, thus laying the foundations for the superb achievements of Germanic craftsmen in the Migration period. These changes did not come about all at once in every part of Germania. Isolation, whether cultural or geographic, is the enemy of all change, and certain regions did not share to the full extent in the general advance plotted in these pages. This does not, however, disguise the plain fact that the first four centuries A.D. were a time in which the great technological backlog of northern Europe in the Iron Age was largely eradicated.

## References

1. Eggers, H. J. (1964), 15ff.
2. Nylen, E. (1968).
3. *Årbøger*, 1900, 140. Brøndsted, J. (1960), 73.
4. *Årbøger*, 1900, 140ff. A. Ouvaroff, *Recherches sur les antiquités de la Russie méridionale* (Paris, 1855), 38f.
5. Bo: Nylen, E. (1968), 84f.; Hede: Stenberger, M. (1964), Fig. 160.
6. This influence from the Black Sea regions is commonly invoked but rarely discussed in detail. The subject requires further examination.
7. Eggers, H. J. (1964), 40ff.
8. Schulz, W. and Zahn, R. (1933).
9. Thorsbjerg: Raddatz, K. (1957), 77ff.; Skedemosse: Hagberg, U. E. (1967), 22ff.; Stráže: V. Ondrouch, *Bohaté hroby z doby rímskej na Slovensku* (Prague, 1957), Tab. 47; Häven: Schach-Dörges, H. (1969), Taf. III, 1–3.
10. Werner, J. (1941) and (1966), 22ff.
11. E. Oxeustierna, *The World of the Norseman* (London, 1967), Pl. 19.
12. H. Hildebrand, in *Kungl. Vitterhets Historie Antikvitets Akad. Månadsblad* (Stockholm, 1873). Later discussed by Raddatz, K. (1957), 120ff. and Hagberg, U. E. (1967), 9ff.
13. Stenberger, M. (1956).
14. Raddatz, K. (1957), 120ff.
15. Roes, A. (1947).
16. Munksgaard, E. (1953).
17. Forssander, J. E. (1937).
18. W. Holmqvist in Eggers, H. J. *et al.* (1964), 172ff.
19. op. cit. 77ff.
20. Oxenstierna, E. (1956), discussed by Ellis Davidson, H. R. (1967), 84ff.
21. *Germania* 5, 4.
22. Eggers, H. J. (1950), 86ff.

23. Werner, J. (1941), 55; Eggers, H. J. *et al.* (1964), 57f.

24. Holmqvist, W. (1951), 68ff.

25. op. cit. 71ff.

26. *Germania* 6, 1.

27. Pleiner, R. (1964) is fundamental on this subject. See also Pleiner, R. (1962).

28. Pleiner, R. (1964), 20ff.

29. H. F. Cleere in *Antiquaries Journal*, lii (1972) 8ff. for a recent account of furnace types.

30. I. Peškař in *Přehled výzkumů*, 1961 (Brno, 1962).

31. Pleiner, R. (1964), 21f. J. A. Jíra in *Obzor praehistoricky*, 1–2 (1910–11).

32. Pleiner, R. (1964), 24.

33. Z. Trňáčková in *Arch. Rozhledy*, viii (1956), 507, 515.

34. Bielenin, K. (1964).

35. K. Bielenin and M. Radwan in *Materialy Arch.* (Crakow), i (1959), 279ff.

36. H. Hingst in *Offa*, xi (1952), 28ff. and in W. Krämer (Ed.), *Neue Ausgrabungen in Deutschland* (Berlin, 1958), 258ff.

37. W. Wegewitz in *Nachrichten aus Niedersachsens Urgeschichte*, xxvi (1957), 3ff.

38. Tacitus, *Annals* xiii, 57, 1–3.

39. E. A. Thompson in *Hermes*, lxxxiv (1956), 376.

40. K-H. Otto and H. Grünert in *Jahresschrift für mitteldeutsche Vorgeschichte*, xli-ii (1958), 389ff. T. Voigt in *Alt-Thüringen*, vi (1962–3), 383.

41. R. von Uslar in *Germania*, xix (1935), 249ff. Schulz, W. (1953), 55ff. Schach-Dörges, H. (1969), 83 and map 13.

42. L. Gajewski in *Arch. Polski*, iii (1959), 101ff. and in *Sprawozdania Archeologiczne*, v (1959), 281ff.

43. Brøndsted, J. (1960), 37ff.

44. Schmid, P. (1969a), 140ff and Abb. 10.

45. On entire subject, Trier, B. (1969).

46. Petersen, H. (1888); Klindt-Jensen, O. (1949), 87ff.

47. Hayen, H. (1957).

48. Hayen, H. (1971).

49. Among several major studies, the following may be singled out: Hald, M. (1950); W. von Stokar, 'Spinnen und Weben bei den Germanen', *Mannus-Bibliothek*, lix (1938); W. La Baume, *Die Entwicklung des Textilhandwerks in Alteuropa* (Bonn, 1955); J. P. Wild, *Textile Manufacture in the Northern Roman Provinces* (Cambridge, 1970) adduces a good deal of comparative material from the Roman world.

50. cf. *Germania* 17, 3.

51. K. Schlabow in *Festschrift für G. Schwantes* (Cologne, 1951), 176ff., and *Trachten der Eisenzeit aus Moorfunden in Schleswig-Holstein* (Neumünster, 1961).

52. K. Schlabow in *Oldenburger Jahrb.*, lii (1952–3), 160ff.

53. Hagberg, U. E. (1967), 116ff.

54. ibid.

# 5 | Armament and warfare

To the Romans the Germanic peoples were first and foremost warriors and their historians were naturally interested in barbarian armament and barbarian conduct of war. Despite this interest, however, the information which those historians provide does not amount to very much. A principal reason is that, with the notable exception of Ammianus Marcellinus, the Roman writers who discuss, or even mention, early German warfare and armament had no opportunity for personal observation. Even a writer like Ammianus who knew the Germans at first hand, inevitably knew much more about the peoples living near the Imperial frontiers than about the inhabitants of remoter regions such as Poland and Scandinavia. Indeed it is very doubtful whether any of the writers whose work we possess knew anything in detail about the warfare of peoples settled in lands so far removed from the Roman Empire. On these matters even Tacitus has little that is precise to say.

There are other limitations to the available literary sources. First, they throw light only upon the early Roman Iron Age and the last century of that period. There is virtually nothing on the centuries before the time of Julius Caesar or, more pertinently, on the second and third centuries A.D. Secondly, the ancient writers, and especially Tacitus, tended to regard the armament and warfare of all the Germanic peoples as homogeneous. There is very little trace in the *Germania* of regional differences which are apparent in the archaeological material, the weapons and the other equipment of the warrior, with which this chapter is chiefly concerned. This material provides a much more complete picture than the literary sources, but it must be admitted that even the archaeological evidence is not of consistent depth and quality. In certain regions at certain times few weapons or assemblages of equipment have been recorded. Often these gaps in the record occur because at certain times it was not the custom to include the warrior's equipment among his grave-goods. In some cases, the gaps reflect nothing more than neglect by modern students. The information provided by archaeology, however, is both greater and more detailed than that offered by ancient writers and it has the further advantage of covering a wider geographical scope.[1]

The importance of the great peat-bog deposits of Denmark and Schleswig for this study will be obvious. Warrior-graves, however, also provide an immense quantity of weapons and offer a more even chronological spread than the great votive deposits. In one other respect graves containing weapons are of more use than massive accumulations of equipment dedicated to the gods. Warrior-graves can demonstrate *combinations* of weapons as no other find can, and can locate them securely in a particular region. It may well be that much of the German, as well as the Roman, equipment which ended its useful life in the peat-bogs had been carried far from its place of origin to its place of deposition in the north. This is less likely to happen in the case of grave furnishings, though the possibility of exotic weapons occasionally being buried with the dead must clearly be allowed for.

It has already been remarked that archaeology sheds more light on some periods than on others. For the earlier La Tène phase, for example, the sum of archaeological finds is very small and limited in geographical scope. In the middle of the pre-Roman Iron Age the picture becomes clearer as warrior-graves became commoner and votive deposits like Hjortspring and Krogsbølle occur. For the late pre-Roman Iron Age, numerous large cemeteries provide fairly adequate testimony to the warriors' equipment, particularly in northern Germania. From the early Roman period, the stock of information steadily grows to reach its peak in the unparalleled panoply of armament provided by the deposits at Nydam, Thorsbjerg, Vimose and Ejsbøl.[2]

As in so many other fields, the armament of the Germanic peoples, and particularly those in the western territories, was always open to influence from outside Germania. In the second and first centuries B.C. several important innovations were made as a result of contact, or rather mingling, with the inhabitants of the Celtic lands. There were, of course, many circumstances in which German and Celtic warriors met, either in combat or alliance. The great train of Cimbri and Teutones on its long progress through central Europe drew Celtic warriors along with it. The host of Ariovistus brought Celt and German together, as did the short-lived empire of Maroboduus. Borrowings from Celtic armament and the import of weapons from areas where La Tène culture flourished are therefore only to be expected. Such borrowings are evident in Denmark[3] and to a lesser extent in northern Germany, particularly in swords, scabbards, spears and shields, but the degree of Germanic dependence upon Celtic armament and weapon types has been exaggerated in the past. Such influence as there was made itself felt during the later pre-Roman Iron Age.

In the sphere of weapons, a much more powerful influence was at work on the early Germans, the influence of their many-sided contact with the Roman Empire. From the earlier Roman Iron Age it is possible to see Roman and Germanic armament drawing gradually closer together, until by the late fourth century in certain parts of Europe it is frequently impossible to assign the weapons in a grave or votive deposit with perfect confidence to the Roman or the barbarian side.[4] Various factors brought about this change. One of these was the steady flow, through various channels, of Roman equipment into barbarian Europe. A certain amount, naturally, reached Germania in the form of loot from Roman forts in the frontier provinces or from Roman armies operating in barbarian territory. Occasionally, this Roman military gear betrays its origins by the makers' stamps on swords or by punched centurial and other inscriptions on spears and armour. No doubt illicit traffic in arms carried some equipment into barbarian hands, though we have no way of knowing how much.

Just as important as the import of actual Roman weapons was the introduction of Roman standards of war equipment. The main agents here will have been those numerous barbarians who served in the Roman armies and afterwards returned to their own people. These included a fair number of chieftains and other influential warriors as well as an untold host of rank-and-file Germans. Several of the chieftains later demonstrated what apt pupils of the Roman military machine they had been by their effective opposition to their old masters. The list includes some formidable names; Arminius, probably Maroboduus, Gannascus and Civilis. There is no actual proof that men like these and their

F

humbler followers made far-reaching improvements to Germanic armament. But in view of their experience in the Roman world, they can hardly have remained unaware of the superior standards of Roman equipment and organization. It is impossible to estimate how many barbarians served in the Imperial forces from the time of Julius Caesar to the late fourth century but they must have numbered many thousands. Those who returned to Germania may have left their equipment behind them, but their notions about the kind and quality of weapons they wanted to possess and use will have gone home with them.

We may now begin to trace the history of northern armament from the earlier phases of the Iron Age as best we can from the weapons themselves. In the period of the earliest Hallstatt culture, the sword clearly played a decisive role in northern armament, the other important weapons being lances and axes. The swords, both bronze and iron, and the iron lance-heads indicate that the weapon types were essentially homogeneous over a very wide area and this area appears in later historical sources as the territory of the Germanic peoples. At this early time, however, the armament of northern Europe displays close affiliation with that of the Celtic lands in central Europe and the Alpine Foreland, as the bronze swords plainly demonstrate.

The earlier Hallstatt bronze swords include several clearly marked types. The Hallstatt bronze sword *par excellence* was the Gündlingen type, a rather short weapon, some 70–75cm long, which might have been used both by mounted men and infantry alike. The Mindelheim sword was a somewhat longer weapon, with a heavy blade and a blunt point. This was a slashing weapon, better suited to the cavalryman. The reasons behind the introduction of slashing weapons at this period are not absolutely clear. One opinion recently expressed[5] is that the new weapon, and a new style of combat, was developed to counter a new enemy in northern and central Europe, the nomadic Cimmerians or Scythians, horsed warriors whom no infantry could hope to oppose. Other scholars derive the Hallstatt swords from Urnfield prototypes without involving nomadic or other external threat as the stimulus.

Whatever the reason for it, the relative importance of cavalry warfare in the early and middle Hallstatt phases is underlined by certain other weapon types. A cemetery at Gorczewice, north of Posen in Poland, for example, contained twelve graves with axes among their contents, in some cases associated with horse harness.[6] These warriors were thus equipped in a manner strikingly similar to those of the east Alpine Hallstatt homeland itself. Another important feature of northern armament at this time is the occurrence of unusually heavy weapons, spears as well as swords. At Billerbeck (Kr. Pyritz) for instance, a huge spear-head nearly 73cm in length accompanied two heavy iron swords. A peat-bog deposit at Klemensker on Bornholm included several massive iron weapons, among them a spear-head nearly 40cm long.[7] Other finds of heavy iron weapons link Poland with the Baltic islands and northern Germany at this period, but their use was not long-lived and they were afterwards not matched until the later pre-Roman Iron Age.

In the later Hallstatt period, profound changes occurred in armament in the north, and, it may be inferred, in tactics also. The sword diminished sharply in importance and in some regions it may have vanished altogether for a time. Its place was taken by a light single-edged knife, generally termed a *Kampfmesser* (fig. 23, d–e), which could be used in close combat. But this was by no means a weapon of great tactical significance. The normal equipment of the warrior now comprised a lance and a shield. Clearly the infantryman had come back into his own, and from now until well into the medieval period his requirements were to determine the essential character of northern armament. Unfortunately the total number of weapon finds of any kind from this period is very small. Weapons were not commonly included among grave-goods in the period so that there is little information available about the combinations of weapons which were employed. Those finds that have been recorded suggest that there was a considerable amount of regional variation in weapons. For examples, axes are rather commoner in the hoards and graves of eastern Germania than further to the west, while daggers some 20–25cm in length seem to be characteristic of the Altmark and Mecklenburg. In Pomerania, graffiti on certain pottery vessels of the Face-urn culture supplement the meagre finds of actual weapons. The most interesting of these graffiti show throwing spears apparently equipped with slings.[8]

The extreme scarcity of the sword in northern Europe at this time is in sharp contrast to its increasing importance among the Celtic peoples in the same period. The great two-edged La Tène swords were now beginning to be widely current in central and western Europe. There is no trace of imports or imitations of these in the north. No doubt a scarcity of iron had much to do with the northern emphasis upon spears and daggers. From now on, until the end of the pre-Roman Iron Age, the warfare of the northern peoples underwent no notable change and appears to have been influenced only to a moderate extent by contact with the Celtic world.

From the earlier Jastorf period (broadly La Tène I), a relatively small number of weapons have been recorded, principally because grave-goods still rarely include war gear. But it is clear enough that the emphasis still lay on weapons designed for combat at close quarters. The spear, the lance and the shield comprised the armament of most warriors. Long swords seem to have been virtually unknown at this period, though a few

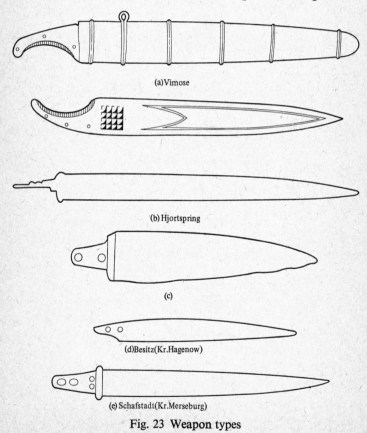

(a) Vimose

(b) Hjortspring

(c)

(d) Besitz (Kr. Hagenow)

(e) Schafstadt (Kr. Merseburg)

Fig. 23 Weapon types

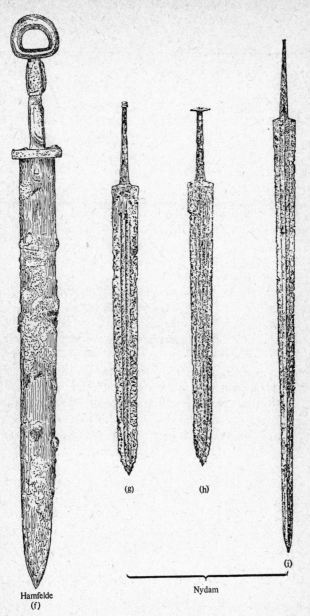

Hamfelde
(f)

(g)

(h)

(i)

Nydam

Fig. 23 Weapon types

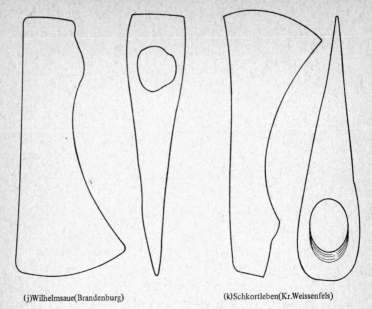

(j)Wilhelmsaue(Brandenburg)          (k)Schkortleben(Kr.Weissenfels)

Fig. 23 Weapon types

short-bladed swords, daggers and *Kampfmesser* do occur. The spear-heads are extremely varied in form and in size, ranging from about 12cm to as much as about 26cm in length. The longer, heavier types, however, are not common. The slight amount of material which can be assembled indicates that, as earlier, the Oder–Vistula area was linked to the Baltic islands and to northern Germany in its weapon types, but within this immense territory local or regional variants are clearly apparent.

The armament of the middle period of the pre-Roman Iron Age is above all revealed in the deposits of war equipment found at Hjortspring and Krogsbølle.[9] These deposits reveal that by the later third and earlier second century B.C. there have been but few changes in northern weaponry, and these of minor significance. The totals of weapons from the two finds speak for themselves. At Hjortspring, the earlier of the two, there were 169 spear- and lance-heads, 138 of iron and 31 of bone, about 150 shields, and only 6 swords, one of which is so short (33cm) as to be properly classed as a *Kampfmesser* (fig. 23, c), The much smaller deposit at Krogsbølle tells a broadly similar story, except that no shields were here represented: 43 spear- and lance-heads, of which 24 were of iron and 19 of bone, and only 7 swords.

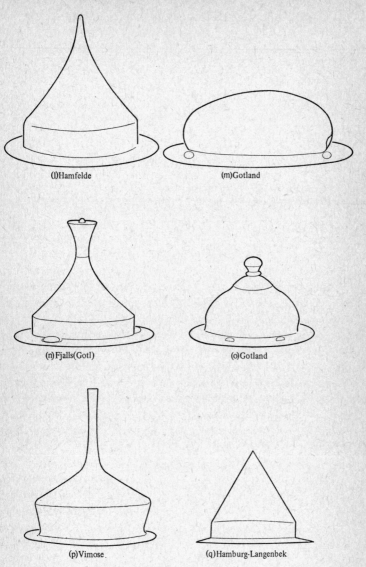

(l)Hamfelde       (m)Gotland

(n)Fjalls(Gotl)       (o)Gotland

(p)Vimose       (q)Hamburg-Langenbek

**Fig. 23 Weapon types**

Grave-finds of this period confirm the relative scarcity of swords compared with spears and lances.

All the swords from Hjortspring and Krogsbølle are short, broad-bladed weapons between 30cm and 40cm long. The sole exception is a fragment of a two-edged La Tène sword from Krogsbølle, but this is so far the only example recorded in the north at this time. The Hjortspring shields were represented mainly by fragments, but a small number were recovered entire. There are two types, one long oval form, 88cm by 50cm, the other rectangular and measuring some 66cm by 30cm. The latter type was by far the commoner. Some of the shields, including their bosses, were made from a single piece of soft wood, normally alder or lime. Others had a board made up from three pieces of wood fastened together and had a separate wooden boss. On none of the shields was there any trace of metal fittings. The surviving bosses have a distinctive 'barleycorn' shape, the prototype for which is found on some La Tène shields. Another almost complete shield of this date comes from Vaedebro near Skanderborg. This belongs to the long oval type also represented at Hjortspring and is particularly interesting in that it bears traces of paint, recalling the remark of Tacitus that German shields were decorated with selected colours, presumably to distinguish men from different fighting units. The Vaedebro shield-board has a feature which those from Hjortspring lack. It has been bored with a large number of small holes which might have taken thongs to stiffen the board.

The Hjortspring shields are not the only relics of contact with distant regions of Europe. The same deposit also contained, most surprisingly, some twenty complete mail garments, all of them unfortunately too poorly preserved for their original form to be reconstructed. These are indeed exotic in northern Europe and must have come to the island of Als from the Celtic or even from the Mediterranean world. They are the only mail garments of this date yet recorded in the north and by far the largest group of body armour from any period of the Iron Age. Their presence, and the presence of the famous ship, must link Hjortspring with the highest level of Germanic warrior society and its contents should not colour our view of what the majority of warriors were familiar with. The smaller deposits, like Krogsbølle, Vaedebro, Tidavad and Wöbs[10] give a clearer picture of the equipment of the rank and file. These finds bespeak above all else infantry forces, equipped with spears, lances and shields.

Throughout the later stages of the pre-Roman Iron Age, no major changes were wrought in the general character of Germanic armament nor, it may be supposed, in fighting methods. There were, however, developments in the forms of the weapons. The most remarkable was the introduction of the short one-edged slashing sword. One of the earliest known occurrences of this sword type is in the wagon-grave at Langå on Fyn, dating from the second century B.C., and from now on it remained a characteristic German weapon until well into the Roman period (fig. 23, a). In some areas its use may have extended into the third century A.D. Its origins have never been satisfactorily explained, for there is no obvious prototype. The view that it was imported from the Celts or modelled on their one-edged knives has little or nothing to support it. In the absence of obvious models and antecedents, it is much likelier that the one-edged sword was invented and developed by Germanic smiths for their own warrior masters.

Alongside the slashing swords, the two-edged La Tène sword put in an appearance, more commonly (as is to be expected) in areas closer to the Celtic territories of central Europe, It was not, however, a common weapon and when it occurs in graves it sometimes does so unaccompanied by other weapons, suggesting that its users were specialists. Away from regions where close contact with the Celts is evidence, the less specialized one-edged sword and the *Kampfmesser* remained in relatively common use.

Another significant feature of armament in the last two centuries B.C. is the increased importance of the javelin. Javelin-heads with barbs now frequently occur in graves, in some areas commonly in pairs. This change too seems likely to have been a purely northern innovation and not a borrowing from the Celts. But some elements in Germanic arms at this time do reveal the hand or the influence of the Celtic smith, especially the iron shield-bosses and certain forms of spear-head.

There is virtually no evidence that body armour was known at this date, even in the form of imported items like the mail coats from Hjortspring. The main means of defence remained the shield and the increased use of iron shield-bosses no doubt also greatly aided use of the shield as an instrument of offence. Other accoutrements included leather belts, some of which bore unusually ornate mounts. The finest series of these are the so-called Holstein belts (*Holsteiner Gürtel*) of which about eighty are known, virtually all of them being found north of the lower Elbe.[11] Their distinctive features are richly ornamented and heavy iron mounts. The Holstein belts do not continue into the Roman period and they appear to have no later counterparts with such massive fittings.

To summarize, during the last two centuries B.C., Germanic weaponry continued to be dominated by the arms of the infantryman, the spear and dagger, with throwing weapons steadily increasing in significance. All the weapons are light and sparing in the amount of iron used. Stocks of the vital metal were plainly limited. Certain outside influences can be detected, that from the areas of La Tène culture being especially noticeable, but a wholesale adoption of Celtic weapons and fighting methods certainly did not take place.

Roman literary sources of the early Empire provide the best starting point for an examination of Germanic warfare in the Roman Iron Age. Tacitus put it succinctly thus:

Only very few have swords or spears. The lances that they carry— *frameae* is the native word—have short and narrow heads, but are so sharp and easy to handle that the same weapon serves for fighting hand to hand or at a distance. The horseman demands no more than his shield and spear, but the infantryman has also javelins for throwing, several to each man, and he can hurl them to a great distance.[12]

This is fully in accord with the state of affairs outlined by the archaeological evidence. The barbarian armies which faced the Roman legions in the first and second centuries A.D. were largely infantry armies, equipped with lances, spears, shields and, to a lesser degree, with swords. The limited role of the sword in the early Roman period is reflected in the relative fewness of graves which contain specimens, even if we allow for the possibility that the sword was so valued a weapon that it was not commonly assigned to the dead.

Sword-bearing warriors at this time probably made up a larger proportion of the war bands than at the time of the Hjortspring deposit, but even now they can scarcely have been a potent military force. It has been estimated that for every swordsman in this period there were ten or more warriors armed with lances. But, assuming that we accept the basis of this calculation, there must be allowance for local and regional variation. The picture is by no means uniform. For example, in Angeln swords hardly ever occur in graves, whereas about the mouth of the Elbe they are consistently present in the richer burials, often along with imported Roman utensils and ornaments. On the island of Gotland and elsewhere in Scandinavia, notably in Jutland, a few wealthy graves[13] have yielded high-quality imitations of Roman *gladii*, fairly certainly the products of a local workshop, while in the Elbe valley there have been found a few specimens of a light sword also deriving from a Roman prototype, of a kind which might have been favoured by mounted men. Actual Roman weapons are occasionally encountered in the north at this time but in no region were they common. The short single-edged sword of the pre-Roman Iron Age was still in use, especially in the eastern and northern parts of Germania. In the west the two-edged thrusting sword was by now the normal type.

Body armour and helmets have still not made their appearance in the archaeological record and it is very unlikely that anyone but a few chieftains possessed them. The rank and file fought either naked or very lightly clad. Roman sculptured reliefs and bronze figurines of the period frequently show German warriors wearing only trousers, or a short cloak, and shoes, but never wearing armour.[14] Some of the figurines show men wearing conical caps, almost certainly of leather, not metal, and these recall the leather cap of the man from the Tollund bog. It follows that against well armoured Roman troops speed and mobility were the essence of barbarian tactics. Their main hope of success against disciplined legionaries with vastly superior equipment rested on the lightning strike against an unsuspecting or ill-prepared foe, operating far from his base in difficult terrain. It is small wonder that the most telling of German victories were won against the less capable of Roman commanders.

In the absence of body armour, the shield assumed importance and, as earlier, it could be used in a limited offensive role, the boss being thrust against the head or body of the foe. No actual examples of shields have survived from the early Roman period but Roman sculptured reliefs provide a plentiful source of illustrations. Triumphal monuments of the early Empire show several types of shields associated with German warriors, round, rectangular and sexagonal forms being the most common. A remarkable series of reliefs from Neumagen, near Trier,[15] shows German prisoners sitting amid a mass of round, sexagonal and half-cylindrical shields, the latter equipped with prominent projecting bosses. German auxiliaries on Trajan's Column carry oval shields, but it is not clear whether these are Roman or barbarian in origin. Finds of actual shields are not recorded again until the third century. The best preserved is a round shield-board from Thorsbjerg (Pl. 4b), just under 1m in diameter. Part of a shield from Vimose is plainly from a rectangular board, though its original size cannot be estimated. The sum of this evidence is, then, that there was a multiplicity of types. Our evidence, however, is of a very general kind and we lack specific information from individual regions of Germania. On the construction of the shield, too, there is little to say. The round shield from Thorsbjerg is made up from several narrow pieces of wood fastened together. In the centre is a hole over which the boss was originally fitted on one side and the hand-grip on the other. Leather coverings are indicated by certain grave-finds and bronze or iron binding of the edges is frequently attested from the early Roman period onward. Whether wickerwork shields were used, as one Roman general hopefully asserted, is uncertain.

Roman monuments suggest that the longer oval, rectangular and sexagonal shields were normally carried by infantry, the round and smaller oval shields by mounted troops. This is entirely credible and may be an early indication that Germanic armament was undergoing change under the influence of Rome, for a broadly similar distinction was observed in the Roman army.

The role of cavalry during the early Roman Iron Age, as earlier, was distinctly limited. There are nevertheless references to numbers of horsemen in the hosts led by Ariovistus and Arminius, and from the time of Julius Caesar onward German cavalry units were employed in the Imperial forces. Caesar clearly found his German horsemen more than useful, though on one occasion at least he felt obliged to remount them on Roman horses, their own mounts being presumably too small. Later, Tacitus pays tribute to the outstanding equestrian skill of certain peoples, notably the Tencteri.[16] Once again, it is the tribes nearer to the Roman frontiers on whom the literary sources concentrate; the archaeological record must provide a more extensive view. We have already noted that weapons such as the slashing sword, which was well suited to use by the cavalryman, was not a common component of free German armament at this time. But there are nevertheless clear indications that some warriors, probably mainly chiefs and their retinues, did form mounted units or led their infantry war bands from the back of a horse.

A major source for these mounted warriors is a series of richly furnished graves, containing among other grave-goods spurs, harness sets or other items of horse gear. Most of these graves have been recorded in Denmark, north-west Germany and the Baltic islands, but they extend eastwards into Mecklenburg, Pomerania and East Prussia,[17] and there are outliers between the Oder and the Vistula. An interesting group of these horsemen's graves occurs in Angeln, beginning at the end of the pre-Roman Iron Age. This group includes burials at Sörup, Husby and Scheersberg bei St Quern, all of these including spurs among their grave-goods. Another group is evident in Jutland and on the islands of Öland and Gotland, the spurs in these graves being almost invariably inlaid with fine silver wires. From Jutland come the two examples from Dollerup and Lynghojgaard, from Gotland the graves at Endre, Linde, Hemse and Stanga, and from Öland Gräsgard and Köping (Pl. 4a). Spurs of the same kind are also known in southern Norway.

This remarkable group of Scandinavian spurs clearly emanated from local craftsmen working for warrior chiefs. Now and again, however, there is a hint of that wider contact which warfare seems often to have stimulated in the north. For example, a bronze spur from Martofte (Odense) is closely paralleled among spurs from the Celtic territories and among the equipment of Celtic auxiliaries serving in the Roman army.

Other examples of inlaid spurs are met with further east. In Mecklenburg, several graves at Hagenow and Körchow contained specimens and a grave at Schwedt (Kr. Kolberg) in Pomerania included one with silver inlay. The lower Elbe valley, too, had its horsed chieftains, as several graves in the Lüneburg region testify. The most striking are the two *Fürstengräber* from Marwedel.[18] Equally rich burials continue into the third century, most notably in Scandinavia, where richly inlaid spurs are found in graves at Essunga (Västergötland) and Vogn (Jutland).[19]

Rich burials containing sets of harness, or bridles and bits, are found over roughly the same areas of northern Germania. Scandinavia is represented by graves at Rønslunde (Aarhus), Gudbjerg (Svendborg), Troelstrup (Aarhus) and Martofte (Odense), the lower Elbe valley by Harsefeld, and the eastern territories by Klein-Fliess in East Prussia.[20] The dating of some of these burials is not clear, but the earlier Roman period should include most of them.

Although this equipment makes a brave show, its importance should not be overemphasized. It does not imply that from the second century onward mounted warriors were playing a significant role in Germanic warfare. If that were the case, it would surely be reflected in the *common* weapons found in the north and in these there was no basic change. No specifically cavalry arms were developed, although the long, two-edged sword did become more widespread in the third century. The graves containing harness sets and handsome spurs more probably represent warriors of a high social standing, chiefs and their followers, who demonstrated their eminence by this somewhat flashy equipment.

There is no evidence that the relative importance of cavalry over infantry forces had increased more than slightly since the time of Caesar. In his day, Ariovistus had some 6000 horsemen in his host. A half-century later, we hear that Maroboduus had only about 4000 horsemen against about 70 000 infantry.[21] Even when barbarian armies did include sizeable contingents of horsed warriors, they were not always used to full effect in battle. Among the Suebic peoples, it is reported, the cavalry dismounted after battle had been joined and fought on foot, keeping their horses ready in case a rapid retreat was necessary.[22]

### The later Roman Iron Age

It is clear enough that the first two centuries of contact between the Germans and the Romans had remarkably little effect upon Germanic armament and tactics. Roman weapon types were not widely adopted and there was no attempt to emulate the standards of Roman body armour. From the later second century, however, one might say from the time of the Marcomannic Wars, there came important changes, as a result of which Germanic and Roman armament were drawn closer together. This time of change is heralded by the appearance of certain kinds of Roman equipment in the north. The most numerous class of these pieces of equipment are the *Ringknaufschwerter*, distinctive Roman swords with a ring at the end of the hilt. (fig. 23, f). These have been found mainly in Jutland, Fyn and the Elbe basin,[23] and in the same general area local imitations of the type also appear. Interestingly, in the same relatively limited part of Germania and at the same time, graves and votive deposits contained a number of Roman mail garments. The dating of the armour and the *Ringknaufschwerter* lies in the middle and later second century, more precisely between 140 and 180, and Dr Raddatz with good reason brings this equipment into relation with the Marcomannic Wars,[24] during which German warriors could have come by Roman equipment either as victors over Roman troops or as auxiliaries in the Imperial service.

There were other developments in northern armament. Iron axes become more frequent in graves from the second century onward, especially in the Elbe basin (fig. 23, j–k), and henceforward the axe, particularly the throwing axe, was to play an increasingly important role in Germanic warfare. Sets of arrowheads, usually in threes, also begin to appear in princely burials in central Germania in the third century. They are, however, usually of silver or bronze and probably are marks of rank rather than skill with the bow.[25] From humbler contexts there is evidence that the bow and arrow were achieving a wider currency, but the bows of the period before the fourth century have not yet been revealed in peat-bog deposits or graves. One authority has suggested that the Germans adopted the bow after seeing its effectiveness in the hands of Sarmatian and Iazygian archers in the Marcomannic Wars. But we still do not know what kind of bow was used in third-century Germania and it should not be assumed to be of Sarmatian origin. When the bow is revealed in the north, in the later fourth century, it is a longbow, which cannot have been derived from a nomadic source. More probably the north Germans invented the longbow for themselves as their Neolithic forebears had done long before. These longbows, in particular the forty or so from Nydam, were some 2m in length and made of yew.[26] They resemble fairly closely not only the English medieval longbow but also the earliest European bows, those of the Neolithic cultures. Their strings were held in notches cut near the ends and the stave ends were tipped with iron or antler ferrules. The hand grip in the centre of the stave could be bound with fine thread.

It is possible, since so many occur among the masses of war gear at Nydam, that the longbows were primarily weapons of war and not of the chase. It is also highly likely that contingents of skilled bowmen were being used in Germanic warfare towards the end of the Roman Iron Age. Bundles of pine-wood and hazel arrows, 68–85cm in length, had also been deposited at Nydam, and most of the other large votive deposits of the late Roman period contain arrow-heads. The Nydam arrow-heads, of which there are 125 surviving examples (111 of iron and 14 of bone), fall into two main classes: a flat type with or without barbs, and a narrow, heavy type with a square, triangular or rhomboidal section.[27] The latter would be admirably suited for use against armoured troops. From now on, then, some German warriors could engage a Roman force in a standing fight, albeit at a range.

The swords of the late Roman Iron Age show a marked tendency to imitate Roman types. The short, single-edged slashing sword had by now virtually disappeared. It can never have been effective against Roman infantry. The commonest sword type used by German warriors was now the long two-edged sword, the *spatha*, which Roman auxiliaries had been using for more than two centuries. A rarer and more specialized form of sword was a long, rapier-like weapon with a narrow flexible blade (fig. 23, 1). This, like the *spatha*, was also a Roman type and the barbarians probably adopted it for its penetrative powers. Other sword forms were current alongside these, for instance the short, broad-bladed weapon modelled on the *gladius* and already in use in the early Roman period.[28] The import of Roman swords markedly increased from the early third century. These weapons manifest themselves by means of makers' stamps on the blade, or by inlaid ornament, or by the form of their hilts. They occur more commonly in the area between the Oder and Vistula and in Scandinavia than elsewhere, but the reasons for this distribution pattern are obscure.[29]

Other Roman sword blades found in *Barbaricum* are distinguished by the technique of 'damascening' or pattern welding. This was a method of twisting bands and wires of iron together and forging harder steel edges on to it. The faces of the sword were then etched and polished so that the pattern produced by the forging process was clearly visible. (fig. 23, g–h).[30] The fourth-century deposits at Nydam, Vimose and Illerup, and contemporary graves in Poland, have produced the earliest pattern-welded swords yet known in the barbarian word, but the origins of the technique lie in Roman workshops about or before A.D. 200. Illicit trade or warriors returning with loot carried the swords northwards and by so doing introduced into northern Europe a technique which was to produce the splendid pattern-welded Frankish and Viking swords.

Unfortunately only the crudest calculations can be made, which can probably never be refined, of the relative number of sword-bearing warriors in the barbarian armies at this time. It has sometimes been argued that since in some of the later peat-bog deposits the proportion of swords to spears is 1:12 at the highest and occasionally as low as 1:16 there were therefore at least twelve spearmen to every sword-bearer. That this is an unreliable calculation is clear when we examine the recently excavated deposit at Ejsbøl.[31] Here were found a total of 380 spear-heads and 60 swords, a ratio of about 1:6. If allowance is made for the known fact that barbarian spearmen each carried two spears into battle, the ratio, on this evidence, would be about 1:3. The evidence of the Ejsbøl North find suggests, further, that the figure of 1:3 is probably nearer the truth than 1:12. This deposit appears to represent the equipment of about 170 to 200 warriors, on the grounds that there were about 160 shields, 191 spears and 203 or more barbed javelins. There were also 60 swords, 60 belts and 62 knives, indicating a sizeable contingent of infantry swordsmen. Calculations of this kind cannot be pressed too far, but for this kind of speculation a deposit made all at one time, such as Ejsbøl North, is a much better guide than the far less homogeneous Vimose or Nydam.

Even in the later phases of the Roman Iron Age body armour and helmets rarely put in an appearance. Mail coats found at Vimose and Thorsbjerg, and in graves elsewhere in northern Germania, are most probably Roman in origin. A few imported Roman helmets, such as those from Thorsbjerg and Hagenow,[32] found their way to the north but they stimulated no change in barbarian equipment. Probably the few imported helmets served as badges of rank rather than armour, the Thorsbjerg and Hagenow examples being showy parade helmets. It is not until the fifth century that we find barbarian leaders beginning to regard the helmet as a vital piece of armour, and even then it seems to have retained a significance as a mark of prestige. The helmet type which they adopted was the distinctive *Spangenhelm*, a helmet made up from a number of bronze or iron plates (usually six or four) riveted to a bronze or iron framework. Cheek-pieces and often a mail neck guard could also be provided. This type of helmet was ultimately of eastern, possibly Parthian, origin, although by the late fourth century it had been adopted by the armies of the eastern Roman Empire. In the fifth century, Ostrogothic workshops in Italy were producing *Spangenhelme* and their products were later copied by craftsmen north of the Alps.[33] They were, however, by no means common and there is no sign that anyone but chieftains and leading warriors possessed them.

The shield remained the principal item of defensive gear. The surviving examples are very rare but the few recorded specimens make it plain that the shield-board had undergone little change since the early Roman period (Pl. 4b). The spiked boss of the early Roman Iron Age, however, largely disappeared in the west, being replaced by a hemispherical type derived from Roman models (fig. 23, l–o). A few of the finer shields were given very ornate bosses inspired by the elaborate equipment of Roman officers. One of the finest is the iron spiked boss from Lilla Harg in Östergötland, which was covered with gilded silver foil and further adorned with precious stones set *en cabochon*. The silver-covered boss from Herpály in Hungary, often quoted as a Germanic product, is more probably to be assigned to a Roman workshop on the middle Danube.[34]

There is still no sign of a greater reliance on cavalry among the Germanic peoples in the late Roman period. It is true that Ostrogothic horsemen played a major part in the Gothic victory at Adrianople, but the chief credit for that triumph goes to the Visigothic infantry—and they were equipped like their forefathers with spear and shield. In late Roman sources the Alamanni figure as a people who fought superbly on horseback, but the archaeological evidence does not suggest that they had any more cavalry than the other barbarians, though they may have used what they had more effectively. Probably it was the retinues of chiefs who rode into battle, at the head of mainly infantry forces.

Siege warfare was naturally not highly developed among peoples who had few fortified settlements over most of their territory. When Germanic peoples began to invade the Roman provinces in the third century, they therefore had virtually no experience of the engines and contrivances which were required to reduce a walled city. Their attempts to learn siege-craft seem usually to have been doomed to disaster from the outset. It must be remembered that all our sources for their conduct of sieges are Roman, and the Romans scarcely ever gave barbarian peoples credit for skill in siege-craft. Nevertheless, the picture presented by Greek and Roman writers is a credible one.[35]

The fundamental disadvantage on the barbarian side was their lack of skill in making the all-essential siege engines. Efficient *onagri* and *balistae* were clearly beyond their technical capabilities and even the elementary towers and mantlets posed great difficulties for them. Even the Batavian auxiliaries, who had already served for some years in the Roman army when besieging the fortress of Vetera on the lower Rhine in A.D. 69, had to rely upon Roman prisoners and deserters to show them how to make siege engines. Their devices, however, had a brief and inglorious career, since the Roman defenders shot them to pieces before they could be brought into operation.[36] Some of the German warbands who poured into Gaul in the later third century had built or acquired war engines, but they did not always need them, for many of the towns they attacked had no walls. The Goths who assaulted Thessalonica in Greece in 269 had machines of some kind, but it cannot be assumed that the invaders made the engines themselves.[37] At least some German war-leaders were well aware that in sieges the barbarians were particularly at a disadvantage. The Visigothic leader Fritigern in 376 tried to prevent his warriors from wasting their energies on sieges that were bound to be fruitless. He was 'at peace with walls', he said.[38] A band of Alamanni viewed walled towns as 'tombs surrounded by nets'. Not until the serious weakening of the Roman frontiers and the accompanying degeneration in the quality of the defenders of towns early in the fifth century did walled cities in the western provinces fall easy prey to barbarian attackers, and even as late as the sixth and seventh centuries, some cities found it possible to hold out for lengthy periods or to frustrate entirely their Germanic besiegers.

This review of barbarian armament suggests that for a lengthy period, from the third century B.C. to the second century A.D., very little change occurred. Thereafter, Germanic weaponry was increasingly influenced by prolonged contact with Rome, so that by the fourth century the armament of the western peoples, especially the Franks and Alamanni, is difficult to distinguish from that of the frontier armies of Rome. Indeed, such a distinction may not realistically be attempted since the Roman forces were themselves largely composed of barbarian troops. But although weapons underwent certain changes in the later Roman Iron Age, in most other respects Germanic warfare, as practised beyond the Roman frontiers, appears to have made no notable advance during the first four centuries A.D. Body armour remained a rarity which only the wealthier warriors and chiefs could hope to possess. Tactics made no progress from the rudimentary level of the ambush, the hit-and-run raid and the headlong onrush against the enemy's line. Any form of commissariat was probably rarely organized. Siege warfare on a serious scale was beyond their competence. In all these respects the armies of the fifth and sixth centuries were scarcely better off than those of Ariovistus and Arminius. The shortcomings stem largely from the character of leadership in war. Individual kings and warleaders rarely enjoyed the authority which would enable them to train an army and hold it together in pursuit of some clearly defined aim. When such a leader, a Maroboduus or an Arminius, did emerge, Rome learnt how formidable German warriors were when well organized and intelligently led. Some modern writers have stressed the great gap between the Roman conduct of war and that of the early Germans, and rightly so. The gap, however, lay not in the equipment of the fighting forces, but rather in organization for war.

## References

1. Jahn, M. (1916), although outdated on many points, is still a useful collection of material. Valuable recent contributions are Raddatz, K. (1966) and (1967b), Schirnig, H. (1965), Steuer, H. (1968). Thompson, E. A. (1965), ch. 4, discusses the literary sources.

2. Engelhardt, C. (1863), (1865), (1867) and (1869).

3. Klindt-Jensen, O. (1949), 41ff. Not everyone would agree with the extent of this 'Celtic', or, better, La Tène, influence.

4. Raddatz, K. (1967b), 14ff.

5. J. D. Cowen in *PPS*, xxxiii (1967), 377ff.

6. *Fontes arch. posnanienses,* iv (1953), 101ff.

7. Billerbeck: G. Dorka, *Urgeschichte des Kreises Pyritz* (Hamburg, 1936), Taf. 46. Klemensker: O. Klindt-Jensen, *Bornholm i folkevanderingstiden* (Copenhagen, 1957), 81, Fig. 64, 8.

8. La Baume, W. (1963), Taf. 23, 1060; Taf. 27, 1261.

9. Hjortspring: Rosenberg, G. (1937). Brøndsted, J. (1960), 35ff. The dating is still being debated; Becker, C. J. (1948) and Hachmann, R. (1960), 184. Krogsbølle: *Årbøger*, 1901, 41ff. Becker, C. J. (1948), 166ff.

10. Raddatz, K. (1966), 437.

11. Hingst, H. (1962).

12. *Germania* 6, 1–2.

13. Nylen E. (1963).

14. cf. K. Schumacher, *Germanendarstellungen* (Mainz, 1935), nos. 69, 70 and 108.

15. op. cit. 68–70.

16. *Germania* 32, 2.

17. This material has not been brought together. On Angeln, H. Jankuhn and K. Raddatz in *Reallexicon germanischer Altertumskunde*[2] (Berlin) Lieferung 3, 298. Holmqvist, W. (1951), 71ff. on some of the Scandinavian evidence. Eggers, H. J. (1951), 113ff. on Mecklenburg. On spurs in general, Jahn, M. (1921).

18. Krüger, F. (1928).

19. Essunga: S. Müller in *Årbøger* 1920, 107; Vogn: B. Nerman in *Fornvännen*, 1937, 109.

20. Danish finds discussed in Klindt-Jensen, O. (1949), 80ff. Harsefeld: Wegewitz, W. (1937), 118; Klein Fliess: W. Gaerte, *Urgeschichte Ostpreussens* (Königsberg, 1929), 169, Abb. 119.

21. Velleius Paterculus ii, 109, 2.

22. Romans knew that German horses were inferior to their own: Zosimos iv, 22, 1–3; Orosius vii, 34, 5. Archaeological evidence suggests that the majority of horses reared in Germania would be too small to be used as cavalry mounts; above, p. 119. Bökönyi, S. (1968).

23. *Offa*, xvii–xviii (1959–61), 22ff.

24. Raddatz, K. (1967b), 8.

25. Werner, J. (1955); Schulz, W. and Zahn, R., (1933), 42 and (1953), 49ff.

26. *Offa*, xx (1963), 39ff.

27. *Offa*, xx (1963), 49ff.

28. Raddatz, K. (1967b), 10f.

29. Dabrowski, K. and Kolendo, J. (1972).

30. *Pays Gaumais* (1949), 19ff. *Med. Arch.*, v (1961), 71ff.

31. M. Ørsnes in Jankuhn, H. (1970), 172ff.

32. Engelhardt, C. (1863), 23ff and Pl. 5. Asmus, W. D., (1938), 83f

33. Werner, J. (1950).

34. Lilla Harg: Oxenstierna, E. (1958), 54ff; Herpály: Fettich, N. (1930).

35. Thompson, E. A. (1965), 131ff.

36. Tacitus, *Histories* iv, 23.

37. Eusebius 101 F2, 2.

38. Ammianus Marcellinus xxxi, 6, 4; cf. also xvi, 4, 2.

# 6 | Gods and sanctuaries

Our ability to comprehend the world of early Germanic religion is severely limited.[1] Not only are the sources of information available to us very restricted, they also contain many contradictions, notably between the evidence provided by classical writers and that brought forward by archaeology. We cannot hope, therefore, to reconstruct anything like a complete picture of Germanic religious affairs during the Roman Iron Age. The literary sources give us an entirely random sample of information about the regional and lesser cults of the period, They say something about Nerthus and Tamfana, but we can never know whether these deities were matched by others in different parts of Germania. The epigraphic evidence from the Roman frontier provinces, especially from the Rhine valley, indicates that a very large number of minor deities were worshipped there, often in tightly localized areas. The same was probably true of pre-literate free Germany, although our meagre sources give little impression of this.

There is another limiting factor. Roman writers and their public were rather more interested in the lurid and sensational aspects of barbarian peoples than in commonplace beliefs and customs, an attitude towards primitive man not unknown in the civilized world today. The ancient literary record thus displays a certain bias towards the more savage rituals associated with the Germanic war gods, and has less to say about the cults of fertility and life.

## The gods of war

It is not surprising, nor coincidental, that the references of Greek and Roman writers to the early Germanic gods have most to say about the war gods and the observances with which they were honoured. Throughout the northern Iron Age and until the conversion to Christianity of the Danes, Swedes and Prussians in the Middle Ages, the gods of war dominated the northern heaven. The descriptions in Strabo, Tacitus, Procopius and Jordanes[2] of horrific rites in honour of the war deities bring home to us the terror aroused in men's minds by the powers which decided the fortunes of battle. Throughout our period we come across references to rituals which involved the sacrifice of a beaten foe, together with his arms, equipment and horses, to the gods of war. When, in the first century A.D., the Chatti and Hermunduri clashed over the possession of a stretch of river which flowed between their territories, both tribes vowed that they would sacrifice the enemy and all his accoutrements to the lord of battle if victory were theirs. This was no mere war of words before hostilities: the Hermunduri won and fulfilled their vow.

Describing the rites practised by the Cimbri a century and a half earlier, Strabo paints a still more hideous picture. The Cimbri suspended their wretched war prisoners over great bronze bowls. Priestesses, aged women dressed in white, climbed up ladders to the hanging men and cut their throats so that their life blood was caught in the bowls beneath. Another people, the Heruls, sacrificed not only their prisoners of war but also men of their own kin who were close to death through old age or illness. Fortunately for us, there are many clear archaeological traces of these savage rituals, but first let us review the earliest literary sources for the Germanic gods.

When the Hermunduri and Chatti vowed to sacrifice each other to the war gods, it was to two gods that the vow was made. These two the Romans could identify as Mars and Mercury. Romans assumed that the deities of other peoples did not differ in essence from those of their own pantheon, so that they must have been able to discern something of the power and attributes of Mars and Mercury in those two barbarian deities. Mercury was held by Tacitus to be the god particularly honoured by the Germans, a god who might receive on fixed days the sacrifice of human beings as well as animals.[3] This was the deity whom the Germans called Wodan, the god of storm and wind as well as war. The identification of the pacific Mercury with a war god may seem surprising, but it is supported by a wide range of evidence. Several later writers, including the author of the *Vita Columbani* and Paul the Deacon say as much.[4] When the later Germans translated the *dies Mercurii* (French, *mercredi*), it became *Wodan-stag* (English, Wednesday). The identification can be explained by reference to the part played by both Mercury and Wodan in leading to the underworld the spirits of the dead. Again, like Mercury, Wodan was concerned with trade and the protection of traders.

The other war god honoured in the Roman period was Tiwaz (Tiw or Tyr in later sources), identified by the Romans with Mars. Originally a sky god, by the time the Romans got to hear of him Tiwaz appears to have had two main spheres of influence, the battlefield and the realm of law and order. One of his titles used on inscriptions set up in the Roman provinces was *Mars Thingsus*, indicating a connection with the *Thing* or people's assembly. Like Wodan, Tiwaz was honoured in later Germanic heathenism, but several of the attributes of both deities had by then been taken over by the great warrior god, Odin. We know scarcely anything about cult ceremonies connected with the worship of Tiwaz, though a yearly assembly of the Semnones and their related tribes in a sacred wood may have been in his honour.[5] Tacitus called the god worshipped at this ceremony *regnator omnium deus*, which has suggested to some scholars that Wodan is here in question. On the whole Tiwaz seems more likely. The deity was first offered a human sacrifice. All those who entered the sacred wood were bound as a sign of submission to the presiding deity. The precise meaning of this ritual binding is, however, not clear, and while later Scandinavian references to binding and to a 'Fetter-grove' hint at the survival of the practice, they throw no light on its significance.

Another Germanic god whom Romans could identify with their own was Donar, the predecessor of Thor, who seemed to have much in common with Hercules. This god was possessed of great physical strength and was, like Hercules, involved constantly in arduous journeyings and battles against monstrous beings. The resemblances between Donar and Hercules do seem close, even extending to the favoured weapon of both gods: the hammer of Donar and the club of Hercules.[6] Unlike Hercules, however, Donar was a god of thunder and, according to some medieval accounts, of the sky. He had strong associations with forest groves and particularly with oak woods, for example a forest in the Weser region was particularly sacred to Donar. This recalls the fact that other peoples of northern and central Europe,

Celts, Slavs and Balts, all worshipped the god of thunder in forests. In the sixteenth century the heathen Prussians still honoured their thunder god *Perkuno* before a sacred oak, and it is quite possible that Donar was worshipped in a similar fashion in the Imperial period.

## Twin gods

There are few other literary traces of early Germanic deities, although among some peoples at least there is evidence for the worship of twin deities. The tribe of the Naharnavali in eastern Germania honoured youthful twins, the Alcis, in a sacred wood.[7] Tacitus was struck by the resemblance of the Alcis to Castor and Pollux but was certain that the cult was native and uninfluenced by external contacts. There are other echoes of the cult of twin gods among the Germans,[8] and a number of Germanic peoples honoured pairs of heroic rulers among the ancestors of their leading families. The Vandal tradition spoke of the Hasdings Raos and Raptos, and Ambri and Assi. The Lombards had the two heroes Aio and Ibor, the early Swedes Alrik and Eirck. There is little evidence, however, that any of these were connected with the cult of the Alcis.

## Fertility deities

The clearest picture of a fertility cult is provided by Tacitus' account of the cult of the goddess Nerthus observed among the tribes at the base of the Jutland peninsula.[9] Tacitus represents Nerthus as a manifestation of Mother Earth and, like other earth goddesses, she visited her devotees at particular times in a sacred wagon which only her own priest might touch or look inside. The wagon was kept in a sacred wood on an island in the western Baltic, perhaps Fyn or Zealand. At a certain time, probably in the spring, the priest sensed that the goddess was present in her wagon and thereupon it was towed through the countryside among welcoming worshippers. War and the taking up of arms was forbidden during Nerthus' progress. Afterwards, the wagon, its cover and perhaps a cult image of the deity were washed in a hidden lake by slaves, who were drowned when the task was completed.

The associations with other fertility deities are obvious. The secrecy surrounding the shrine of the goddess, the banning of war and the carrying of weapons during her festival, the spring progress amid adoring devotees, all these are shared with one or other of the fertility cults of the Mediterranean world. Tacitus was no doubt aware of the similarities between the cult of Nerthus and that of Cybele, but there are no grounds for thinking that he simply invented a cult for the Jutland deity on the basis of what he knew about the worship of Cybele. Similar progresses on a wagon are recorded in Scandinavia during the later heathen period.[10] The Nerthus cult is entirely acceptable, as described by Tacitus, as a major regional cult of fertility, and it is the only cult named in classical sources which may plausibly be linked with features in the archaeological record. At Dejbjerg in west Jutland two small wagons richly ornamented with openwork sheet bronze were found sunk in a peat-bog, relics of cult ceremonial, not burial. The place of origin and the dating of the wagons are alike problematic, some scholars arguing for Gaul about 100 B.C., others for the Danube lands somewhat later.[11] But there is general agreement that these beautifully made vehicles had been employed in cult progresses like those of Nerthus and her priests. A recent find of parts of much more workaday wagons seems to belong to the same milieu as Dejbjerg, though at a humbler level. This was made at Rappendam on the island of Zealand, where a bog deposit yielded up many wagon parts, including some forty wheels, as well as three plough-shares, a female skeleton and the remains of many animal sacrifices.[12] The Rappendam deposit, like that at Dejbjerg, plainly belongs to the sphere of west Baltic fertility rites of which the cult of Nerthus was one manifestation, but a final and conclusive association with Nerthus, though tempting and highly likely, is not possible.

Other deities who receive mention are scarcely more than names, for instance Baduhenna among the Frisii, and Tamfana who was honoured by several tribes in a temple or sanctuary somewhere in the region of the Ruhr and the Lippe.[13] The devotees of Tamfana honoured her in a great autumn festival, presumably connected with harvest rites, and so her general sphere would seem to have been that of fertility. The sky and fertility god Ull, later well known in Scandinavian tradition, is commemorated in a number of early place names in central Sweden and southern Norway, and a tiny fragment of written evidence suggests that he was worshipped in the Roman Iron Age. This is a runic inscription on a scabbard-chape from Thorsbjerg in Schleswig, which reads WUL*Þ*U*Þ*EWAR. This is a twofold name, the first part apparently containing the name of Ull.[14] This inscription will give some impression of how piecemeal and scrappy is our literary evidence for early Germanic deities.[15]

## The archaeological record

The most celebrated cult places of the early Germans are the rich and in many respects well preserved votive deposits which have been recovered from peat-bogs in Denmark and Schleswig. The extraordinary series of these deposits excavated by Conrad Engelhardt between 1858 and 1865 at Thorsbjerg, Nydam, Vimose and Kragehul have until recently claimed most of the attention given to finds of this sort and interpretation of the deposits did not for a long time advance far beyond that generally accepted in the nineteenth century. That the material from the deposits tended to overshadow and obscure the meaning of the deposits themselves is hardly surprising, for by any standards the contents of the four bog deposits excavated by Engelhardt were spectacular: masses of war equipment both Roman and Germanic, two complete ships, elaborately decorated personal ornaments, clothing of outstanding quality, Roman imported goods and hundreds of more humdrum objects in pottery, wood and leather. After Engelhardt's work, which was fortunately well ahead of its day both in execution and in record, knowledge of these and other bog deposits was not significantly increased for more than sixty years. Recently, a stimulus to fresh thought about them has been provided by re-examination of the material from one site, Thorsbjerg,[16] and by the discovery of two further deposits in Denmark, at Illerup near Skanderborg and at Ejsbøl near Haderslev,[17] and a related deposit at Skedemosse[18] on the Swedish island of Öland. Armed with this new material, the problems posed by these fascinating sites can be analysed afresh, beginning with the earliest known deposits which date from the middle of the pre-Roman Iron Age.

The earliest of the large votive deposits of war gear is that found at Hjortspring on the island of Als.[19] The deposit has been made in an insignificant bog but the importance of the site cannot be obscured by its humble surroundings. The centrepiece of the Hjortspring deposit is a small ship, the earliest clinker-built vessel yet known in Europe. This was 19m long and had been constructed from five large planks held together without the aid of iron nails. The craft would have lain low in the water and been none too stable in a heavy sea, but in the sheltered inlets of the western Baltic it could have proved a serviceable vessel for about twenty-four men. About the ship lay a mass of weapons and equipment, the most striking items being about 150 wooden

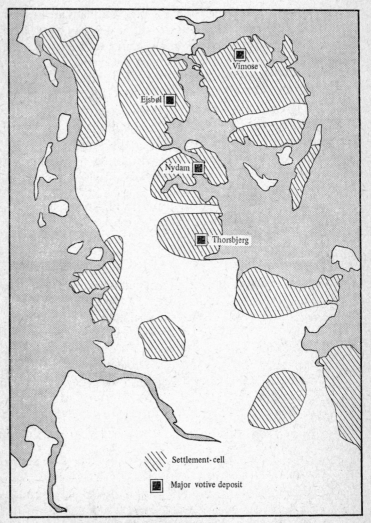

Fig. 24 Distribution of the major votive deposits

shields, or parts of them, 138 spear-heads of iron and thirty-one of bone and antler, at least twenty mail garments—perhaps the most exotic of all the Hjortspring material—and at least six one-edged swords and their wooden scabbards. There were domestic items too, including a fine series of wooden vessels, bowls, dishes, lidded boxes and a bucket. Since Rosenberg's original publication it has been generally assumed that all these objects were deposited at one time, though there is nothing in the excavator's observations which precludes the possibility that objects were thrown into the bog at various times. On balance, however, a large proportion of the war gear, if not all of it, may be taken to represent a single deposition, though dating is beset with difficulty (see p. 166). In the most recent discussion of Hjortspring Hachmann places it about 200 B.C., though a still earlier dating is possible.

The other votive finds of the pre-Roman Iron Age are very small by comparison and normally contain only weapons. After Hjortspring the most important deposit is that at Krogsbølle on Fyn with seven swords, twenty-four iron spear-heads and another nineteen of bone. The find from Tidavad in Östergötland and Wöbs (Kr. Eutin) contained only iron spear-heads, while that from Vaedebro near Skanderborg comprised a shield with traces of paint on its board, spear-heads, an arrow and a knife.[20] No deposits of war gear are yet known which date exclusively from the end of the pre-Roman Iron Age and the early Roman period. In fact it is not until the late second century A.D. that large votive offerings to the gods of war are again encountered, the outstanding instances of this date being two of the four excavated by Engelhardt, namely Vimose and Thorsbjerg.[21]

Some of the contents of the Thorsbjerg find have of late been intensively studied and made accessible by publication; it will therefore be examined first. The site of the Thorsbjerg bog lies close to Süderbrarup, about 19km north-east of Schleswig and 5km north of the Sliförde which gives access to the sea. The objects lay in a fairly limited area beneath some 2·5m to 3m of peat. There were finds of other objects here after Engelhardt's work and there is a strong possibility that more still remains to be found.

A large proportion of the material recovered consisted of weapons and armour, but there were also personal ornaments, clothing and agricultural tools. The most unusual items were substantial parts of two Roman army parade helmets, one of bronze, the other of silver partially covered with gold foil, an outstanding representative of its type and here gaining in splendour in a spot so remote from its land of origin. The helmets were accompanied by other Roman objects, shields, swords, javelins, belts, mail garments and brooches. There were also two discs of bronze covered with silver-gilt foil, their decoration later augmented by figures and animals and birds in a native manner (see p. 138). The bulk of the Germanic contribution to the Thorsbjerg deposit, however, lay in weapons: longbows, bundles of arrows, literally stacks of shields, ash spears, horse harness and other accoutrements. Finally, there were at least five items of clothing, comprising two pairs of trousers, two fine cloaks and a handsome long-sleeved shirt. Many of the objects, especially the weapons and clothing, had clearly been deliberately destroyed before being thrown into the bog. Sword blades, javelins and spear-heads had been bent, twisted or even broken, shield-bosses had been crushed or split open, and some of the garments had been slashed with a knife. These marks of destruction were also apparent in the other large deposits, notably Vimose and Nydam.[22]

Engelhardt and his immediate successors believed that the mass of the deposit was homogeneous and had been thrown into the peat at the same period of time. Thirty-seven Roman denarii, ranging from Nero to Septimius Severus, appeared to provide a secure *terminus post quem* for the deposition of shortly after 200 and suggested that the deposit as a whole belonged to the first half of the third century. Not until 1912 was it pointed out that the brooches from Thorsbjerg ranged from the second century B.C. to the fourth century A.D., though they were commonest in the third century.[23] The pottery in the find, which Engelhardt was not in a position to discuss at all fully, helps to give further precision to the dating of the deposit.[24] The bulk of the vessels belong to the first century B.C. and the beginning of the Roman period, though appreciable numbers of sherds date from the first and second centuries A.D. The inference must be that offerings of some kind were already being made in the late pre-Roman Iron Age and the early Roman period and that these were different in character from the offerings of the late second century onward. What the earlier offerings were can be established partly by analogy with the other large peat-bog deposits, partly on the evidence of innumerable small deposits from Denmark and northern

Germany. The pottery vessels were used as containers for various kinds of animal sacrifice, sometimes an entire young creature, more often a joint from a mature animal. Pigs, sheep, cattle and horses all fulfilled this sacrificial role, especially pigs and cattle. The vessels also seem to have contained such animal products as milk and butter, and occasionally even human bones and hair. The offerants of the pre-Roman and the Roman Iron Age were, then, depositing mainly animal sacrifices, no doubt to fertility deities in the hope of securing fruitfulness for land and crops. There is at this time no trace of a warlike strain in the offerings. Those responsible were first and foremost farmers, not warriors.

The mass of weapons and war equipment was deposited in the bog in the late second century and the earlier part of the third. The forces of fertility and life have clearly given way to the gods of war, this change no doubt reflecting developments within the Germanic social order. The terminal date for the main deposit of war gear at Thorsbjerg lies within the third century, but there was at least one further ceremony here after that time, in which a small group of sword and scabbard parts was deposited.[25]

Observations allowed from the Thorsbjerg material provide fresh insight into the nature and the history of this large deposit at least. First of all, the use of the same peat-bog over such a lengthy period should indicate that Thorsbjerg played a special role in the religious life of Angeln (see p. 195). Secondly, there is clear evidence that the character of the deposit changed considerably during the three centuries over which it accumulated, the most striking change, from a peasant milieu to one in which warriors called the tune, occurring in the second century. Finally, although many weapons and other objects were certainly deposited on the same occasion (as the stacks of shields and bundles of arrows make clear), it cannot be assumed that *all* the war gear was consigned to the ground in a single ceremony.

The most famous of all the votive deposits is that at Nydam near Østersottrup, which lies some 32km north of Thorsbjerg in a narrow marshy valley close to the strait which separates Als from the mainland.[26] The material was recovered from under a peat deposit at depths varying between 1m and 2m. In all, the votive objects were scattered over an area measuring about 1000 sq.m. Although the find is chiefly celebrated for the splendid ship dating from the later fourth century,[27] there were actually three ships in the deposit. One still lies in the peat and another was successfully recovered but later fell a victim to the Danish–German war of 1864. The two excavated ships had been deliberately sunk, apparently after they had been laden with war equipment and other goods. The equipment included 100 or more swords, 93 of them pattern-welded, and some bearing the name-stamps of Roman makers, more than 550 spears and javelins, at least 40 bows, 170 arrow-heads. As at Thorsbjerg, some of the material had been grouped or bundled together before being immersed in the bog. Once again most of the weapons had been damaged or broken into pieces. The accompanying goods included brooches, belts, pottery and wooden vessels, agricultural implements, the remains of animal sacrifice, and Roman coins of which the latest is a denarius of 218.

Unlike Thorsbjerg, the material from Nydam has not yet been restudied in detail, but it does not appear to cover quite so wide a time span as Thorsbjerg. Deposition began in the late second century and extended into the mid fifth. The date of the weapons in the find ranges from the late second onward, but the great bulk date from the third and fourth centuries. They may have been deposited on two or three occasions at the end of the Roman period. Later, in the fifth century, the last offering was made at Nydam. This was a small group of sword parts, usually called Nydam II, as it lay about 45m away from the large nucleus of objects.

Attention is bound to be held by the three Nydam ships and it is particularly unfortunate that one has largely perished while another cannot now be located in the ground. The fragmentary remains of the second Nydam ship seem to be those of a vessel which is considerably older than the complete ship of the fourth century.[28] That second ship might indeed be closer in date to the Hjortspring vessel than to its companion at Nydam and the fact that Hjortspring itself is only a few kilometres away across the Als sound might suggest that in this part of the western Baltic there presided a deity whose particular concern or whose symbol was the ship.[29] On the other hand, both the Hjortspring vessel and the intact Nydam ship appear to be warships rather than anything else, although even a warship might end its days in the service of a god.

The third of the great deposits of the Roman period excavated by Engelhardt is that at Vimose in the north-west of the island of Fyn.[30] This deposit resembles Thorsbjerg in that it begins in the late pre-Roman Iron Age with offerings of animal remains in pots. But from an early date in the Roman period weapons were deposited at Vimose. Most of the warrior equipment, however, once again dates from the late second and early third centuries. It includes a complete mail garment, and a fine range of both Roman and Germanic weapons. Brooches, agricultural and other tools, and wooden vessels augment the catalogue. The final deposition, a group of sword parts, dates from about A.D. 400.

After Engelhardt's work almost a century elapsed before other large deposits of the Roman period were located and excavated, the oustanding recent discoveries being made at Illerup, of which only a brief notice has been published, and Ejsbøl, of which detailed interim accounts have already appeared.[31] The Ejsbøl deposits have much in common with Nydam and the rest. There is the same emphasis upon weaponry, much of which has been bent, broken or even burnt before deposition. There were two quite distinct concentrations within the bog, a large one near the centre, and one smaller close to the shore. Since Ejsbøl is the first major deposit to be virtually completely dug, the history of its accumulation is of unusual importance. The excavator adduces good grounds for believing that the larger group of objects, some 500 in all, was deposited all at one time in the later fourth century. The smaller concentration, too, appears to be a homogeneous deposit, dating from the early fifth century. As we noted above, the larger deposit might be interpreted as the equipment of a force of about 200 men, sixty of whom were heavily armed and nine mounted. The smaller deposit belongs to the same category as Nydam II and the late deposit at Vimose, containing mainly scabbard and sword parts along with three superb silver buckles and three swords.

The votive deposits found in Sweden are much more heterogeneous than those of Denmark, and north Germany. By and large, they are smaller and contain such things as rings and other ornaments, animal remains, or occasionally weapons. One interesting group contains only horse trappings, reins, bridles and parts of saddles. A few are more complex than the rest, containing pots, wooden and wicker vessels, weapons, ornaments and the almost inevitable animal bones. The distribution of these northerly votive sites centres on Skåne, Öland and Gotland. The only votive deposit in a peat-bog which can so far rival the great finds in Denmark is that at Skedemosse on Öland.[32]

G

This deposit accumulated over several centuries, starting in the third century A.D. and receiving offerings until the early sixth. The majority of the objects, however, were deposited in the fourth and fifth centuries. The most striking are seven gold snake-headed rings and two gold finger-rings. The remainder of the deposit has a more warlike aspect: swords and sword attachments, spear-heads, arrows, axes, shield parts, belt fittings and horse trappings. A few personal adornments such as beads and combs were also present. Large quantities of bone point to animal sacrifices, the usual cattle, horses, sheep, pigs and dogs being represented. The horse appears to have been the animal most commonly sacrificed, there being more than 100 identifiable individual beasts in the excavated material (see p. 198). Since horse trappings as well as horse bones were very much to the fore at Skedemosse, it has been suggested that a horse-god held sway in this part of the Baltic and the idea has a fair measure of support from other finds (see p. 199).[33] Human sacrifices, too, were offered at Skedemosse, some fifty individuals of both sexes and all ages.

Thus, it is clear that sacrifices could be made at the same spot over a considerable period, as at Thorsbjerg and Vimose, or within a comparatively short space of time, as at Nydam, Illerup and Ejsbøl. It is also now widely appreciated, from the deposits laid down over a lengthy time, that the character of the objects sacrificed could vary considerably from period to period. The evidence from Thorsbjerg suggests that offerings to a fertility deity in the later pre-Roman Iron Age were later supplanted by offerings of brooches and other ornaments to a god with another sphere of interest. Later still, from the beginning of the late Roman Iron Age, the accent was very much on fine and costly war gear and imported goods, to the exclusion of almost all else. These new cult observances clearly reflect the influence and aspirations of ambitious and outward-looking warriors, at this time by far and away the most thrusting element in society.

## The situation of the cult places

Apart from Skedemosse on Öland, which in any case differs in many respects from the others, the five major deposits of the Roman Iron Age lie in the Jutland peninsula or on the adjacent islands. No deposits remotely resembling them are known from the shores of the North Sea or the Baltic, or from any other part of Germania. Their local distribution and their relationship with settlement areas is equally remarkable (fig. 24). Thorsbjerg lies at the heart of the clearly defined settlement area of Angeln, Ejsbøl in the territory of the Oberjersdal *Kreis*, Nydam at the centre of the 'island' of settlement north of the Eckernförde and Vimose likewise in northern Fyn. These central positions suggest strongly that the cult places held a strong significance for an entire population group, and not merely for a single ruling

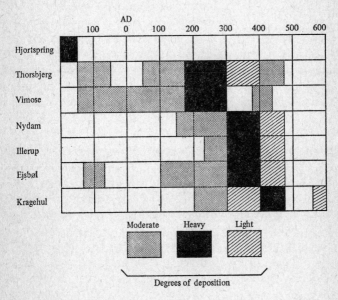

Fig. 25 Chronology of the major votive deposits

family or large community. Whether those population groups were entire tribes, cult associations or other kinds of social grouping the evidence does not allow us to determine.

The existence of an enormous number of small votive sites alongside the great peat-bog deposits suggests that individual communities, clans or families had their own sacred places, commonly marshes, pools or springs. The great majority of the recorded examples lie in Denmark and Schleswig-Holstein but this northern preponderance probably does not reflect faithfully their original distribution. They certainly existed in other parts of Germania, including Lower Saxony, Thuringia and Silesia. The offerings placed in these rustic deposits are extremely various and not all are easy to interpret. There is a natural emphasis upon fertility, expressed in animal sacrifices, but other phenomena such as human sacrifice and the presence of wooden idols in human shape are not always easily explained.

The wooden idols have now been recorded from a considerable number of peat-bog sanctuaries. They are mostly crude but vigorously carved anthropomorphic figures (Pl. 3), usually male, occasionally female, and now and then occurring in pairs. The most imposing are the male and female figures found at Braak in Holstein, the male deity being ten feet high, his consort somewhat shorter.[34] On both figures the sexual characteristics were originally fully emphasized. Another striking idol is the ithyphallic figure from Broddenbjerg in Jutland.[35] This northern Priapus stood about one metre high and he had been set upon a heap of stones in the middle of a peat-bog. Around the little cairn lay the remains of pottery vessels containing food offerings. A similar situation had been chosen for a rather earlier idol found at Rosbjerggaard in Jutland and these stone cairns may have been more than mere pedestals for the idols. In Old Norse the term *hǫngr* can mean 'sanctuary' as well as 'cairn'.

Two small sanctuaries in Thuringia[36] contained idols of different forms. At Possendorf near Weimar an asexual wooden figure with upraised arms stood in a peat-bog. Nearby lay a human skeleton and a number of bronze objects, some of which had been broken before deposition. At Oberdorla near Mühlhausen, the idol was no more than a tall pole thrust into the peat, at its base the skull and foot bones of a man. In a later phase of this cult place several poles had been erected and about them lay the bones of horses, pottery vessels and a set of carpenters' tools. Figures of gods or spirits were also set up in places where men might be in danger. For example, in the marsh of Wittemoor near Oldenburg,[37] at a point where a timber roadway crossed a particularly dangerous stretch of bog, a number of stylized figures, both male and female, were set up to give what protection they could to travellers.

Other kinds of sacred place recall those familiar in Celtic Europe. Springs, wells and streams containing small votive offerings are recorded from all over Germania. Mineral springs appear to have been particularly revered and a number, e.g. the Brodelbrunnen at Bad Pyrmont[38] in Lower Saxony, received offerings over several centuries. Cult shafts and pits are also recorded from parts of

Germania, though they do not appear to have been common. The most interesting is an example found at Greussen (Kr. Sonderhausen) in Thuringia.[39] This was a shaft cut 3–3·5m deep into the chalk bedrock and containing six or more cult vessels. One of these was in the form of a boar, another of a bird of prey, and a third had applied boar masks on its sides. Other zoomorphic vessels have been noted from Thuringia and their date, like that of the Greussen shaft, can be confidently placed in the Roman Iron Age. Rather later, in the fifth century, a pot in the shape of a boar was used as a cremation container in a grave at Liebenau in Lower Saxony and a figure of a boar surmounts the lid of a slightly later Saxon vessel from the cemetery at Issendorf near Stade.[40] There is a great deal of other evidence that the boar was an important religious symbol, particularly in the realm of fertility, as well as a commonly sacrificed animal.[41] But there are no solid grounds for speaking of a cult of the boar. More probably the animal symbolized certain qualities of one or more deities, as it did for Freyr and Freyja in later times.

That cult places and sanctuaries existed on dry ground as well as in marshes and pools must be assumed, though identification of such sites poses many problems, since so many of the adjuncts of simple ceremonies will have been in normally perishable materials. A small number of these sites, however, have been located. A notable instance is the site at the Rote Maass near Damp in Schleswig.[42] This took the form of a circle of nine large stones some 7·5m in diameter. Immediately adjacent to the circle to the south lay a rectangle marked out by 'walls' a single stone wide. At the centre of this lay another rectangular space, about 6m by 4·5m with smaller rectangles around it. The circle and the rectangular settings probably date from the Roman Iron Age but later in its history, in the late fourth and early fifth centuries, the site was used as a cremation cemetery. There is no close analogy to the Rote Maass in northern Europe or anywhere else, although square and rectangular enclosures in the realm of cult and burial are familiar enough in the Celtic regions.

*Animal and human sacrifice*

The sacrifice of living things, including men, played an important role in the religious observances of the early Germans.[43] The animals most commonly sacrificed were horses, cattle, sheep and goats, pigs, dogs, and occasionally wild animals. In a striking number of votive deposits the bones of horses outnumber those of other animals. At Skedemosse, for example, 35 per cent of the great quantity of animal bones was of horse, 28 per cent of cattle, 22·7 per cent of sheep or goat, with much smaller proportions of pig, dog and wild creatures. The animals were deposited in peat-bogs, streams or pools entire, or with their bones cut or split into small fragments. They might also be represented by certain carefully selected parts of the skeleton, notably the skull, feet and tail. This is particularly true of the horse.[44] It is apparent therefore that the animals were commonly eaten in sacrificial meals and the remains, or on occasion the less edible parts, later deposited. There is also some evidence that the entrails were offered in sacrifice.

The principal source of information about animal sacrifices are bog and pool deposits found in the Danish peninsula and islands, with outliers in Germany and southern Sweden. But it is known that sacrifices were offered in settlements and cemeteries as well as besides pools and marshes. The commonest type of site at which animals were sacrificed was a small bog; these occasionally contain the remains of sacrificed human beings as well as animals. A good example is the find at Rislev on the island of Zealand.[45] This contained the remains of eleven horses, seven cattle, five sheep, three dogs and a few pig bones. The skeletons of two women and a child, and the scattered bones of a fourth individual, were also recovered from the lowest levels of the peat. Scraps of pottery date this deposit to the late fourth or early fifth century. The horse bones, once again mainly skulls, feet and tails, lay in one part of the bog, the other animals being more scattered. Both young and old beasts had been slaughtered, the normal means of despatching them being a heavy blow on the forehead. Most of the bones, except those of the dogs, bore marks of cutting, indicating that the animals had normally been eaten after the sacrifice.

On a large number of bog votive sites, pottery vessels occur in the peat, in some cases with animal remains inside them.[46] Probably these pots were usually employed as containers for selected parts of animals, especially the soft parts, heart, liver and intestines. Finds containing such vessels are particularly common in Denmark, more especially in Jutland, in the pre-Roman and earlier Roman Iron Age, though the practice can be traced back to the Neolithic Age in this part of Europe. The Iron Age finds are very various in character. Some consist of large groups of pots with bones both inside them and scattered on all sides. At some sites the vessels contain the bones of complete animals, at others masses of small fragments. In a small number of cases, particular kinds of animals accompanied the pots, dogs, cows or sheep. Animal bones are not, however, invariably present on sites of this kind. At Skaeringe (Zealand) a pit had been dug into the peat to contain four pottery vessels and a few stones, but no animal remains. Over the site of this ceremony a cairn of stones had been erected. Occasionally other objects were included with the pots. At Forlev Nymølle (Jutland), a branch roughly formed into the shape of a woman was surrounded by fragments of pottery, bones and a bundle of flax.

The prominence of the horse in the animal sacrifices deserves special notice. Commonly only the skull, tail and feet are represented, the rest of the body having served as a ritual meal. This rite of burying the skull and extremities of the skeleton links the Germanic world with the Baltic regions and the Steppes, where until comparatively recent times nomads sacrificed chosen horses and afterwards hung up the skin, skull and legs on a pole. There are later echoes of this rite in the sagas and in medieval English traditions, though there the connection is with cursing or insult. Apart from the evidence of the votive deposits, there are other sources for the role of horses in cult ceremonies. One of the gold horns from Gallehus, dating to about the early fifth century, has scenes of a horse sacrifice in which a priest holds a horn, containing perhaps the blood of the victim.[47] Ritual horse-racing and horse-fights are attested in Migration-period Scandinavia and these probably had their counterparts in earlier tradition.

Another animal which figures frequently in votive contexts of all kinds is the dog. In some deposits more dogs had been sacrificed than any other animal. Unlike the other domesticated creatures, however, there is no evidence that the dogs had been eaten in a sacrificial meal. More probably they were connected with fertility cults like that of Nehallenia on the island of Walcheren in the Rhine delta, a goddess who is known from abundant sculptural evidence on Roman altars to have a dog as her constant companion.[48] Another possibility is that a dog could be substituted for a man in a sacrifice, for it is noticeable that dogs and humans occur in the same kinds of ritual deposit.

Occasional sacrifice of human beings is attested in the northern
Bronze Age, usually in connection with funerary rites. Such
sacrifices were very much commoner in the pre-Roman and Roman
Iron Age, though now apparently divorced from a cult of the
dead. From various references in ancient writers the sacrifice of
humans is known to have taken place in at least the following
circumstances.[49] First, and probably most commonly, prisoners
of war were sacrificed to the war gods by the victors after a
successful battle. Secondly, among the Semnones and probably
other Suebic peoples, a god (perhaps Tiwaz) was offered a human
sacrifice in ceremonies held in a sacred wood. Thirdly, after the
cult progress of Nerthus among her worshippers, the slave
ministrants who washed the sacred cart and its vestments were
drowned in a hidden lake. There may well have been other
occasions on which human sacrifices were made, but these ceremonies were surely accompanied by the rite during the early
Imperial period. The archaeological evidence offers a certain
amount of confirmation for the written sources but cannot bear
a straightforward and uniform interpretation and at some points
appears to carry us out of the sphere of religion altogether.

The fact that human remains occur in some of the large peat-
bog deposits, for instance Nydam and Skedemosse, is likely
support for the accounts of Strabo, Orosius and Jordanes which
describe the slaughter of war prisoners. Much smaller votive
offerings, consisting mainly of animal bones and pottery, not
infrequently contain human skeletons or parts of them, indicating
that further occasions when human sacrifice was thought appropriate were humble rustic ceremonies honouring fertility deities.
The votive deposit at Rislev (see p. 198) is only one out of many
known in northern Germania.

There is a further potentially major source on the subject
of human sacrifice in the more or less well preserved human
corpses found in varying circumstances in the northern peat-
bogs.[50] By far the greatest number of these have been recorded
in the peat regions of Denmark, Schleswig-Holstein and Lower
Saxony and the majority of those that can be dated belong to the
period from 100 B.C. to A.D. 500. A strenuous debate continues
about the significance of many of these corpses in the peat.[51] If
we exclude a number which seem to be victims of accident or
murder, many remain who have plainly been done to death in
ceremonies with a brutal conclusion. Men, women and children

are all represented, though adults appear to outnumber the young. They met their deaths in various ways, by hanging, strangulation, decapitation, stabbing, and some perhaps by drowning. Some went into the peat naked or virtually so, others fully clad. Some were accompanied by other offerings or objects, pottery, wooden vessels, animals. Others lay alone.

There is obviously no need to assume that all the bog corpses were victims of religious rites. A famous passage in the *Germania* tells us that those found guilty of treason, cowardice or sexual perversion were put to death by being immersed in a marsh with a hurdle placed over them,[52] and in later law codes there are references to forcible drowning as atonement for serious offences. On the other hand, one school of opinion argues that the great majority of the corpses represent sacrifices to fertility gods. To establish a basis for discussion, let us therefore examine some of the more interesting of recent finds.

After the famous corpse of the man from Tollund, which has been exhaustively described elsewhere, one of the best preserved of these finds is that of a man from Graubålle in Jutland, found in 1952.[53] He lay about 32m from dry ground in an old peat cutting in a small cauldron-bog. The man had been killed at the age of about thirty by having his throat cut. The corpse was naked and unaccompanied by other objects. As with the corpses from Tollund and Borremose, the internal organs were well enough preserved for the stomach contents to be identified, and like the Tollund and Borremose men his last meal had consisted of a gruel to which many different kinds of seeds had been added.

Some bogs have yielded more than one Iron Age body. The cauldron-bog at Windeby in Schleswig[54] contained at least two, a young girl of about fifteen and, 4·8m away, a man. They had not met their deaths in the same way. The man had around his neck a springy hazel branch with which he had apparently been strangled. The girl's body bore no marks of violence and we must conclude that she had been drowned. Both bodies had been held down in the mud and water by branches, and a large stone in the case of the girl. Both the Windeby bodies had gone into the bog without any clothing on them, except that the girl wore an ox-hide collar round her neck and a bandage covering her eyes.

One of the most recent finds of a bog corpse is that from Dätgen also in Schleswig.[55] This was of a thirty-year-old man,

H

killed by a thrust through the heart. He had then been decapitated (the head lay nearby) and his skin removed. He was naked and the only object found with him was a woollen thread attached to one ankle. Like the Windeby bodies, he had been held down in the marsh by branches.

Not all the bog corpses have been found entire. Parts of the human body too, especially the head, hands and feet, occur as isolated finds. Heads are particularly common, both of men and women. The head of an old man from Osterby in Schleswig had been wrapped up in a deer-skin cape before being thrown into the peat.[56] On the right side of the head, the long hair had been gathered up into a large knot, the 'Suebian' knot of Tacitus. The presence of this hair style on bog corpses (the man from Dätgen also sported it) is interesting, for Tacitus explains that this knot was a mark of free birth among the Suebi.[57] Other writers make it plain that the hair-knot was worn among non-Suebic peoples as well, but at least in the cases of these corpses we are certainly dealing with free-born Germans, and not menials slain after taking part in a religious rite. Some observers have made much of the fact that a large number of the corpses, especially the men, have ropes, thongs or withies around their necks. The man from Tollund bore a hide noose round the neck and there are many other cases of throttling or hanging. It is dubious whether much significance should be attached to this phenomenon. The truth is that although the number of cases of hanging and strangulation is large, it is not overwhelmingly so. It must also be taken into account that in a large number of instances the corpse is too poorly preserved for identification of the means of death.

What relation have the corpses to religious ceremonies? The punishment of serious crimes and sacrifices to fertility gods must account for many of them, but it is difficult, and in many cases impossible, to single out the appropriate cases. Also, it is not certain that we are dealing with only two categories, with criminals and sacrificial victims. Dr K. W. Struve[58] has recently suggested that some were the victims of the community rather than of public law, condemned to die because for some reason they were objects of fear, to be cast out of their community and kept out where they could do no harm to their fellows. The suggestion has its attractions, not least because some of the practices in evidence are apotropaic in character,[59] as though the dead might still have power to harm. There are then at least three possible categories of bog corpses and the truly sacrificial instances may not be as numerous as has been thought.

## Divination

The early Germans were much given to divination, the leading role in which was taken by seeresses. These had so exalted a place in barbarian society that their honours were almost on a par with those of the gods. Some of them wielded considerable political influence. Veleda, who issued her prophecies from a tower in which she hid away from mortal eyes, played a significant part in the revolt of the Batavi and other lower Rhine Germans against Rome in A.D. 69. The leader of the rebellion, Julius Civilis, relied heavily on her support, allowing her representative equal diplomatic status with himself when Roman embassies were being received. Several other seeresses achieved fame far outside Germania, the most favoured being perhaps Ganna who uttered her prophecies for the emperor Domitian.

In the *Germania* we hear of three methods of taking auspices.[60] In one, the branch of a fruit-tree was broken into fragments, each one given marks or symbols, and all then thrown on to a white cloth. The prophecy was then made by the priest (or head of the family if the occasion was private) taking up three of the sticks one by one and interpreting the symbols of them. This reference to marks on pieces of wood inevitably recalls the runic alphabet but it is not safe to assume that Tacitus' evidence provides grounds for dating the origins of the runic script to the first century A.D. Another means of predicting events was by observing the flight or songs of birds, a form of divination recorded among other primitive peoples. But the most interesting, and Tacitus believed the most favoured, means of German divination involved certain sacred white horses kept in groves. When guidance for a course of action was required, these horses were yoked to a sacred chariot by the king or chief priest, who then walked alongside them to record their snorts and neighs. Yet another method of divining the outcome of events, in this case the fortunes of a battle, was to pit a champion in single combat against a captive taken from the enemy of the moment. The way the duel was decided indicated the final outcome of the battle or war.

To the sphere of divination and magic belonged the early use of runic signs. The geographical origins of runes are still keenly debated but there is now a widespread measure of agreement as to when runes were introduced into Germania. The earliest runic inscriptions occur on objects which can be dated to about the end of the second century or the beginning of the third.[61] By that time, however, the runic script appears to have been fully developed. Philologically the beginning of the Roman period seems more appropriate than the second century for the beginning of the *futhark*, since the early Germanic forms *ei* and *ī* are both found in the names for the *i* and *ī* runes. The archaeological evidence, however, will not take us back so far.

The early inscriptions occur on shield-bosses, scabbards, sword mounts, spear-heads, brooches and combs. They are generally short, giving only the name of the owner of the object, of the person whose gift it was, or of the rune-master. A rather longer inscription than usual is that on the gold ring in the Pietroassa treasure, which reads in Gothic 'Property of the Goths, dedicated and inviolable'.[62] Many of the inscriptions are magic formulae or invocations, the intention of which was to guard a warrior in battle, weaken an enemy, make a weapon invincible, ward off or cure a disease. Each of the twenty-four main signs in the *futhark* had its own name and behind this name lay a meaning, often symbolic. Thus, the *u* rune ∩ stood for the auroch or its strength, the ᛈ (or *th*) rune for giant, the *b* rune ᛒ for birch twig, a fertility symbol. Two signs represent divine beings, ↑ or *t* for Tiwaz and ◊ (*ng*) for Ingwaz, god of the fruitful year.

Two views on the origins of runes are current.[63] The first of these derives the *futhark* from the Latin alphabet, though the various proponents of the view suggest different areas in which the Latin letters were transformed into runes. At first sight the thesis seems to be supported by the unquestionable fact of Rome's deep influence in free Germany and, to a certain extent, by the closeness of the runes for *b*, *f*, *g*, *m* and *r* to their Latin counterparts. On the whole, however, philological opinion does not favour the Latin script as a source for runes.

The other hypothesis sees the north Italic (or north Etruscan) script as the most likely model for the runic *futhark*, its main support being the correspondence between no less than nine north Italic letters and the appropriate runes. This may seem a cogent argument, but it must be noted that we still have no runic inscriptions from southern Germania (i.e. from an area into

which north Italic letters might reasonably have been trans-
mitted) which date from before the fifth century A.D. A direct
link between north Italic and runes is thus still not established.
The events and the persons who brought these signs to northern
Europe remain (and perhaps always will remain) unexplained.
As it appears at present, the earliest inscriptions are concentrated

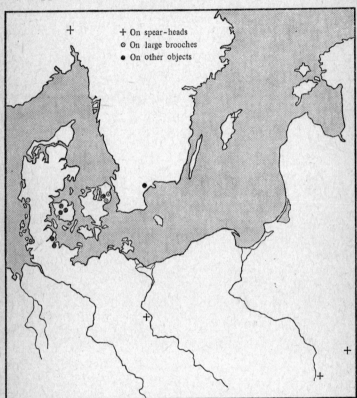

Fig. 26 Distribution of runic inscriptions of the third and
fourth centries

in the Jutland peninsula and the west Baltic islands, and it is
likely that it was here that a series of magic signs was transformed
into a formal script (fig. 26).[64]

Despite the close dealings between most parts of Germania and
the Roman frontier provinces, Germanic paganism betrays no
trace of the influence of Rome. Roman and Oriental cults gained

no devotees beyond Rome's northern frontier. Even the Christian religion did not reach the barbarians until the later fourth century, and its impact was slight. The task of missionary work beyond the Roman frontiers was taken up very slowly by the Church and it was not until the fifth century that organized missions went to work. In the absence of missions, the Christian gospel could only spread to the barbarians through the initiative of individuals. Some Germans became Christians while serving in the Roman army and thereafter returned home taking their faith with them. Others were converted through contact with Christian prisoners seized in raids on Roman territory. Even these sporadic conversions belong to the fourth century or later.

Among the Visigoths alone of the major peoples was the progress of conversion to Christianity before 400 notable. This was largely due to the work of Ulfila,[65] himself the child of a Gothic father and a Christian mother who had been carried off into Gothic territory in a late third-century raid. Born about A.D. 311, Ulfila became a 'reader' of the Church in Gothia, the members of which were probably mainly captured Roman provincials. In 341 he went to Constantinople as a member of a Gothic embassy, was consecrated bishop and charged with the task of serving the Church among the Goths. Later driven out of Gothia by a persecution, he spent the remaining thirty-three years of his life in the Empire. During this period, Ulfila invented an alphabet for the Gothic language and translated the Bible into that tongue. This extraordinary career belongs more to medieval Christendom than to the barbarian world. Down to the end of the fourth century civilized eyes were still focused upon the ring of lands around the Mediterranean. Christian missions were not sent into northern Europe for their message seemed wasted on a warrior society. 'How can Christian virtues live among the barbarians?' asked one Christian notable. The work of Ulfila showed how, although it did not shatter the conviction that Christianity could only flourish within an urban society.

### References

1. Good general accounts are J. de Vries, *Altgermanische Religionsgeschichte*, 2nd ed. (Berlin, 1956–7) and G. Dumézil, *Les dieux des Germains* (1959). Ellis Davidson, H. R. (1964) and (1967) contain much of value on the Roman Iron Age as well as on later periods.

2. Strabo, *Geography* vii, 2, 3; Tacitus, *Annals* xiii, 57; Procopius,

*History of the Wars* 11, 15; Jordanes, *History of the Goths*, tr. C. C. Mierow (Princeton, 1915), vol. iv, 61.

3. *Germania* 9, 1.

4. On these and other medieval references, F. Ström, *On the Sacral Origin of the Germanic Death Penalties* (Stockholm, 1942), 179f.

5. *Germania* 39, 3.

6. J. Werner, in *JRGZM*, xi (1964), 176ff.

7. *Germania* 43, 4.

8. Ellis Davidson, H. R. (1967), 88ff.

9. *Germania* 40, 2.

10. And in the Bronze Age. Ellis Davidson, H. R. (1967), 55f. and 73f. Later Scandinavian sources refer to Njord, a male counterpart of Nerthus (the names are philologically linked). Whether Nerthus and Njord were siblings, worshipped side by side in the Roman Iron Age, is uncertain. The later pairing of Freyr and Freyja might be a parallel case.

11. Petersen, H. (1888); Klindt-Jensen, O. (1949), 87ff.

12. G. Kunwald in *Präh. Zeitschr.*, xlv (1970), 42ff.

13. Baduhenna: Tacitus, *Annals* iv, 73; Tamfana: Tacitus, *Annals*, 51.

14. Krause, W. and Jankuhn, H. (1966), 53f, no. 20.

15. *Germania* 9, 3.

16. Raddatz, K. (1957) and in Jankuhn, H. (1970), 188ff.

17. Illerup: H. Andersen in *Kuml*, 1951, 9ff. and 1956, 7ff.; Ejsbøl: Ørsnes, M. (1963) and in Jankuhn, H. (1970), 172ff.

18. Hagberg, U. E. (1967).

19. Rosenberg, G. (1937). Conveniently in Brøndsted, J. (1960), 31ff.

20. On these, see above p. 168.

21. Vimose: Engelhardt, C. (1869); Thorsbjerg: Engelhardt, C. (1863), Jankuhn, H. in Klose, O. (1966), 377ff.

22. The damage or destruction of objects before consignment to votive deposits is also widely known in the Celtic world. The breaking of the weapons presumably symbolizes the breaking of the power of a defeated foe.

23. Blume, E. (1912), 178, n. 3.

24. K. Raddatz in Jankuhn, H. (1970). 188ff.

25. This dates from the end of the fourth century.

26. Engelhardt, C. (1865).

27. H. Shetelig in *Acta Arch.*, i (Copenhagen, 1930), 1ff.

28. Jankuhn, H. (1970b).

29. cf. *Germania* 9, 2.

30. Engelhardt, C. (1869).

31. Ørsnes, M. (1963) and in Jankuhn, H. (1970), 172ff.

32. Hagberg, U. E. (1967).

33. op. cit. 79ff.

34. A recent radiocarbon date, however, suggests that these may be as late as the sixth century.

35. A. Feddersen in *Årbøger* 1881, 269ff. Brøndsted, J. (1960), 117.

36. Behm-Blancke, G. (1958) and (1960).

37. Hayen, H. (1971).

38. Jacob-Friesen, K. H. (1928).

39. Neumann, G. (1958).

40. Liebenau: A. Genrich in *Präh. Zeitschr.*, xlvii (1972), 94ff. (This dates from the seventh century.) Issendorf: *Jahrb. des Prov. Museums in Hannover*, iii (1928), 69ff. The urn is now lost.

41. Beck, H. (1965).

42. C. Ahrens in *Offa*, xxiii (1966), 92.

43. H. Jankuhn in *Nachrichten der Akad. Wissen. Göttingen*, 1967, 115ff. Behm-Blancke, G. (1965).

44. Hagberg, U. E. (1967), 79ff.

45. C. J. Becker in Jankuhn, H. (1970), 119ff.

46. op. cit. 146ff.

47. Ellis Davidson, H. R. (1967), 86. This emphasis upon the horse in ritual appears to have begun in the late Roman Iron Age.

48. See now *Deae Nehalleniae*, Middelburg and Leiden 1971, *passim*. A. Hondius-Crone in *Spiegel Historiael*, v (1970), 619ff.

49. Orosius v, 16. *Germania* 39, 1; 40, 2.

50. These finds are collected together in Dieck, A. (1965). General account in Glob, P. V. (1969).

51. H. Jankuhn in *Nachrichten der Akad. Wissen. Göttingen*, 1967, 115ff.

52. *Germania* 12, 1.

53. Tollund: K. Thorvildsen in *Årbøger*, 1950, 302ff. Graubålle: P. V. Glob in *Kuml*, 1956, 99ff.

54. Dieck, A. (1965), no. 658.

55. Struve, K. W. (1967).

56. Dieck, A. (1965), no. 632. K. Schlabow in *Offa*, viii (1949), 3ff.

57. *Germania* 38, 2.

58. op. cit. 68ff.

59. e.g. decapitation, flaying, and possibly castration. Struve, K. W. (1967), 48ff.

60. *Germania* 10.

61. Krause, W. and Jankuhn, H. (1966), 6f.

62. T. Capelle in *Frühmittelalterliche Studien*, ii (1968), 228ff. The Pietroassa treasure may, however, be of the fifth century.

63. Krause, W. and Jankuhn, H. (1966), 6ff.

64. Wener, J. (1966), in which a link between the introduction of runes and the origins of figured art is suggested.

65. Thompson, E. A. (1966).

# 7 | Towards civilization

This book describes a pre-literate culture and thus its subject would not be classed by Samuel Johnson as 'authentick history'. There are several things in such a study that we must forgo. The impact of great events, of individual leaders, the sense of change and diversity in society which is usually present in historical periods, all are perforce missing from our knowledge of the early Germanic world. We must be content with a general picture of early Germanic culture and remain conscious of the many gaps which our sources do not allow us to fill. A general picture, however, is still very important, for when we study the early Germans and their relations with the Roman world, we witness the birth of medieval Europe. One of the themes of the earlier part of this book is what happened to a primitive, remote, barbarian society after it came into contact with an outward-looking civilized power. One of the main strands of the later history of Europe was woven during this period, the powerful attraction which drew the northern barbarians to the south and the west towards the Roman provinces and their wealth. When Tacitus wrote 'we show our homes and our farms [to the Hermunduri] and they do not covet them' (*Germania* 41, 2), he was utterly mistaken. What Rome showed to the barbarians in the earlier Roman Empire was to determine what happened in western Europe for the next few centuries.

The impact of Rome on the barbarians has recurred frequently in this book. By far and away the main motor of technical change for the early Germans was the Roman Empire. During the Roman Iron Age there was a gradual levelling-up of barbarian technology towards Roman standards, until by the fourth century the cultural gap between barbarians and Romans had appreciably closed, and for some Germans may have been altogether eliminated. From Tacitus onward Germanic technical

H*

attainments have been generally underestimated. The advances made in the first three centuries A.D., particularly in the extraction and manufacture of iron and the working of gold, silver and bronze, are now clear for all to see. In textile manufacture it has long been known that the barbarians had little or nothing to learn from the craftsmen of the Roman world.

Other seeds were sown in the period of contact with Rome, including those whose germination led in due course to the development of figured art and to the introduction of writing. As for the spread of less tangible ideas about such things as kingship, law, the bonds of society, kinship, this is not the place to begin a necessarily arduous inquiry, but that the paradigm of Rome was ever in the background cannot be doubted.

By the end of the third century we have reached a turning-point in the history of the Germanic peoples. In the earlier Roman period, the German tribes were more or less effectively held in check by the Roman forces stationed along the Rhine and Danube, partly by force, partly by diplomacy and subsidy. Trouble broke out from time to time but this never spread to affect other areas of the Roman world. This balance was maintained down to the Marcomannic Wars, fought in the reign of Marcus Aurelius (A.D. 161–80). These campaigns ended in a precarious victory for Rome, but they marked the end of clear Roman ascendancy over her northern neighbours. From the late second century onward, there was greatly increased pressure first on the Danube frontier, later on the Rhine also, culminating in the massive and devastating invasions into the Balkans and Gaul shortly after the middle of the third century.

How are we to explain this shift of the military initiative from Rome to the barbarians? The weakness and distraction of the Roman central government in the third century naturally holds part of the answer. But there were more profound changes on the barbarian side. The numerous smaller tribes which from time to time had formed short-lived, fissile confederations under leaders such as Maroboduus and Arminius by now had given way to larger groupings; among them Franks beyond the lower Rhine, Alamanni south of the Main and Saxons on the sea coast and about the lower Elbe and Weser. In the east, the name Goth was now applied not to a small and remote people in the lower Vistula valley but to a formidable power which threatened the Balkan provinces from across the lower Danube. In central

Germania, too, there were signs of major changes in political geography, leading eventually to the emergence of the supra-tribal groupings of the Thuringians and Burgundians. The tendency of all these peoples was to press southwards, thus impelling tribes nearer the Roman frontiers to spill over into Roman territory, which was for most of them the best thing that could happen.

There was at least one further reason for change in the military balance during the third century, namely the considerable improvement in barbarian armament, particularly in those weapons which would enable them to engage well armoured infantry in combat (see p. 176). Though this improvement had its limits (there was, for instance, no contemporary development of body armour) it must have gone a long way towards closing the yawning gap which existed between Roman and Germanic war equipment in the early years of contact.

The war bands of the third century were to become the *gentes* of the fourth and fifth. But it may not be assumed that when such groupings as the Alamanni, Franks and Saxons are first mentioned in the third century they were already distinct political entities. This is not borne out by the slender evidence and is in any case highly unlikely. Even in the fourth century, most of the barbarian groups which threatened the Roman frontiers acted under the command of war-leaders with limited and usually immediate objectives in view. To take Rome or Aquileia was not their aim. A short campaign and perhaps a lodgement in the rich provincial countryside would suffice. They came in seeking Roman land and to become Roman provincials or as like them as possible; many of them succeeded. In most, perhaps all, of the Roman provinces settled by barbarians the sub-Roman provincial population was greatly in the majority over the migrants— a fact too often overlooked. It follows that to resist the acquisition of Roman ways would have required sustained effort, and that was not their intention. They came in seeking not to overthrow an urban civilization but to find their own place in what survived.

There was nothing new in all this land-seeking. The Roman Empire had a long experience of dealing with barbarians, whether Celts, Germans or nomads, who wanted to settle in Roman territories. The Ubii crossed the Rhine, with Roman approval, either in Julius Caesar's day or some twenty-five years later. When in the mid-first century A.D. a band of Frisii crossed the lower Rhine and established themselves on the Roman bank, they promptly set about tilling the soil. 40 000 Germans are said to have been settled by Tiberius on the Rhine and in Gaul, 100 000 Bastarnae by Probus, and 300 000 Sarmatians by Constantine in the Balkan provinces. Although these figures are improbably large, what the events imply for cultural mixing is clear enough. After the period of severe conflict between Roman and German in the middle decades of the third century, there are signs of the growth of a symbiosis between the civilized and some of the barbarian powers. When the Goths moved into the abandoned Roman province of Dacia at the end of the third century, they found there a substantial Roman provincial population. Though the encounter is unlikely to have been entirely without bloodshed, the two populations mingled to an extent surprising to Englishmen, whose conception of Germanic settlement tends to be formed by Gildas and the Anglo-Saxon Chronicle. Dacia, however, was a province given up by Rome.

Territories still under Roman administration also received an admixture of barbarian settlers. Saxons settled in eastern Britain before Britannia ceased to be a Roman province. No ancient writer records this, but the ceramic evidence cannot now be seriously challenged and it continues to increase. Before the end of the third century Salian ('salty') Franks occupied the Betuwe, the land between the Rhine and the Waal, and thus became subject to Roman control. Shortly afterwards, groups of barbarians, including Suebi and Sarmatians as well as Franks, were settled in certain devastated areas of northern Gaul to till the land and provide men for the Roman army. These settlers, *laeti* as they were termed, are first heard of in 294 but it is an early fifth-century document, the *Notitia Dignitatum*, which gives us our first and only clear evidence as to where they were stationed by listing the headquarters of the prefects set in charge of them. These headquarters lay deep within the provinces, mostly between the Meuse and Seine but with a few outliers in Normandy and Brittany.

Thus the history of the Germanic peoples in the fourth and fifth centuries, particularly in western Europe, is inextricably bound up with that of the declining Roman provinces. But the tale is by no means always one of destruction and waste. Barbarians were by this time better equipped for life inside the Empire than most ancient writers believed.

# Bibliography

The following abbreviations have been used in the Bibliography and reference lists.

| | |
|---|---|
| *Acta Arch.* | *Acta Archaeologica* (Copenhagen) |
| *Arch. Geographica* | *Archaeologia Geographica* |
| *Arch. Polona* | *Archaeologia Polona* |
| *BROB* | *Berichten van de Rijksdienst voor het Oudheidkundig Bodemonderzoek* |
| *Diss. Arch. Gandenses* | *Dissertationes Archaeologicae Gandenses* |
| *Hist. Zeitschr.* | *Historische Zeitschrift* |
| *JRGZM* | *Jahrbuch des Romisch-Germanischen Zentralmuseums Mainz* |
| *JRS* | *Journal of Roman Studies* |
| *Phil-Hist. Kl.* | *Philosophisch-Historische Klasse* |
| *Präh. Zeitschr.* | *Prähistorische Zeitschrift* |

ALBRECHTSEN, E. (1954–68), *Fynske Jernaldergrave*, vols. 1–3, Copenhagen and Odense.

ALMGREN, O. (1923), 'Studien über nordeuropäische Fibelformen', *Mannus-Bibliothek*, xxxii.

ALMGREN, O. and NERMAN, B. (1914 and 1923), *Die ältere Eisenzeit Gotlands*, 2 vols., Stockholm.

ASMUS, W. D. (1938), *Tonwaregruppen und Stammesgrenzen in Mecklenburg während der ersten beiden Jahrhunderte nach der Zeitwende*, Neumünster.

BANTELMANN, A. (1955), *Tofting. Eine vorgeschichtliche Warft an der Eidermündung*, Neumünster.

BANTELMANN, N. (1971), *Hamfelde. Ein Urnenfeld der römischen Kaiserzeit in Holstein*, Neumünster.

BECK, H. (1965), *Das Ebersignum im Germanischen*, Munich.

BECK, H. (Ed.) (1970), 'Spätkaiserzeitliche Funde in Westfalen', *Bodenaltertümer Westfalens*, xii.

BECKER, C. J. (1948), 'Die zeitliche Stellung des Hjortspringfundes innerhalb der vorrömischen Eisenzeit in Dänemark', *Acta Arch*, xix, 145.

—— (1961), *Førromersk Jernalder i Syd- og Midtjylland*, Copenhagen. (The pre-Roman Iron Age in south and central Jutland.)

—— (1965), 'Ein früheisenzeitliches Dorf bei Grøntoft, West-Jütland', *Acta Arch.*, xxxvi, 209.

—— (1968), 'Das zweite früheisenzeitliche Dorf bei Grøntoft, West-Jütland', *Acta Arch.*, xxxix, 235.

—— (1971), 'Früheisenzeitliche Dörfer bei Grøntoft, West-jütland', *Acta Arch.*, xlii, 79.

BECKHOFF, K. (1963), 'Die eisenzeitliche Kriegsbogen von Nydam', *Offa*, xx, 39.

BEHAGHEL, H. (1943), *Die Eisenzeit im Raum des rechtsrheinischen Schiefergebirges*, Wiesbaden.

BEHM-BLANCKE, G. (1956), 'Die germanischen Dörfer von Kablow bei Königs Wusterhausen', *Ausgrabungen und Funde*, i, 161.

—— (1958), 'Ein westgermanisches Moor- und Seeheiligtum in Nordwestthüringen), *Ausgrabungen und Funde*, iii, 264.

—— (1960), 'Latenezeitliche Opferfunde aus dem germanischen Moor- und Seeheiligtum von Oberdorla, Kr. Mühlhausen', *Ausgrabungen und Funde*, v, 232.

—— (1965), 'Das germanische Tierknochenopfer und sein Ursprung', *Ausgrabungen und Funde*, x, 233.

BEHREND, R. (1969), 'Die bronze- und spätlatenezeitliche Besiedlung der Alteburg bei Arnstadt', *Alt-Thüringen*, x, 97.

BELTZ, R. (1910), *Die vorgeschichtliche Altertümer Mecklenburg-Schwerin*, Schwerin.

BENINGER, E. (1937), *Die germanische Bodenfunde in der Slowakei*, Reichenberg and Leipzig.

BENINGER, E. and FREISING, H. (1933), *Die germanische Bodenfunde in Mähren*, Reichenberg.

BERSU, G., HEIMBE, G., LANGE, H. and SCHUCHHARDT, C. (1926), 'Der Angivarish-Cheruskische Grenzwall [etc.]' *Präh. Zeitschr.*, xvii, 100.

BIELENIN, K. (1964), 'Das Hüttenwesen in Altertum im Gebiet der Gory Swietokrzyskie', *Präh. Zeitschr.*, xlii, 77.

BLUME, E. (1912), 'Die germanischen Stämme und die Kulturen zwischen Oder und Passarge zur römischen Kaiserzeit', i, *Mannus-Bibliothek*, viii.

—— (1915), 'Die germanischen Stämme und die Kulturen [etc.]', ii, *Mannus-Bibliothek*, xiv.

BOELES, P. C. J. A. (1951), *Friesland tot de elfde eeuw*, The Hague.

BÖHNER, K. (1963), 'Zur historischen Interpretation der sogenannten Laetengräber', *JRGZM*, x, 139.

BOHNSACK, D. (1938), *Die Burgunden in Ostdeutschland und Polen während des letzten Jahrhunderts vor Christus*, Leipzig.

BÖKÖNYI, S. (1968), 'Data on Iron Age horses of Central and Eastern Europe', *Bull. American School of Prehistoric Research*, xxv.

BOLIN, S. (1926), *Fyndan av romerska mynt i det fria Germanien*, Lund. (Finds of Roman coins in free Germany.)

—— (1930), 'Die Funde römischer und byzantinischer Münzen im freien Germanien', *Bericht der Röm-Germ. Kommission*, xix, 86.

BÖNFER, L., STIEREN, A. and KLEIN, A. (1936), 'Eine germanische Siedlung in Westick bei Kamen, Kr. Unna, Westfalen', *Westfalen*, xxi, 410.

BRANDT, J. (1960), *Das Urnengräberfeld von Preetz in Holstein*, Neumünster.

BRØNDSTED, J. (1954), *Guldhornene*, Copenhagen. (Gold horns.)
—— (1960), *Danmarks Oldtid. III Jernalder*, Copenhagen. (Denmark's prehistory.)

CAPELLE, T. (1971), *Studien über elbgermanischen Gräberfelder in der ausgehender Latenezeit und der älteren römischen Kaiserzeit*, Münster.

COBLENZ, W. (1955), *Das Gräberfeld von Prositz*, Leipzig.

DABROWSKI, J. (1962), 'Recent research on the early Iron Age in the territory to the east of the Lower Vistula', *Arch. Polona*, iv, 181.

DABROWSKI, K. and KOLENDO, J. (1972), 'Les épées romaines découvertes en Europe centrale et septentrionale', *Arch. Polona*, xiii, 59.

DANNHEIMER, H. (1962), *Die germanischen Funde der späten Kaiserzeit und des frühen Mittelalters in Mittelfranken*, Berlin.

DE BOONE, W. J. (1954), *De Franken van hun eerste optreden tot de dood van Childerik*, Amsterdam.

DETLEFSEN, D. (1904–9), *Die Entdeckung des germanischen Nordens im Altertum*, Berlin.

DIACONU, G. (1965), *Tirgşor. Necropola din secolele III–IV e.n.*, Bucharest.

DIECK, A. (1965), *Die europäischen Moorleichenfunde*, vol. i, Neumünster.

DOPPELFELD, O. and BEHM, G. (1938), 'Das germanische Dorf auf dem Bärhorst bei Nauen', *Präh. Zeitschr.*, xxviii–ix, 284.

ECK, T. (1891), *Les deux cimetières gallo-romains de Vermand et de St-Quentin*, Paris.

EGGERS, H. J. (1950), *Lübsow, ein germanischer Fürstensitz der älteren Kaiserzeit*, *Präh Zeitschr.*, xxxiv–v, 58.
—— (1951), *Der römische Import im freien Germanien*, Hamburg.
—— (1959), *Einführung in die Vorgeschichte*, Munich.

EGGERS, H. J., WILL, E., JOFFROY, R. and HOLMQVIST, W. (1964), *Kelten und Germanen in heidnischer Zeit*, Baden-Baden.

EICHHORN. G. (1927), 'Der Urnenfriedhof auf der Schanze bei Grossromstedt', *Mannus-Bibliothek*, xli.

ELLIS DAVIDSON, H. R. (1964), *Gods and Myths of Northern Europe*, Harmondsworth.
—— (1967), *Pagan Scandinavia*, London.

ENGELHARDT, C. (1863), *Thorsbjerg Mosefund*, Copenhagen.
—— (1865), *Nydam Mosefund 1859–63*, Copenhagen.
—— (1867), *Kragehul Mosefund*, Copenhagen.
—— (1869), *Vimose Fundet*, Copenhagen.

ERDNISS, J. (1939), *Die Chauken, Ihre raumliche Abgrenzung auf Grund der Bodenfunde*, Würzburg.

FETTICH, N. (1930), 'Der Schildbuckel von Herpály', *Acta Arch.*, i, 221.

FORSSANDER, J. E. (1937), 'Provinzialrömisches und Germanisches: Stilstudien zu den schonischen Funden von Sösdala und Sjörup', *Meddelanden fran Lunds Univ. Historiska Museum*, 1937.

GENRICH, A. (1943), 'Neue Gesichtspunkte zum Ursprung der

Sachsen', *Archiv für Landes- und Volkskunde von Niedersachsen*, xvi, 83.

—— (1954), *Formenkreise und Stammesgruppen in Schleswig-Holstein nach geschlossenen Funden des 3 bis 6 Jahrhunderts*, Neumünster.

—— (1965), 'Zur Geschichte der Altsachsen auf dem Kontinent', *Die Kunde*, xvi, 107.

—— (1969), 'Der gemischt-belegte Friedhof bei Liebenau, Kr. Nienburg', *Nachrichten aus Niedersachsens Urgeschichte*, xxxviii, 3.

—— (1970), Der Ursprung der Sachsen, *Die Kunde*, xxi, 66.

GESCHWENDT, F. (1972), *Der vor– und frühgeschichtliche Mensch und die Heilquellen*, Hildesheim.

GIMBUTAS, M. (1971), *The Slavs*, London.

GLOB, P. V. (1951), *Ard og Plov i Nordens Oldtid*, Aarhus. (Ard and plough in northern prehistory.)

—— (1969), *The Bog People*, London.

GODŁOWSKI, K. (1962), 'Ein Gräberfeld aus der späten Kaiserzeit in Opatów (Kr. Kłobuck)', *Arch. Polona*, iv, 295.

—— (1968), 'Die Przeworsk-Kultur der mittleren und späten Kaiserzeit', *Zeitschr. für Archäologie*, ii, 256.

—— (1970), *The Chronology of the Late Roman and Early Migration Periods in Central Europe*, Crakow.

GRAMBACH, B. (1968), *Germanen-Slawen-Deutsche. Forschungen zu ihrere Ethnogenese*, Berlin.

GREMPLER, W. (1887–8), *Der Fund von Sakrau*, Breslau.

GROHNE, E. (1953), *Mahndorf. Frühgeschichte des bremischen Raumes*, Bremen.

GUTHJAHR, R. (1934), *Die Semnonen im Havelland zur frühen Kaiserzeit*, Greifswald.

HAARNAGEL, W. (1940), 'Die Marschsiedlungen in Schleswig-Holstein und in linkselbischen Küstengebiet', *Probleme der Küstenforschung im südlichen Nordseegebiet*, i, 87.

—— (1956), 'Vorläufiger Bericht über die Wurtengrabung auf der Feddersen Wierde bei Bremerhaven', *Germania*, xxxiv, 125.

—— (1957a), 'Vorläufiger Bericht über das Ergebnis der Wurtengrabung auf der Feddersen Wierde bei Bremerhaven im Jahre 1956', *Germania*, xxxv, 275.

—— (1957b), 'Die spätbronze-früheisenzeitliche Gehöftsiedlung Jemgum bei Leer auf dem linken Ufer der Ems', *Die Kunde*, viii, 2.

—— (1961a), 'Zur Grabung auf der Feddersen Wierde 1955–59', *Germania*, xxxix, 42.

—— (1961b), 'Probleme der Siedlungforschung in Küstengebiet zwischen Elbe und Weser in der Spätlatenezeit', *Jahrb. der Männer vom Morgenstern*, xlii, 74.

—— (1963), 'Die Ergebnisse der Grabung Feddersen Wierde im Jahre 1961', *Germania*, xli, 280.

—— (1965a), 'Die Untersuchung einer spätbronze-, ältereisenzeitlichen Siedlung in Boomborg-Hatzum, Kr. Leer [etc.])', *Neue Ausgrabungen und Forschungen in Niedersachsen*, ii, 132.

—— (1965b), 'Die Grabung auf der Heidenschanze bei Wesermünde im Jahre 1958', *Studien aus Alteuropa*: *Beihefte 10–11 der Bonner Jahrb.*, Teil ii, 142.

HACHMANN, R. (1951), 'Die Gliederung des Gräberfelds von Gross Romstedt', *Arch. Geographica*, i, 17.

—— (1956), 'Zur Gesellschaftsordnung der Germanen in der Zeit um Christi Geburt', *Arch. Geographica*, v, 7.

—— (1961), 'Die Chronologie der jüngeren vorrömischen Eisenzeit', *Bericht Röm-Germ. Kommission*, xli, 1.

—— (1970), *Die Goten und Skandinavien*, Berlin.

—— (1971), *The Germanic Peoples*, London.

HACHMANN, R., KOSSACK, G. and KUHN, H. (1962), *Völker zwischen Germanen und Kelten*, Neumünster.

HAGBERG, U. E. (1967), *The Archaeology of Skedemosse*, 2 vols., Stockholm.

—— (Ed) (1972), *Studia Gotica, Handlingar Kungl. Vitterhets Historie och Antikvitets Akademiens*, xxv, Stockholm.

HALBERTSMA, H. (1963), *Terpen tussen Vlie en Eems*, Groningen.

HALD, M. (1950), *Olddanske Tekstiler*, Copenhagen. (Early Danish textiles.)

—— (1962), *Jernalderens Dragt*, Copenhagen. (Iron Age dress.)

HATT, G. (1949), *Oltidsagre*, Copenhagen. (Prehistoric fields.)

—— (1957), *Nørre Fjand. An early Iron Age Village Site in West Jutland*, Copenhagen.

HAYEN, H. (1957), 'Zur Bautechnik und Typologie der . . . hölzernen Moorwege und Moorstrassen', *Oldenburger Jahrb.*, lvi, 83.

—— (1971), 'Hölzerne Kultfiguren am Bohlenweg XLII (Ip) im Wittemoor (Ldkr. Wesermarsch)', *Die Kunde*, xxii, 88.

HINGST, H. (1962), 'Zur Typologie und Verbreitung der Holsteiner Gürtel', *Offa*, xix, 69.

HÖFLER, O. (1934), *Kultische Geheimbünde der Germanen*, Frankfurt-am-Main.

HOFMEISTER, H. (1930), *Die Chatten I. Mattium, Die Altenburg bei Neidenstein*, Frankfurt-am-Main.

HOLMQVIST, W. (1951), *Tauschierte Metallarbeiten des Nordens aus Römerzeit und Völkerwanderung, Handlingar Kungl. Vitterhets Historie och Antikvitets Akademiens*, Stockholm.

—— (1964), *Filigran och Granulation i nordiskt Guldsmide*, Stockholm. (Filigree and granulation in northern goldsmithing.)

IONITA, I. (1971), 'Das Gräberfeld von Independenta', *Saarbrücker Beiträge zur Altertumskunde*, x.

JACOB-FRIESEN, K. H. (1928), *Der altgermanische Opferfund im Brodelbrunnen zu Pyrmont*, Hannover.

JAHN, M. (1916), 'Die Bewaffnung der Germanen in der älteren Eisenzeit', *Mannus-Bibliothek*, xvi.

—— (1921), 'Der Reitersporn', *Mannus-Bibliothek*, xxi.

JANKUHN, H. (1955), 'Klima, Besiedlung und Wirtschaft der älteren Eisenzeit im westlichen Ostseebecken', *Arch. Geographica*, ii, 23.

—— (1963), 'Terra . . . silvis horrida', *Arch. Geographica*, x–xi, 19.

—— (1964), *Nydam und Thorsbjerg. Moorfunde der Eisenzeit*, Neumünster.

—— (1966), 'Archaeologische Bemerkungen zur Glaubwürdigkeit des Tacitus in der *Germania*', *Nachrichten Akad. Wissen. Göttingen*, Phil-Hist. Kl., 1966, 409.

—— (1969), *Deutsche Agrargeschichte I Vor- und Frühgeschichte vom Neolithikum bis zur Völkerwanderungszeit*, Stuttgart.

—— (Ed.) (1970a), *Vorgeschichtliche Heiligtümer und Opferplätze in Mittel- und Nordeuropa*, *Abhandlungen Akad. Wissen. Göttingen*, Phil-Hist. Kl., lxxiv.

—— (1970b), *Das zweite Nydamboot, Frühe Menschheit und Umwelt*, Teil i in *Fundamenta*, Reihe A, Band 2, Ed. H. Schwabedissen, Cologne-Vienna.

JANSSEN, W. (1972), *Issendorf: Ein Urnenfriedhof der späten Kaiserzeit und der Völkerwanderungszeit*, Teil i, *Die Ergebnisse der Ausgrabung*, 1967, Hildesheim.

JAZDZEWSKI, K. (1965), *Poland*, London.

JONES, A. H. M. (1964), *The Later Roman Empire*, Oxford.

KASZEWSKA, E. (1964), 'Materialy z cmentarzyska w Zadowicach, pow. Kalisz', *Prace i Materialy*, xi, 101. (Material from the cemetery at Zadowice.)

KEILING, H. (1965), 'Ein neues Gräberfeld der vorrömischen Eisenzeit von Brahlstorf, Kr. Hagenow', *Jahrb. für Bodendenkmalpflege in Mecklenburg*, 1965, 177.

KIETLINSKA, A. and DABROWSKA, T. (1963), 'Cmentarzysko z okresu wplywow rzymskich we wsi Spicymierz, pow. Turck', *Materialy Starozytne*, ix, 143. (A cemetery of the Roman Iron Age at Spicymierz.)

KLINDT-JENSEN, O. (1959), 'Foreign Influences in Denmark's Early Iron Age', *Acta Arch.*, xx, 1.

KLOSE, J. (1934), *Roms Klientel-Randstaaten am Rhein und an der Donau*, Breslau.

KLOSE, O. (Ed.) (1960–6), *Geschichte Schleswig-Holsteins*, Neumünster.

KMIECIŃSKI, J. (1962), 'Problems of the so-called Gotho-Gepidian culture in the light of recent research', *Arch. Polona*, iv, 270.

—— (1968), *Odry. Cmentarzysko kurhanowe z okresu rzymskiego*, Lodz. (Odry: a barrow cemetery of the Roman period.)

KÖRBER-GROHNE, U. (1967), *Geobotanische Untersuchungen auf der Feddersen Wierde*, Berlin.

KÖRNER, G. (1939), *Der Urnenfriedhof von Rebenstorf im Amte Lüchow*, Hildesheim.

KOSSACK, G. (1966a), 'Beiträge zur Ur- und Frühgeschichte Mecklenburgs. Ein Forschungsbericht', *Offa*, xxiii, 7.

—— (1966b), 'Zur Frage der Dauer germanischer Siedlungen in der römischen Kaiserzeit', *Zeitschr. der Gesellschaft für Schleswig-Holsteins Geschichte*, xci, 13.

KOSSINNA, G. (1897), 'Die ethnologische Stellung der Ostgermanen', *Indogermanische Forschungen*, vii, 276.

—— (1902), 'Die indogermanische Frage archaeologisch beantwortet', *Zeitschr. für Ethnologie*, xxxiv, 161.

—— (1911), 'Die Herkunft der Germanen', *Mannus-Bibliothek*, vi.

—— (1936), *Ursprung und Verbreitung der Germanen in vor- und frühgeschichtlicher Zeit* (3rd ed.), Leipzig.

KOSTRZEWSKI, B. (1947), 'Cmentarzysko z okresu rzymskiego w Koninie', *Przegląd Archeologiczny*, vii, 192. (A cemetery of the Roman Iron Age at Konin.)

KOSTRZEWSKI, J. (1919), *Die ostgermanische Kultur der Spätlatenezeit*, Würzburg.

—— (1962a), *The Ancient Polish Culture*, Warsaw.

—— (1962b), 'Le problème du séjour des Germains sur les terres de Pologne', *Arch. Polona*, iv, 7.

KRAUSE, W. and JANKUHN, H. (1966), *Die Runeninscriften im älteren Futhark*, Göttingen.

KRÜGER, F. (1928), 'Das Reitergrab von Marwedel', *Lüneburger Festblätter*, i, 1ff.

KUCHENBUCH, F. (1938), 'Die altmärkisch-osthannöverschen Schalenurnenfelder der spätrömischen Zeit', *Jahresschrift für die Vorgeschichte der sächsisch-thüringischen Länder*, xxvii.

KUHN, H. (1968), 'Die Nordgrenze der keltischen Ortsnamen in Westdeutschland', *Beiträge zur Namenforschung*, iii, 311.

—— (1973), 'Das Rheinland in den germanischen Wanderungen', *Rheinische Vierteljahresblätter*, xxxvii, 276.

LA BAUME, P. (1971), 'Besonders wertvolle römische Funde in Niedersachsen, Bremen und Hamburg', *Die Kunde*, xxii, 129.

LA BAUME, W. (1961), *Frühgeschichte der europäischen Kulturpflanzen*, Giessen.

—— (1963), *Die pommerellischen Gesichtsurnen*, Mainz.

LAMMERS, W. (Ed.) (1967), *Entstehung und Verfassung des Sachsenstammes*, Darmstadt.

LASER, R. (1965), *Die Brandgräber der spätrömischen Kaiserzeit in nördlichen Mitteldeutschland*, Teil i, Berlin.

LÜDERS, A. (1955), 'Eine kartographische Darstellung der römischen Münzschätze im freien Germanien', *Arch. Geographica*, ii, 85.

MACKEPRANG, M. B. (1943), *Kulturbeziehungen im nordischen Raum des 3 bis 5 Jahrhunderts*, Leipzig.

MÄHLING, W. (1944), *Die Bodenbacher Gruppe. Zur Frage der latenezeitlichen elbgermanischen Landnahme in Nordböhmen, Abhandlungen der deutschen Akad. Wissen Prag*, Phil-Hist. Kl., xv.

MAJEWSKI, K. (1960), *Importy rzymskie w Polsce*, Warsaw. (Roman imports in Poland.)

MELIN, B. (1965), *Die Urheimat der Kimbern*, Uppsala.

MEYER, E. (1966), 'Das germanische Gräberfeld von Zauschwitz (Kr. Borna)', *Arbeits- und Forschungsber. zur sächsischen Bodendenkmalpflege*, Beiheft vi.

—— (1971), 'Die germanischen Bodenfunde der spätrömischen Kaiserzeit und der frühen Völkerwanderungszeit in Sachsen'

(I, Katalog), *Arbeits- und Forschungsber. zur sächsischen Boden-denkmalpflege*, Beiheft ix.

MILDENBERGER, G. (1966), 'Vor- und Frühgeschichte der böhmischen Länder', in Bosl, K. (Ed.), *Handbuch der Geschichte der böhmischen Länder*, 20 Stuttgart.

—— (1970), *Die thüringische Brandgräber der spätrömischen Zeit*, Cologne and Vienna.

—— (1972), *Sozial- und Kulturgeschichte der Germanen*, Stuttgart.

MITREA, B. and PREDA, C. (1966), *Necropole din secolul al IV-lea e.n. in Muntenia*, Bucharest.

MOTYKOVA-SNEIDROVA, K. (1963), 'Die Anfänge der römischen Kaiserzeit in Böhmen', *Fontes Arch. Pragenses*, vi.

—— (1965), 'Zur Chronologie der älteren römischen Kaiserzeit in Böhmen', *Berliner Jahrb. für Vor- und Frühgeschichte*, v, 103.

—— (1967), 'Weiterentwicklung und Ausklang der älteren römischen Kaiserzeit in Böhmen', *Fontes Arch. Pragenses*, xi.

MUCH, R. (1898), 'Der germanische Himmelsgott', *Abhandlungen zur germanischen Philologie: Festschrift für R. Heinzel*, 189, Halle.

—— (1967), *Die Germania des Tacitus* (3rd ed.) with archaeological commentary by H. Jankuhn, Heidelberg.

MÜLLER-WILLE, M. (1965), *Eisenzeitliche Fluren in den festländischen Nordseegebieten*, Münster.

MUNKSGAARD, E. (1953), 'Collared Gold Necklets and Armlets. A remarkable Danish fifth century group', *Acta Arch.*, xxiv, 67.

NENQUIN, J. A. E. (1953), 'La nécropole de Furfooz', *Diss. Arch. Gandenses*, i.

NERMAN, B. (1935), *Die Völkerwanderungszeit Gotlands*, Stockholm.

NETOLITZKY, F. (1931), 'Unser Wissen von den alten Kulturpflanzen Mitteleuropas', *Veröffentlichungen Röm-Germ. Kommission*, xx, 14.

NEUMANN, G. (1958), 'Der germanische Kultfund von Greussen, Ldkr. Sondershausen', *Jahresschrift für mitteldeutsche Vorgeschichte*, xli–ii, 486.

NIERHAUS, R. (1966), *Das swebische Gräberfeld von Diersheim*, Berlin.

—— (1969), 'Der Silberschatz von Hildesheim', *Die Kunde*, xx, 52.

NORDEN, E. (1959), *Die germanische Urgeschichte in Tacitus' Germania* (4th ed.), Darmstadt.

NYLEN, E. (1963), 'Early Gladius Swords found in Scandinavia', *Acta Arch.*, xxxiv, 185.

—— (1968), 'Die älteste Goldschmiedekunst der nordischen Eisenzeit und ihr Ursprung', *JRGZM*, xv, 75.

OHLHAVER, H. (1939), *Der germanische Schmied und sein Werkzeug*, Leipzig.

ØRSNES, M. (1963), 'The Weapon Find in Ejsbøl Mose at Haderslev', *Acta Arch.*, xxxiv, 232.

OXENSTIERNA, E. (1945), *Die Urheimat der Goten*, Leipzig.

—— (1956), *Die Goldhörner von Gallehus*, Lindingö.

—— (1958), *Die ältere Eisenzeit in Östergötland*, Lindingö.

PERNICKA, R. M. (1966), 'Die Keramik der älteren römischen Kaiserzeit in Mähren', *Opera Univ. Brunensis (Brno): Facultas Phil.*, cxii.

PESCHECK, C. (1939), *Die frühwandalische Kultur in Mittelschlesien*, Leipzig.

PETERSEN, H. (1888), *Vognfundene i Dejbjerg Praestegaardsmose*, Copenhagen. (Wagon-find in the Praestegaard bog at Dejbjerg.)

PIC, J. L. (1907), *Die Urnengräber Böhmens*, Leipzig.

PIGGOTT, S. (1965), *Ancient Europe*, Edinburgh.

PIRLING, R. (1966), *Das römisch-fränkische Gräberfeld von Krefeld-Gellep*, Berlin.

PLEINER, R. (1962), *Staré evropské kovářství*, Prague. (Ancient smithing in Europe.)

—— (1964), 'Die Eisenverhüttung in der *Germania Magna* zur römischen Kaiserzeit', *Bericht Röm-Germ. Kommission*, xlv, 11.

PLETTKE, A. (1921), *Ursprung und Ausbreitung der Angeln und Sachsen*, Hildesheim.

PLETTKE, F. (1940), *Der Urnenfriedhof von Dingen, Kr. Wesermünde*, Hildesheim.

RADDATZ, K. (1957), *Der Thorsberger Moorfund: Gürtelteile und Körperschmuck*, Neumünster.

—— (1960a), 'Römische Axte aus dem freien Germanien', *Offa*, xvii–xviii, 17.

—— (1960b), 'Ringknaufschwerter aus germanischen Kriegergräbern', *Offa*, xvii–xviii, 26.

—— (1963), 'Pfeilspitzen aus dem Moorfund von Nydam', *Offa*, xx, 49.

—— (1966), 'Die germanische Bewaffnung der vorrömischen Eisenzeit', *Nachrichten Akad. Wissen. Göttingen*, Phil-Hist. Kl., 1966, 427.

—— (1967a), *Das Wagengrab der jüngeren vorrömischen Eisenzeit von Husby, Kr. Flensburg*, Neumünster.

—— (1967b), 'Die Bewaffnung der Germanen in der jüngeren römischen Kaiserzeit', *Nachrichten Akad. Wissen. Göttingen*, Phil-Hist. Kl., 1967, 1.

RAJEWSKI, Z. (1959), *Biskupin. Polnische Ausgrabungen*, Warsaw.

RANGS-BORCHLING, A. (1963), *Das Urnengräberfeld von Hornbek in Holstein*, Neumünster.

REINERTH, P. (Ed.) (1940), *Vorgeschichte der deutschen Stämme*, Leipzig–Berlin.

REINHARDT, W. (1965), 'Studien zur Entwicklung des ländlichen Siedlungsbildes in den Seemarschen der ostfriesischen Westküste', *Probleme der Küstenforschung im südlichen Nordseegebiet*, viii, 73.

ROEREN, R. (1960), 'Zur Archäologie und Geschichte Südwestdeutschlands im 3 bis 5 Jahrhunderts n. Chr.', *JRGZM*, vii, 214.

ROES, A. (1947), 'Some Gold Torcs found in Holland', *Acta Arch.*, xviii, 175.

RÖHRER-ERTL, O. (1971), 'Untersuchungen am Material des Urnenfriedhofes von Westerwanna, Kr. Land Hadeln', *Hamburger Reihe zur Kultur- und Sprachwissenschaft*, viii.

ROOSENS, H. (1967), 'Laeti, Foederati und andere spätrömische Niederschläge im belgischen Raum', *Die Kunde*, xviii, 89.

ROSENBERG, G. (1937), 'Hjortspringfundet', *Nordiska Fortidsminder*, iii, 1.

RYBAKOV, B. A. (Ed.) (1960), 'Chernyakhovskaya Kultura', *Materialy i Issledovaniya po Arkh. SSSR*, lxxxii. (The Chernjakov culture).

RYBOVA, A. (1970), 'Das Brandgräberfeld der jüngeren römischen Kaiserzeit von Pňov', *Archeologické Studijní Materiály*, ix.

SAKAŘ, V. (1970), 'Roman Imports in Bohemia', *Fontes Arch. Pragenses*, xiv.

SANDER, E. (1939), 'Die Germanisierung des römischen Heeres', *Hist. Zeitschr.*, clx, 1.

SCHACH-DÖRGES, H. (1969), *Das jungkaiserzeitliche Gräberfeld von Wilhelmsaue in Brandenburg, Berliner Beiträge zur Vorgeschichte*, xiii.

—— (1970), *Die Bodenfunde des dritten bis sechsten Jahrhunderts n. Chr. zwischen unterer Elbe und Oder*, Neumünster.

SCHINDLER, R. (1940), *Die Besiedlungsgeschichte der Goten und Gepiden im unteren Weichselraum*, Leipzig.

—— (1955), 'Eine germanische Siedlung des 1 bis 5 Jahrhunderts in Hamburg-Farmsen', *Hammaburg*, iv, 173.

—— (1958), 'Eine frühgeschichtliche Siedlung in Hamburg-Bramfeld', *Hammaburg*, v, 145.

SCHIRNIG, H. (1965), 'Waffenkombinationen in germanischen Gräbern der Spätlatene- und älteren Kaiserzeit', *Nachrichten aus Niedersachsens Urgeschichte*, xxxiv, 19.

—— (1969), *Die Keramik der Siedlung Böhme, Kr. Fallingbostel, aus der römischen Kaiserzeit*, Neumünster.

SCHLABOW, K. (1965), *Der Thorsbjerger Prachtmantel*, Neumünster.

—— (1967), *Trachten der Eisenzeit*, Schleswig.

SCHLÜTER, O. and AUGUST, O. (1958), *Atlas des Saale- und mittleren Elbegebietes* (2nd ed.).

SCHMID, P. (1957), 'Die vorrömische Eisenzeit in nordwest-deutschen Küstengebiet', *Probleme der Küstenforschung im südlichen Nordseegebiet*, vi, 49.

—— (1965), 'Die Keramik des 1 bis 3 Jahrhunderts n.-Chr. im Küstengebiet der südlichen Nordsee', *Probleme der Küstenforschung im südlichen Nordseegebiet*, viii, 9.

—— (1969a), 'Die vor- und frühgeschichtliche Grundlagen der Besiedlung Ostfrieslands nach der Zeitwende', in *Ostfriesland im Schutze des Deiches*, Band I, Leer.

—— (1969b), 'Bemerkungen zur Datierung der jüngsten Siedlungsphase auf der Dorfwurt Feddersen Wierde, Kr. Wesermünde', *Neue Ausgrabungen und Forschungen in Niedersachsen*, iv, 158.

SCHMIDT, L. (1934), *Geschichte der deutschen Stämme bis zum Ausgang der Völkerwanderung, 1. Die Ostgermanen* (2nd ed.), Munich.

—— (1938), *2. Die Westgermanen* (2nd ed.), Munich.

—— (1942), *Geschichte der Wandalen* (2nd ed.), Munich.

SCHMIDT-THIERLBEER, E. (1967), *Das Gräberfeld von Wahlitz, Kr. Burg.*, Berlin.

SCHÖNBERGER, H. (1952), 'Die Spätlatenzeit in der Wetterau', *Saalburg Jahrbuch*, xi, 21.

—— (1969), 'The Roman Frontier in Germany: an archaeological survey', *JRS*, lix, 144.

SCHRICKEL, W. (1964), 'Die Nordgrenze der Kelten im rechtsrheinischen Gebiet der Spätlatenzeit', *JRGZM*, xi, 138.

SCHUBART, H. (1955), 'Die Funde der frühen römischen Kaiserzeit in Vorpommern', *Wissenschaftliche Zeitschr. der Univ. Greifswald*, iv.

—— (1957), 'Eine Karte zur Besiedlung Mecklenburgs in der älteren römischen Kaiserzeit, *Forschungen zur Vor- und Frühgeschichte*', ii, 112, Leipzig.

SCHULDT, E. (1955), Pritzier. *Ein Urnenfriedhof der späten römischen Kaiserzeit in Mecklenburg*, Berlin.

SCHULZ, W. (1939), *Vor- und Frühgeschichte Mitteldeutschlands*, Halle.

—— (1953), *Leuna. Ein germanischer Bestattungsplatz der spätrömischen Kaiserzeit*, Berlin.

SCHULZ, W. and ZAHN, R. (1933), *Das Fürstengrab von Hassleben*, Berlin and Leipzig.

SCHÜTTE, G. (1927), *Ptolemy's Maps of N. Europe*, London.

SCHWANTES, G. (1951), 'Die Jastorf-Zivilisation', *Festschrift für P. Reinecke*, 119, Mainz.

—— (1952), 'Die Seedorf-Stufe', *Corolla Archaeologica in honorem C. A. Nordmann*, 58, Helsinki.

STENBERGER, M. (1933), *Öland under äldre järnalderen*, Stockholm. (Öland in the early Iron Age.)

—— (1948), *Det forntida Öland*, Lund. (Prehistoric Öland.)

—— (1956), 'Tuna in Badelunda. A grave in central Sweden with Roman vessels', *Acta Arch.*, xxvii, 1.

—— (1964), *Det forntida Sverige*, Stockholm. (Prehistoric Sweden.)

STENBERGER, M. and KLINDT-JENSEN, O. (1955), *Vallhagar*, 2 vols., Stockholm.

STEUER, H. (1968), 'Zur Bewaffnung und Sozialstruktur der Merowingerzeit', *Nachrichten aus Niedersachsens Urgeschichte*, xxxvii, 18.

STJERNQVIST, B. (1955), *Simris. On Cultural Connections of Scania in the Roman Iron Age*, Bonn and Lund.

STROHEKER, K. F. (1961), Alamannen im römischen Reichsdienst, *Eranion: Festschrift für H. Hommel*, Tübingen.

STRÖMBERG, M. (1961), *Untersuchungen zur jüngeren Eisenzeit in Schonen*, Teil i–ii, Lund.

STRUVE, K. W. (1967), 'Die Moorleiche von Dätgen. Ein Diskussionsbeitrag zur Strafopferthese', *Offa*, xxiv, 33.

SWOBODA, B. (1972), 'Neuerworbene römische Metallgefässe aus Stráže bei Pieštàny', *Archaeologica Slovaca Fontes*, xi.

SZYDŁOWSKI, J. (1962), 'Ein neues Gräberfeld des Dobrodzien-Typus in Olsztyn, pow. Częstochowa', *Arch. Polona*, iv, 306.

TACITUS, *Germania* (Ed. J. G. C. Anderson), Oxford, 1938.

TACKENBERG, K. (1925), *Die Wandalen in Niederschlesien*, Berlin.

—— (1934), *Die Kultur der frühen Eisenzeit in Mittel- und Westhannover*, Hildesheim and Leipzig.

THOMPSON, E. A. (1965), *The Early Germans*, Oxford.

—— (1966), *The Visigoths in the Age of Ulfila*, Oxford.

TIERNEY, J. J. (1960), 'The Celtic Ethnography of Posidonius', *Proc. Irish Academy*, lx, section c, 189.

TISCHLER, F. (1937), *Fuhlsbüttel, ein Beitrag zur Sachsenfrage*, Neumünster.

—— (1939), Der Topf von Eddelaker Typ, *Urgeschichtsstudien beiderseits der Elbe*, 1939, 307.

—— (1954a), 'Der Stand der Sachsenforschung, archäologisch gesehen', *Bericht Röm-Germ. Kommission*, xxxv, 21.

—— (1954b), *Das Gräberfeld Hamburg-Fuhlsbüttel, Beiheft ii zum Atlas der Urgeschichte*, Hamburg.

—— (1955), *Das Gräberfeld Oberjersdal, Kr. Hadersleben, Beiheft iv zum Atlas der Urgeschichte*, Hamburg.

—— (1965), 'Neue Literatur zur Sachsenforschung', *Die Kunde*, xvi, 130.

TRIER, B. (1969), *Das Haus im Nordwesten der Germania Libera*, Neumünster.

UENZE, O. (1953), *Vorgeschichte der hessischen Senke in Karten*, Marburg.

VANA, Z. (1970), *Einführung in die Frühgeschichte der Slawen*, Neumünster.

VAN ES, W. A. (1964), Het Rijengrafveld van Wageningen, *Palaeohistoria*, x, 181.

—— (1966), 'Friesland in Roman Times', *BROB*, xv–xvi, 37.

—— (1967), 'Wijster. A Native Village beyond the Imperial Frontier', *Palaeohistoria*, xi, 29.

VAN GIFFEN, A. E. (1936), 'Der Warf in Ezinge, Prov. Groningen, und seine westgermanische Häuser' *Germania*, xx, 40.

—— (1958), 'Prähistorische Hausformen auf Sandböden in den Niederlanden', *Germania*, xxxvi, 35.

VOIGT, T. (1940), 'Die Germanen des 1 und 2 Jahrhunderts im Mittelelbegebiet', *Jahresschrift Halle*, xxxii.

VON MÜLLER, A. (1956), 'Das frühkaiserzeitliche Gräberfeld von Nitzahn, Kr. Rathenau', *Jahresschrift für mitteldeutsche Vorgeschichte*, xl, 179.

—— (1957), *Formenkreise der älteren römischen Kaiserzeit im Raum zwischen Havelseenplatte und Ostee*, Berlin.

—— (1962), 'Fohrde und Hohenferchesar', *Berliner Beiträge zur Vorgeschichte*, iii.

VON USLAR, R. (1934), 'Die germanische Keramik in den Kastellen Zugmantel und Saalburg', *Saalburg Jahrbuch*, viii, 61.

—— (1938), *Westgermanische Bodenfunde*, Berlin.

—— (1964), *Studien zu den frühgeschichtlichen Befestigungen zwischen Nordsee und Alpen*, Cologne and Graz.

—— (1964b), 'Spätlatenezeitliche Gräber in Leverkusen-Rheindorf', *Germania*, xlii, 36.

—— (1965), 'Stämme und Fundgruppen', *Germania*, xliii, 138.

—— (1972), 'Archaeologische Fundgruppen und germanische Stammesgebiete vornehmlich aus der Zeit um Christi Geburt', in *Zur germanischen Stammeskunde*, 146, Darmstadt.

VULPE, R. (1953), *Sapaturile dela Poineşti din 1949, Materiale arh. privind Istoria Veche*, i. (Excavations at Poineşti in 1949.)

WAAS, M. (1969), *Germanen im römischen Dienst* (2nd ed.), Bonn.

WAHLE, E. (1941), 'Zur ethnische Deutung frühgeschichtlicher Kulturprovinzen', *Sitzungsbericht der Heidelberger Akad. Wissen*, 1940–1.

WALLACE-HADRILL, J. M. (1971), *Early Germanic Kingship in England and on the Continent*, Oxford.

WALLER, K. (1938), *Der Galgenberg bei Cuxhaven*, Leipzig.

—— (1959), *Die Gräberfelder von Hemmoor, Quelkhorn, Gudendorf, und Duhnen-Wehrberg in Niedersachsen, Beiheft viii zum Atlas der Urgeschichte*, Hamburg.

—— (1960), 'Das Gräberfeld von Oxstedt und seine Bedeutung für die Sachsenforschung', *Die Kunde*, xi, 13.

WATERBOLK, H. T. (1961), 'Beschouwingen ... de opgravingen te Tritsum, gem. Franekeradeel', *It Beaken*, xxiii, 216.

—— (1962), 'Hauptzüge der eisenzeitlichen Besiedlung der nördlichen Niederlanden', *Offa*, xix, 9.

—— (1964), 'The Bronze Age Settlement of Elp', *Helinium*, iv, 97.

—— (1966), 'The Occupation of Friesland in the Prehistoric Period', *BROB*, xv–xvi, 13.

WEGEWITZ, W. (1937), *Die langobardische Kultur im Gau Moswidi*, Hildesheim.

—— (1944), *Der langobardische Urnenfriedhof von Tostedt-Wüstenhofen im Kreise Harburg*, Hildesheim.

—— (1965), *Der Urnenfriedhof von Hamburg-Langenbek*, Hildesheim.

—— (1972), *Das langobardische Brandgräberfeld von Putensen, Kr. Harburg*, Hildesheim.

WEISGERBER, L. (1969), *Rhenania Germano-Celtica*, Bonn.

WELLS, C. (1972), *The German Policy of Augustus*, Oxford.

WENSKUS, R. (1961), *Stammesbildung und Verfassung*, Cologne and Graz.

WERNER, J. (1941), *Die beiden Zierscheiben des Thorsberger Moorfundes*, Berlin.

—— (1950), 'Zur Herkunft der frühmittelalterlichen Spangenhelm', *Präh, Zeitschr.*, xxxiv–v, 178.

—— (1951), 'Zur Entstehung der Reihengräberzivilisation', *Arch. Geographica*, i, 23.

—— (1955), 'Pfeilspitzen aus Silber und Bronze in germanischen Adelsgräbern der Kaiserzeit', *Historisches Jahrb*, lxxiv, 38.

—— (1956), *Beiträge zur Archäologie des Attila-Reiches*, Munich.

—— (1958), 'Kriegergräber aus der ersten Hälfte des 5 Jahrhunderts zwischen Schelde und Weser', *Bonner Jahrb*, 158, 372.

—— (1965), 'Zu den alamannischen Burgen des 4 und 5 Jahrhunderts', in *Speculum Historiale* (Ed. C. Bauer, L. Boehm and M. Möller), Freiburg and Munich, 439.

—— (1966), 'Das Aufkommen von Bild und Schrift in Nordeuropa', *Sitzungsberichte der Bayer. Akad. Wissen*, Phil-Hist. Kl., iv, 1.

WILLERDING, U. (1970), 'Vor- und frühgeschichtliche Kulturpflanzenfunde in Mitteleuropa', *Neue Ausgrabungen und Forschungen in Niedersachsen*, v, 287.

ZEMAN, J. (1961), *Severni Morava v mladsi dobe rimske*, Prague. (Northern Moravia in the later Roman Empire.)

ZIMMER-LINNFELD, K. (1960), *Westerwanna I, Beiheft ix zum Atlas der Urgeschichte*, Hamburg.

# Index